品味经典

——高校英语阅读教程

APPRECIATING THE ENGLISH CLASSICS

— A READING COURSEBOOK FOR COLLEGE STUDENTS

张周瑞　张　洁　王　宁　编著

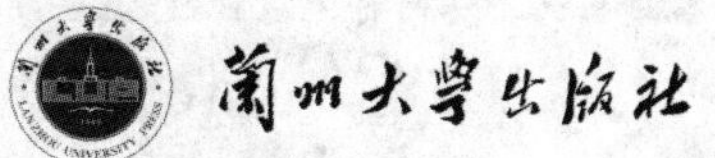

图书在版编目(CIP)数据

品味经典／张周瑞，张洁，王宁编著．—兰州：兰州大学出版社，2013.3

高校英语阅读教程

ISBN 978-7-311-04086-4

Ⅰ.①品… Ⅱ.①张… ②张… ③王… Ⅲ.①英语—阅读教学—高等学校—教材 Ⅳ.①H319.4

中国版本图书馆 CIP 数据核字(2013)第 058486 号

策划编辑 陈红升
责任编辑 锁晓梅 武素珍
封面设计 刘 杰

书　　名 品味经典
——高校英语阅读教程
作　　者 张周瑞 张 洁 王 宁 编著
出版发行 兰州大学出版社 (地址:兰州市天水南路 222 号 730000)
电　　话 0931-8912613(总编办公室) 0931-8617156(营销中心)
0931-8914298(读者服务部)
网　　址 http://www.onbook.com.cn
电子信箱 press@lzu.edu.cn
印　　刷 兰州奥林印刷有限责任公司
开　　本 787 mm×1092 mm 1/16
印　　张 15.5
字　　数 351 千
版　　次 2013 年 3 月第 1 版
印　　次 2013 年 3 月第 1 次印刷
书　　号 ISBN 978-7-311-04086-4
定　　价 39.00 元

(图书若有破损、缺页、掉页可随时与本社联系)

在阅读中学习语言(代序)

阅读是语言学习的基石,在阅读中触摸文字的律动,感知大师的神韵,徜徉于艺术的河流。阅读能为你打开世界的另一扇门,无论你富贵抑或是贫穷。

任何一种语言的学习都离不开阅读,英语自然也不例外。哲人说,"振叶以寻根,观澜而溯源。"正是基于这种追本溯源的心理,人们渴望阅读到原汁原味的经典著述或者接近原创意蕴的译文。但现实中我们恰恰缺乏这样的东西,对于语言工作者和学习者而言,这不能不说是一种缺憾。但是令我感到欣慰的是,我们身边一些年轻的语言教育工作者已经注意到了这个问题,并付诸于实践和探索当中。张周瑞、张洁、王宁三位老师就是他们当中的优秀代表,他们联袂编撰的《品味经典——高效英语阅读教程》一书,选材于原创经典,着眼于阅读和赏析,涉及散文、诗歌、哲理小品、演讲词、书信、影视台词等六个板块,可以说是一部不可多得的读本和教材。此外,出于辅助阅读和方便教学的考虑,本书还附有精美的译文和独到的注释,满足了不同层次读者的需求,希望大家能喜欢并从中获益。

品味经典就是传承文明,品味经典就是延续文化,而阅读可以充盈人生。那么,还等什么呢？打开书,开始你的精神旅程吧!

2013年3月1日

前　言

语言是人类最基本的交流工具,是文化传承的重要载体,人类的文明借助语言得以衍延和丰富。其中,文学作品作为艺术语言典范,从来就是人们学习语言精华、认识民族历史文化、感受艺术魅力的最佳途径。代表域外文化结晶之一的西方文学,经过历史积淀,其经典文字具有很高的艺术水准,极具鉴赏意义。

《品味经典》是一本关于西方经典文学作品阅读与赏析的教材,目的在于为读者提供文学阅读欣赏范本,以便于其学习借鉴域外文化,提高自身的文化修养和审美能力。

本书从散文、诗歌、哲理故事、演讲词、书信、影视台词等六类文本入手,精选涉及英语国家社会文化、政治历史、宗教、风土人情及科普知识等领域的杰作,以帮助读者对域外文化有较为全面的理解。其中包括英国文艺复兴时期最重要的哲学家、思想家、科学家弗朗西斯·培根的《论读书》、英国杰出的戏剧家和诗人莎士比亚的《十四行诗》、英国政治家、演说家、作家温斯顿·丘吉尔的《致妻子的信》及著名的美国民权运动领袖马丁·路德·金的《我有一个梦想》等公认名作。

阅读西方经典文学作品的过程中,反复吟诵原文,用英语思维逻辑去体会其间的精髓,往往会收到事半功倍的学习效果。如英文诗歌,若只看译作就难以深刻体会诗歌的韵味,只有细品原文才能走进作者创造的独特的诗歌意境。而名人演讲词,则有助于了解其所处的时代背景和不平凡的人生轨迹。

本书具有以下特点:

一、语言优美,主体性强。本书包括散文、诗歌、哲理故事、演讲词、书信、影视台词等章节,每个章节围绕一个主题,有助于学生全面了解各类文学作品,从而提高学生对原作的领悟力和感知力。

二、内容丰富,涉猎面广。本书作品选择时尽量考虑选取不同时代、体裁、主体和文体风格等作品,主要涉及英语国家的社会文化、政治历史、宗教、风土人情及科普知识等领域。

三、欣赏性强,实用性好。本书仔细挑选出语言优美且广为流传的经典作品,有很强的可读性和欣赏性。就赏析而言,本书提供全面系统的导读信息,包括作者简介、创作背景、作品评析,便于学生很好地阅读和理解原作,增加读者的阅读兴趣,提高英语阅读理解能力,增强英语语感,扩大词汇量,增加英语国家文化背景知识,具有很强的实用性和趣味性。

四、简单易懂,方便读者。为方便阅读,书中添加了译文和注释,这样既可以让广大读者能够读懂它们,完整地了解作家及其作品,又可以使读者增长文学知识,陶冶情操,不断开拓视野,拓展思维,提高英语综合水平。

本书适合大学英语语言学习者、具有中级以上英语水平的自学者和广大英语爱好者使用。希望读者带着愉快的心情去阅读这本书,对于读者来说,如果能够理解、感悟到其中语言的奥妙和思想的精髓,并能够对英语学习有帮助,对人生有所启迪,本书的目的就达到了。

由于编者才疏学浅,错漏之处在所难免,在此热切希望有关专家和广大读者批评指正。

编 者

2013 年 1 月 20

目　录

第一章　散文名篇

第二章　名诗精选

第三章 哲理故事

第四章 名人演讲

第五章 名人书信

第六章 经典影片

第一章　散文名篇

原文

1　Of Studies

Sir Francis Bacon

Studies serve for delight, for ornament, and for ability. Their chief use for delight, is **in privateness and retiring; for ornament**, is in discourse; and for ability, is in the judgment and disposition of business.

For expert men can execute, and perhaps judge of particulars, one by one; but the general counsels, and **the plots and marshalling of affairs**, come best from those that are learned.

To spend too much time in studies is sloth; to use them too much for ornament, is affectation; to make judgement wholly by their rules, is the humour of a scholar.

They perfect nature, and are perfected by experience: for natural abilities are like natural plants, that need **proyning** by study; and studies themselves do give forth directions too much at large, except they be bounded in by experience.

Crafty men contemn studies, simple men admire them, and wise men use them; for they teach not their own use; but that is a wisdom without them, and above them, won by observation.

Read not to contradict and confute; nor to believe and take for granted; nor to find talk and discourse; but to weigh and consider.

Some books are to be tasted, others to be swallowed, and some few to be chewed and digested; that is, some books are to be read only in parts; others to be read, but not curiously; and some few to be read wholly, and with diligence and attention.

Some books also may be read by deputy, and extracts made of them by others; but that would be only in the less important arguments, and the meaner sort of books; else distilled books are, like common distilled waters, **flashy** things.

Reading maketh a full man; conference a ready man; and writing an exact man. And therefore, if a man write little, he had need have a great memory; if he confer little, he had need have a present wit; and if he read little, he had need have much cunning, to seem to know that he doth not.

Histories make men wise; poets **witty**; the mathematics subtle; natural philosophy deep; moral grave; logic and rhetoric able to contend. ***Abeunt studia in morses.***

Nay there is no **stond** or impediment in the wit, but may be wrought out by fit studies: like as diseases of the body may have appropriate exercises. Bowling is good for the stone and reins; shooting for the lungs and breast; gentle walking for the stomach; riding for the head; and the like.

So if a man's wit be wandering, let him study the mathematics; for in demonstrations, if his wit be called away never so little, he must begin again. If his wit be not apt to distinguish or find differences, let him study the Schoolmen; for they are **cymini sectores**. If he be not apt to beat over matters, and to call up one thing to prove and illustrate another, let him study the lawyers' cases. So every defect of the mind may have a special receipt.

译文

1 论读书

弗朗西斯·培根

读书足以怡情,足以傅彩,足以长才。其怡情也,最见于独处幽居之时;其傅彩也,最见于高谈阔论之中;其长才也,最见于处世判事之际。

练达之士虽能分别处理细事或一一判别枝节,然纵观统筹,全局策划,则舍好学深思者莫属。

读书费时过多易惰,文采藻饰太盛则矫,全凭条文断事乃学究故态。

读书补天然之不足,经验又补读书之不足,盖天生才干犹如自然花草,读书然后知如何修剪移接;而书中所示,如不以经验范之,则又大而无当。

有一技之长者鄙作书,无知者羡读书,唯明智之士用读书,然书并不以用处告人,用书之智不在书中,而在书外,全凭观察得之。

读书时不可存心诘难作者,不可尽信书上所言,亦不可只为寻章摘句,而应推敲细思。

书有可浅尝者,有可吞食者,少数则须咀嚼消化。换言之,有只需读其部分者,有只需大体涉猎者,少数则须全读,读时须全神贯注,孜孜不倦。书亦可请人代读,取其所作摘要,但只限题材较次或价值不高者,否则书经提炼犹如水经蒸馏,淡而无味矣。

读书使人充实,讨论使人机智,笔记使人准确。因此不常做笔记者须记忆特强,不常讨论者须天生聪颖,不常读书者须欺世有术,始能无知而显有知。

读史使人明智,读诗使人灵秀,数学使人周密,科学使人深刻,伦理学使人庄重,逻辑修辞之学使人善辩;凡有所学,皆成性格。

人之才智但有滞碍,无不可读适当之书使之顺畅,一如身体百病,皆可借相宜之运动除之。滚球利睾肾,射箭利胸肺,慢步利肠胃,骑术利头脑,诸如此类。如智力不集中,可令读数学,盖演题须全神贯注,稍有分散即须重演;如不能辨异,可令读经院哲学,盖是辈皆吹毛求疵之人;如不善求同,不善以一物阐证另一物,可令读律师之案卷。如此头脑中凡有缺陷,皆有特效可医。

（王佐良　译）

注释

1. in privateness and retiring: when alone and away from work. 幽居独处

2. for ornament: for ability. （显得）有才学

3. the plots and marshalling of affairs: the planning and handling of practical matters. 对事物的计划与安排

4. proyning: old spelling for pruning, meaning“cultivating”. 修剪枝叶

5. crafty［'kræfti］*adj.* practical and cunning 狡猾的；灵巧的　◆此处译为“有一技之长的”。

6. flashy［'flæʃi］*adj.* tasteless or insipid 浮华的；瞬间的　◆该处指无味的；无趣的

7. witty［'witi］*adj.* clever or ingenious 诙谐的；机智的

8. Abeunt studia in morses（Latin）: the phrase, quoted from the *Heroides*（XV. 83）by Ovid, means that studies go to make up a man's character. 拉丁文，意为“凡有所学，皆成性格”。

9. stond: obstacle. 障碍，干扰

10. cymini sectores（Latin）: hair - Splitters. 拉丁文，意为“过分讲究细节的人”。

赏析

弗朗西斯·培根（1561—1626），英国文艺复兴时期最重要的哲学家、思想家、科学家。他不但在文学、哲学上多有建树，在自然科学领域里，也取得了重大成就。培根是一位经历了诸多磨难的贵族子弟，复杂多变的生活经历丰富了他的阅历，他的思想成熟，言论深邃，富含哲理。他的整个世界观是现世的而不是宗教的（虽然他坚信上帝）；他是一位理性主义者而不是迷信的崇拜者；是一位经验论者而不是诡辩学者；在政治上，他是一位现实主义者而不是理论家。主要著作有：《新工具》《学术的进步》《新大西岛》《亨利七世本纪》等。

培根还是一位散文家。他在文学方面的代表作就是《随笔》（*Essays*），文笔非常优美，是值得一读的佳作。《随笔》1597年初版时只收有10篇文章，1612年版增至38篇，1625年版（即末版）增至58篇。在培根逝世31年后的1657年，有一个Rawley版将培根的未完稿《论谣言》（*Of Fame*）作为第59篇收入其《随笔》，但由于该篇只有“起承”尚无“转合”，故后来的通行本仍多以五十八篇为标准。《随笔》的内容涉及政治、经济、宗教、爱情、婚姻、友谊、艺术、教育和伦理等，几乎触及了人类生活的方方面面。作为一名学识渊博且通晓人情世故的哲学家和思想家，培根对他谈及的问题

均有发人深省的独到之见。《随笔》语言简洁,文笔优美,说理透彻,警句迭出,几百年来深受各国读者欢迎,据说有不少人的性格曾受到该书的熏陶。于今天的青年读者而言,读《随笔》就像听一位睿智的老人侃侃而谈,因其包含着这位先哲的思想精髓。其中有很多名句:

1. 读史使人明智,读诗使人灵秀,数学使人周密,科学使人深刻,伦理学使人庄重,逻辑修辞之学使人善辩;凡有所学,皆成性格。

2. 真理是时间之产物,而不是权威之产物。

3. 合理安排时间就是节约时间。

本书选取了培根《随笔》中最为脍炙人口的四篇佳作,有《论读书》(*Of Studies*)、《谈美》(*Of Beauty*)、《谈利己之聪明》(*Of Wisdom for a Man's Self*)和《论爱情》(*Of Love*)。本文就是选自《随笔》的第50篇哲理散文。作者探讨了为学为人的经验智慧。文章开篇即是点题,即"读书足以怡情,足以傅彩,足以长才"。这篇随笔的写法不同一般,它论述的范围相当广泛,但语言十分简练,几乎一句就是一个观点。然后从五个方面对中心思想进行论述:(1)合适或不合适的学习方法;(2)不同的人对学习有不同的看法;(3)读书的方法;(4)学习不同的科目可以铸造不同人的性格;(5)有效的学习可以弥补人的缺点。

作者的写作特点:(1)运用比喻说理。例如,"盖天生才干犹如自然花草,读书然后知如何修剪移接",来说明读书对人的天赋的作用。这样写,生动形象、通俗易懂。(2)运用排比说理。例如,"读书足以怡情,足以傅彩,足以长才。其怡情也,最见于独处幽居之时;其傅彩也,最见于高谈阔论之中;其长才也,最见于处世判事之际。"又如,"读史使人明智,读诗使人灵秀,数学使人周密,科学使人深刻,伦理学使人庄重,逻辑修辞之学使人善辩"。这样写,所说的道理十分显豁,读起来富于气势,增强说服力和感染力。(3)运用对比说理。正面说了以后,再从反面来说,使说理更加全面、有力。例如,文章开头从正面说了读书的目的,接着又从反面说了读书的三种偏向。又如,文章的最后一个层次,先从正面说读书可以塑造人的性格,又从反面说读书可以弥补性格、精神上的缺陷。读书贵在运用。应该记一些东西,应精确些,以助谈兴谈资,这是运用;但更重要的运用却是内化,将其融进自己的知识和经验体系之中,成为指导自己工作与生活的"哲学",这才是更高层次的"学以致用"。如果光是为了猎奇与装饰,读书实在是没什么用;如果读成了书呆子,书不读也罢!

这篇文章的风格古朴典雅,简洁而明快,字里行间,屡屡见发人深省的警句和妙语,蕴含着不凡的智慧与经验的哲理。《论读书》一文,应加强诵读,力求熟读成诵。

原文

2 Of Beauty

Sir Francis Bacon

Virtue is like a rich stone, best plain set; and surely virtue is best, in a body that is comely, though not of delicate features; and that hath rather dignity of presence, than beauty of aspect. Neither is it almost seen, that very beautiful persons are otherwise of great virtue; as if nature were rather busy, not to err, than in labor to produce excellency. And therefore they prove accomplished, but not of great spirit; and study rather behavior, than virtue.

But this holds not always: for Augustus Caesar, Titus Vespasianus, ***Philip le Belle* of France**, Edward the Fourth of England, ***Alcibiades* of Athens**, **Ismael the Sophy of Persia**, were all high and great spirits; and yet the most beautiful men of their times. In beauty, that of favor, is more than that of color; and that of decent and gracious motion, more than that of favor. That is **the best part of beauty**, which a picture cannot express; no, nor the first sight of **the life**. There is no excellent beauty, that hath not some strangeness in the proportion. A man cannot tell whether **Apelles**, or **Albert Durer**, were the more trifler; whereof the one, would make a personage by geometrical proportions; the other, by taking the best parts out of divers faces, to make one excellent. Such personages, I think, would please nobody, but the painter that made them. Not but I think a painter may make a better face than ever was; but he must do it by a kind of felicity (as a musician that maketh an excellent air in music), and not by rule. A man shall see faces, that if you examine them part by part, you shall find never a good; and yet altogether do well. If it be true that the principal part of beauty is in decent motion, certainly it is no marvel, though persons in years seem many times more amiable; ***pulchrorum autumnus pulcher***; for no youth can be comely but by pardon, and considering the youth, as to make up the comeliness. Beauty is as summer fruits, which are easy to corrupt, and cannot last; and for the most part it makes a dissolute youth, and an age a little out of countenance; but yet certainly again, **if it light well**, it maketh virtue shine, and vices blush.

译文

2 谈 美

弗朗西斯·培根

德行犹如宝石,朴素最美;其于人也:则有德者但须形体悦目,不必面貌俊秀,与其貌美,不若气度恢宏。人不尽知:绝色无大德也;一如自然劳碌终日,但求无过,而无力制成上品。因此美男子有才而无壮志,重行而不重德。

但亦不尽然。罗马大帝奥古斯提与泰特思,法王菲律浦,英王爱德华四世,古雅典之亚西拜提斯,波斯之伊斯迈帝,皆有宏图壮志而又为当时最美之人也。美不在颜色艳丽而在面目端正,又不尽在面目端正而在举止文雅合度。美之极致,非图画所能表,乍见所能识。举凡最美之人,其部位比例,必有异于常人之处。阿贝尔与杜勒皆画家也,其画人像也,一则按照几何学之比例,一则集众脸形之长于一身,二者谁更不智,实难断言,窃以为此等画像除画家本人外,恐无人喜爱也。余不否认画像之美可以超绝尘寰,但此美必为神笔,而非可依规矩得之者，乐师之谱成名曲亦莫不皆然。人面如逐部细察，往往一无是处，观其整体则光彩夺目。美之要素既在于举止，则年长美过年少亦无足怪。古人云："美者秋日亦美。"年少而著美名，率由宽假，盖鉴其年事之少，而补其形体之不足也。美者犹如夏日蔬果，易腐难存；要之，年少而美者常无行，年长而美者不免面有惭色。虽然，但须托体得人，则德行因美而益彰，恶行见美而愈愧。

（王佐良　译）

注释

1. virtue [ˈvətʃu] excellence of any kind (not merely moral virtue). 指任何美德或德行，不单指道德。

2. Phillip le Belle of France: Phillip the Fair, King of France. 法国国王

3. Alcibiades of Athens: Athenian general and statesman. 雅典将军和政治家

4. Ismael the Sophy of Persia: the first Shah of Persia. 波斯的第一位国王，被称为"沙"。

5. the best part of beauty: the seemly graceful behavior. 指优雅行为之美

6. the life: the reality, the person who is depicted. 这里指亲见或直观。

7. Apelles: Greek painter, 4th century B. C. It was not Apelles but Zuxis, an earlier artist, who, when he wished to paint an ideal face, chose five girls as his models (see Cicero, On Invention. Ⅱ.P.1). 公元前4世纪的希腊画家

8. Albert Durer: German painter in the 15th century. 公元前15世纪的德国画家

9. pulchrorum autumnus pulcher: the autumn of the beautiful. 拉丁文。本义暮秋之色更美，这里意为"美者虽到中年仍是美的"。

10. if it light well: if it alights on a worthy person. 这里意为把爱的形貌与美的德行结合起来。

赏析

自从法国文学家蒙田以尝试的手笔创立"essay（随笔）"这一体裁之后，这种文体便焕发出勃勃生机。培根是英国之艺复兴时期的大哲学家，他用当时知识界流行的学术语言拉丁语，写了多部哲学著作。在英国文学史上，培根的主要贡献在于：(1)将蒙田创立的随笔移植到英国，使之成为英国散文的重要门类；(2)在乔叟、莎士比亚等人之后，进一步巩固和提升了英语的表现力。

本文是选自《随笔》的第43篇哲理散文，是一篇关于"美"的经典之作。它语言简洁，内涵深刻，充满哲理。"美"本身是个很广泛的话题，作者通过谈美，讨论内秀与貌美的辩证关系。文章开篇点题，从四个方面论证中心思想，即外在的美和内在

的美，优雅行为之美，画家关于美的标准和美人的迟暮也是美。篇末重申只有把爱的形貌与美的德行结合起来，美才会放射出真正的光辉。文章的风格古朴典雅，简洁而明快，字里行间，屡见发人深省的警句和妙语，蕴含着不凡的智慧与哲理。

美貌如同双刃剑，但无论如何算是上天的恩赐。但过多地依赖于美貌必然会使人浅薄而成为夏日的鲜果。世界上没有一个人是十全十美的，所以，不要抱怨自己外在的缺陷，只有内在的美才是永恒的美。美德重于美貌，把美的形貌与美的德行结合起来，美才能真正发出光辉。文中有这样一句话："形体之美要胜于颜色之美，优雅行为之美又胜于形体之美。"形体是一个人的整体形象，体形、颜色指五官相貌，主要是脸部，是局部的。而行为之美，指举手投足的动作神态，是后天的，是内在美的折射表现，在三者中最高。如今，有些人只注重外表的美丽，而忽略了内在，他们虽然具有美貌，却由于缺乏优美的修养而不配得到赞美，所以一个打扮并不华贵却端庄严肃而有美德的人是令人肃然起敬的。因此，把美的形貌与美的德行结合起来吧。只有这样，美才会散发出真正的光辉。

原文

3 Of Wisdom for a Man's Self

Sir Francis Bacon

An ant is a wise creature for itself, but it is a **shrewd** thing, in an orchard or garden. And certainly, men that are great lovers of themselves, waste the public. Divide with reason; between self-love and society; and be so true to thyself, as thou be not false to others; specially to thy king and country. It is a poor centre of a man's actions, himself. **It is right earth. For that only stands fast upon his own centre; whereas all things, that have affinity with the heavens, move upon the centre of another, which they benefit**. The referring of all to a man's self, is more tolerable in a sovereign prince; because themselves are not only themselves, but their good and evil is at the peril of the public fortune. But it is a desperate evil, in a servant to a prince, or a citizen in a republic. For whatsoever affairs pass such a man's hands, he crooketh them to his own ends; which must needs be often **eccentric to** the ends of his master, or state. Therefore, let princes, or states, choose such servants, as have not this mark; except they mean their service should be made but **the accessory**. That which maketh the effect more pernicious, is that all proportion is lost. It were disproportion enough, for the servant's good to be preferred before the master's; but yet it is a greater extreme, when a little good of the servant, shall carry things against a great good of the master's. And yet that is the case of bad officers, treasurers, ambassadors, generals, and other false and corrupt servants; which set a bias upon their bowl, **of their own petty ends and envies**, to the overthrow of their master's great and important affairs. And for the most part, the good such servants receive, is after the model of their own fortune; but the hurt they sell for that good, is **after the model of** their master's fortune. And certainly it is the nature of extreme self-lovers, as they will set an house on fire, and **it were** but to roast their eggs; and yet these men many times hold credit with their masters, because their study is but to please them, and profit themselves; and for either respect, they will abandon the good of their affairs.

Wisdom for a man's self is, in many branches thereof, a depraved thing. It is the wisdom of rats, that will be sure to leave a house, somewhat before it falls. It is the wisdom of the fox, that thrusts out the badger, who digged and made room for him. It is the wisdom of crocodiles, that shed tears when they would devour. But that which is specially to be noted is, that those which (as Cicero says of Pompey) are ***sui amantes, sine rivali***, are many times unfortunate. And whereas they have, all their times, sacrificed to themselves, they become in the end, themselves sacrifices to the inconstancy of fortune, whose wings they thought, by their self-wisdom, to have pinioned.

译文

3 谈利己之聪明

弗朗西斯·培根

若论为己营生,蚂蚁可谓一种聪明的动物,但对果园花圃来说,它却是一种祸害;而毋庸置疑,过分自私的人亦会有害于公众。故人应该理智地在私利与公利之间划出界线,不可因利己而有负于他人,尤其不可有负于君王和国家。常人之行为以我为中心实乃不幸,因为那就像地球只绕其轴心而转,而与各重天道有亲和力的所有天体都绕别的中心而运动并有益于它们所围绕的中心。一切以自我为中心,这于帝王君王尚情有可原,因为君王并不仅仅代表其自身,他们的祸福也与公众的安危息息相关;但于普通臣民或公民,一切以自我为中心则是一种大恶,因为凡事经这种人之手,他们都会使其适合自己的目的,而他们的目的往往都与君王和国家的目标背道而驰,由此可见,君王或国家不可选这种人作为臣仆或公仆,除非只让他们做一些无关紧要的琐事。谋私利的更大危害是使纲常失调。置臣利于君利之先已是违常乱纲,而为臣之小利损君之大利则更是大逆不道。然而这正是那些贪官污吏所为,腐败堕落的大臣、司库、使节和将军,无不为其蝇头小利而偏离正道,从而破坏其君王的宏图大业。而总的说来,这些人所获之利通常只与他们的财富相称,可他们为获私利而牺牲的公利则往往与君王的财富成正比。为烤熟自家鸡蛋而不惜烧掉公家房屋,这无疑就是极端利己者的本性;然而这类利己者却往往得到主人的信任,因为他们的心思全在于如何讨好主人,如何替自己捞好处;他们可以为任何一点好处而抛弃主人的利益。

为利己而玩弄的诸多聪明,说到底是一种败坏的聪明。它是老鼠的聪明,因大屋将倾,鼠必先逃之;它是狐狸的聪明,因獾掘洞穴,狐占而居之;它是鳄鱼的聪明,因其欲食之,必先哭之。但值得指出的是，那些除自己之外谁也不爱的人（如西塞罗笔下的庞培），到头来往往都可叹可悲；尽管他们总是为自己而牺牲他人，并自以为已用其聪明缚住了命运的翅翼，但他们终归也会变成无常命运的祭品。

（曹明伦　译）

注释

1. shrewd [ʃrud] *adj.* mischievous. 精明的；狡猾的；机灵的　◆此处译为“聪明的”。

2. It is right earth. For that only stands fast upon his own centre, whereas all things that have affinity with the heavens move upon the centre of another, which they benefit: This sentence means that a man's self is exactly like the earth, for it alone, according to Ptolemaic astronomy, remains fixed while the planetary spheres move around it. 克罗狄斯·托勒密（Claudius Ptolemaeus），古希腊地理学家、天文学家、数学家。他认为地球是宇宙的中心，且静止不动，日、月、行星和恒星均围绕地球运动。本句意为：常人以我为中心，就像其他天体都绕地球为中心而运动并有益于地球一样。

3. eccentric to: different from. 背道而驰

4. the accessory [æk'sɛsəri] n. of assistance only. 配件；附件；从犯　◆此处指做辅助性工作或琐事的人。

5. of their own petty ends and envies: who are diverted from their proper, faithful course in favour of. 为其蝇头小利而偏离正道

6. after the model of: on the scale of, proportionate to. 成比例

7. it were: even if it were only to. 仅仅是为了

8. sui amantes sine rivali: (Latin) lovers of themselves without rival. （拉丁文）只爱自己的人

赏析

本文是选自《随笔》的第23篇哲理散文。作者通过谈论“利己的聪明”，对小人的小智慧进行理性的批判。就拿蚂蚁来说，冬天对于蚂蚁来说是难以度过的，所有工蚁必须努力地汲取食物，并将食物贮存起来。但是，如果有一只蚂蚁，为了满足自己的私欲，只将自己肚子填饱，偷懒不去进行劳动，这势必会影响其他的蚂蚁。当越来越多的蚂蚁开始效仿第一只蚂蚁，那么到了冬天，一整巢的蚂蚁都会因为寒冷，因为当时的偷懒，被自己害死。之所以会有利己的聪明是因为有欲望，有不劳而获的欲望。而这种欲望，最先当是源于人类自己。利己的聪明，真可谓聪明。他们为了煮熟鸡蛋，可以点燃房子。

这种愚蠢的聪明，到现在都没有完全绝迹，还在像蛀虫一样孜孜不倦地啃食这个社会，当社会这个大房子被蛀得千疮百孔之后，必然会崩坍的，到那时这些蛀虫还会有去路？所谓的利己的聪明，那也只不过是一些小聪明罢了。利欲熏心，只为蝇头小利而出卖诚信，出卖朋友，甚至出卖自己的一切，只为与恶魔撒旦做交易，这笔交易的最大赢家当然是恶魔。这些聪明最后只会为自己的成功自掘坟墓。

原文

4 Of Love

Sir Francis Bacon

The stage is more beholding to love, than the life of man. For as to the stage, love is ever matter of comedies, and now and then of tragedies; but in life it doth much mischief; sometimes like a **siren**, sometimes like a **fury**.

You may observe, that amongst all the great and worthy persons (whereof the memory remaineth, either ancient or recent) there is not one, that hath been transported to the mad degree of love: which shows that great spirits, and great business, do keep out this weak passion. You must except, nevertheless, **Marcus Antonius**, the half partner of the empire of Rome, and **Appius Claudius**, the decemvir and lawgiver; whereof the former was indeed a voluptuous man, and inordinate; but the latter was an austere and wise man: and therefore it seems (though rarely) that love can find entrance, not only into an open heart, but also into a heart well fortified, if watch be not well kept.

It is a poor saying of **Epicurus**, *Satis magnum alter alteri theatrum sumus*; as if man, made for the contemplation of heaven, and all noble objects, should do nothing but kneel before a little idol, and make himself a subject, though not of the mouth (as beasts are), yet of the eye; which was given him for higher purposes.

It is a strange thing, to note the excess of this passion, and how it braves the nature, and value of things, by this; that the speaking in a perpetual hyperbole, is comely in nothing but in love. Neither is it merely in the phrase; for whereas it hath been well said, that the arch-flatterer, with whom all the petty flatterers have intelligence, is a man's self; certainly the lover is more. For there was never proud man thought so absurdly well of himself, as the lover doth of the person loved; and therefore it was well said, "That it is impossible to love, and to be wise." Neither doth this weakness appear to others only, and not to the party loved; but to the loved most of all, except the love be reciproque. For it is a true rule, that love is ever rewarded, either with the reciproque, or with an inward and secret contempt.

By how much the more, men ought to beware of this passion, which loseth not only other things, but itself! As for the other losses, the poet's relation doth well figure them: that he that preferred **Helena**, quitted the gifts of Juno and Pallas. For whosoever esteemeth too much of amorous affection, quitteth both riches and wisdom.

This passion has his floods, in very times of weakness, which are great prosperity, and great adversity; though this latter has been less observed: both which times kindle love, and make it more fervent, and therefore show it to be the child of folly. They do best, who if they cannot but admit love, yet make it keep quarters; and sever it wholly from their serious affairs, and actions, of life; for if it check once with business, it troubles men's fortunes, and makes men, that they can no ways be true to their own ends.

I know not how, but martial men are given to love: I think, it is but as they are given to wine; for perils commonly ask to be paid in pleasures.

There is in man's nature, a secret inclination and motion, towards love of others, which if it be not spent upon some one or a few, doth naturally spread itself towards many, and maketh men become humane and charitable; as it is seen sometime in friars.

Nuptial love maketh mankind; friendly love perfecteth it; but wanton love corrupteth, and cmbaseth it.

译文

4 论爱情

弗朗西斯·培根

舞台上的爱情生活比生活中的爱情要美好得多。因为在舞台上,爱情只是喜剧和悲剧的素材,而在人生中,爱情却常常招来不幸。它有时像那位诱惑人的魔女,有时又像那位复仇的女神。

你可以看到,一切真正伟大的人物(无论是古人、今人,只要是其英名永铭于人类记忆中的),没有一个是因爱情而发狂的人,因为伟大的事业抑制了这种软弱的感情。只有罗马的安东尼和克劳底亚是例外。前者本性就好色荒淫,然而后者却是严肃多谋的人。这说明爱情不仅会占领开旷坦阔的胸怀,有时也能闯入壁垒森严的心灵——假如守御不严的话。

埃辟克拉斯曾说过一句笨话:“人生不过是一座大戏台。”似乎本应努力追求高尚事业的人类,却只应像玩偶般地逢场作戏。虽然爱情的奴隶并不同于那班只顾吃喝的禽兽,但毕竟也只是眼目色相的奴隶,而上帝赐人以眼睛本来是有更高尚的用途的。

过度的爱情追求,必然会降低人本身的价值。例如,只有在爱情中,才总是需要那种浮夸谄媚的辞令。而在其他场合,同样的辞令只能招人耻笑。古人有一句名言:“最大的奉承,人总是留给自己的。”——只有对情人的奉承要算例外。因为甚至最骄傲的人,也甘愿在情人面前自轻自贱。所以古人说得好:“就是神在爱情中也难保持聪明。”情人的这种弱点不仅在外人眼中是明显的，就是在被追求者的眼中也会很明显——除非她(他)也在追求他(她)。所以，爱情的代价就是如此，不能得到回爱，就会得到一种深藏于心的轻蔑，这是一条永真的定律。

由此可见，人们应当十分警惕这种感情。因为它不但会使人丧失其他，而且可以使人丧失自己本身，甚至其他方面的损失。古诗人早告诉我们，那追求海伦的人，是放弃了财富和智慧的。

当人心最软弱的时候，爱情最容易入侵，那就是当人春风得意，忘乎所以和处境困窘，孤独凄零的时候，虽然后者未必能得到爱情。人在这样的时候最容易跳入爱情的火焰中，由此可见，"爱情"实在是"愚蠢"的儿子。但有一些人，即使心中有了爱，仍能约束它，使它不妨碍重大的事业。因为爱情一旦干扰情绪，就会阻碍人坚定地奔向既定的目标。

我不懂是什么缘故，使许多军人更容易堕入情网，也许这正像他们嗜爱饮酒一样，是因为危险的生活更需要欢乐的补偿。

人心中可能普遍具有一种博爱倾向，若不集中于某个专一的对象身上，就必然施之于更广泛的大众，使他成为仁善的人，像有的僧侣那样。

夫妻的爱，使人类繁衍。朋友的爱，给人以帮助。但那荒淫纵欲的爱，却只会使人堕落毁灭啊！

(林语堂　译)

注释

1. siren: 古希腊神话，传说地中海有魔女塞壬(Siren)，歌喉动听，诱使过往船只陷入险境。

2. fury: 原文为"Flries"，传说中的地狱之神。

3. Marcus Antonius: 安东尼，恺撒部将。后因迷恋女色而战败被杀。

4. Appius Claudius: 克劳底亚，古罗马执政官，亦因好色而被杀。

5. Epicurus: 埃辟克拉斯(前342—前270年)，古罗马哲学家。

6. Helena: 海伦。古希腊神话，传说天后赫拉、智慧之神密纳发和美神维纳斯，为争夺金苹果，请特洛伊王子评判。三神各许一愿，密纳发许以智慧，维纳斯许以美女海伦，天后许以财富。结果王子把金苹果给了维纳斯。

赏析

培根的58篇《随笔》(Essays, 1625)堪称英国散文史上的经典之作。这些短小精悍的作品务实、准确、清楚、紧凑，是英国随笔的上乘之作。在新古典主义盛行的17—18世纪，随笔的创作更是空前，文学史家称这一时期为随笔的"黄金时代"。代表作家有蒲柏、艾迪生 (Joseph Addison)、斯蒂尔(Richard

Steele)、约翰逊(Samuel Johnson)等人。在19世纪,虽然有了小说的兴起与日趋成熟,但是,随笔的创作并未因此而走向衰落,像兰姆(Charles Lamb)、黑兹利特(William Hazlitt)、亨特(Leigh Hunt)、昆西(De Quincy),美国的爱默生(Ralph Waldo Emerson)、梭罗(Henry David Thoreau)等这样的一些著名作家,都写出了许多优秀的作品。这一时期在文学史上称为随笔的"白银时代"。

本文是选自《随笔》的第10篇哲理散文。文中作者谈到对爱情的认识和思考,以及对爱情的理解,包含许多洞察秋毫的经验之谈,也探讨了爱情哲理。文笔言简意赅、睿智夺目,词句干脆而对比,所以涵义饱满而措辞警策,往往一语中的。但愿读者在阅读时能管中窥豹,领略出培根的文章风采。

原文

5 About Reading Books

Virginia Woolf

It is simple enough to say that since books have classes — fiction, biography, poetry — we should separate them and take from each what it is right that each should give us. Yet few people ask from books what books can give us. Most commonly we come to books with **blurred** and **divided minds**, asking of fiction that it shall be true, of poetry that it shall be false, of biography that it shall be flattering, of history that it shall enforce our own prejudices. If we could **banish** all such **preconceptions** when we read, that would be an admirable beginning. Do not dictate to your author; **try to become him**. Be his fellow-worker and accomplice. If you hang back, and reserve, and criticize at first, you are preventing yourself from getting the fullest possible value from what you read. But if you open your mind as widely as possible, then signs and hints of **almost imperceptible fineness**, from the twist, and turn of the first sentences, will bring you into the presence of a human being unlike any other. **Steep** yourself in this, **acquaint yourself with** this, and soon you will find that your author is giving you, or attempting to give you, something far more definite. The thirty-two chapters of a novel — if we consider how to read a novel first — are an attempt to make something as formed and controlled as a building: but words are more **impalpable** than bricks; reading is a longer and more complicated process than seeing. Perhaps the quickest way to understand the elements of what a novelist is doing is not to read, but to write, to make your own experiment with the dangers and difficulties of words. Recall, then, some event that has left a **distinct impression on** you — how at the corner of the street, perhaps, you passed two people talking. A tree shook, an electric light danced, the tone of the talk was comic, but also tragic, a whole vision, an entire conception, seemed **contained** in that moment.

译文

5 谈读书

弗吉尼亚·伍尔芙

既然书籍有不同的门类,如小说、传记、诗歌等,我们就应该把它们区分开来,并从每种书中汲取它应当给我们提供的正确的东西;这话说起来固然容易,然而,很少有人要求从书籍中得到它们所能提供的东西,通常我们总是三心二意地带着模糊的观念去看书:要求小说情节真实,要求诗歌内容虚构,要求传记阿谀奉承,要求历史能加深我们自己的偏见。如果我们读书时能抛弃所有这些成见,那将是一个极可贵的开端。我们对作者不要指手画脚,而应努力站在作者的立场上,设想自己在与作者共同创作。假如你退缩不前,有所保留并且一开始就批评指责,你就在妨碍自己从你所读的书中得到最大的益处。然而,如果你能尽量敞开思想,那么,书中开头几句迂回曲折的话里所包含的几乎难以觉察的细微的迹象和暗示,就会把你引到一个与众不同的人物的面前去。如果你深入下去,如果你去认识这个人物,你很快就会领悟作者正在给你或试图给你某些明确得多的东西。倘若我们首先考虑怎样读小说,那么,一部小说中的三十二章就是企图创造出像一座建筑物那样既有一定的形式而各部分又受到控制的东西,不过词句要比砖块难以捉摸,阅读的过程要比看一看更费时、更复杂。理解小说家创作工作的各项要素的捷径也许并不是阅读,而是写作,而是亲自试一试遣词造句中的艰难险阻。那么,回想一下给你留下鲜明印象的某些事——比如,你怎样在大街的拐角处从两个正在交谈着的人身边走过,树在摇曳,灯光在晃动,谈话的语气既喜又悲;这一瞬间似乎包含了一个完整的想象,一个整体的构思。

(江治 译)

注释

1. blur[blə:] *vt. & vi.*模糊;使模糊不清
2. divided minds: 意见不统一
3. banish['bæniʃ] *vt.* 流放,放逐
4. preconception[ˌprikən'sepʃən] *n.* 偏见
5. try to become him: 应努力站在作者的立场上。become在这里用作及物动词,解作“配合”“适应”。
6. almost imperceptible fineness : 几乎难以觉察的细微
7. steep[stip] *adj.* 陡峭的
8. acquaint yourself with...: 使(你)自己认识(了解)
9. impalpable [im'pælpəbəl] *adj.* 无形的,难以捉摸的

10. distinct impression on: 给……留下鲜明的影响

11. contained [kən'teind] *adj.* 从容的

赏析

20世纪,随笔的创作日益呈现出多元势态。劳伦斯(D. H. Lawrence)、伍尔芙(Virginia Woolf)、奥威尔(George Orwell)等人的文学随笔,罗素(Bertrand Russell)的哲学、社会学随笔,爱因斯坦(Albert Einstein)的科学随笔,等等,与这一时期成为主流的"期刊随笔(the Journalistic Essay)"构成相互辉映的文化景观。

弗吉尼亚·伍尔芙(Virginia Woolf,1882—1941)。英国女作家、批判家、意识流小说的代表人物之一。《墙上的斑点》是她第一篇典型的意识流作品。她被认为是20世纪现代主义与女性主义的先锋之一。在两次世界大战期间,伍尔芙是伦敦文学界的核心人物,她同时也是布卢姆茨伯里派(Bloomsbury Group)的成员之一。其最知名的小说包括《戴洛维夫人》(*Mrs. Dalloway*)、《灯塔行》(*To the Lighthouse*)、《雅各的房间》(*Jakob's Room*)。

本文主要讨论了书的分类、读书的方法和对作者的了解。作者借助想象与联想,由此及彼、由浅入深、由实而虚依次写来,可以融情于景、寄情于事、寓情于物、托物言志,表达作者的真情实感,实现物我的统一,展现出更深远的思想,使读者领会更深的道理。

弗吉尼亚·伍尔芙曾说过:"关于读书方面,一个人能对另一个人所提出的唯一劝告就是:不必听什么劝告,只要遵循你自己的天性,运用你自己的理智,得出你自己的结论,就行了。如果我们之间在这一点上能取得一致意见,我才觉得自己有权利提出一些看法或建议,因为你们绝不会允许它们去束缚你们自己的独立性,而这种独立性才是一个读者所拥有的最重要的品质。……但是,要享受自由,我们当然也得对自己有一定限制。我们不能徒劳无益地、愚昧无知地浪费掉自己的精力,为了给一个玫瑰花坛浇水,把半个宅子全喷洒得精湿。我们必须在当场准确有力地培养自己的能力。"在这一前提下,伍尔芙给作者的读书建议正如文中所说:不要向作者发号施令,而要设法变成作者自己。做他的合作者和同伙。如果你一开始就退缩不前、持保留态度并且评头论足,你就是在阻止自己、不能从你所读的书中获得尽可能丰富的意蕴。但是,只要你尽可能宽广地敞开你的心胸,那么书一开头的曲曲折折的句子中那些几乎察觉不出的细微征兆和暗示,就会把你带到一个与任何别人都迥然不同的人物面前。

原文

6 Nature(Extract)

Ralph Waldo Emerson

Nature is a setting that fits equally well a comic or a mourning piece. In good health, the air is a **cordial** of incredible virtue. Crossing a bare common, in snow **puddles**, at twilight, under a clouded sky, without having in my thoughts and occurrence of special good fortune, I have enjoyed a perfect **exhilaration**. Almost I fear to think how glad I am. In the woods too, a man casts off his years, as the snake his slough, and at what period soever of life, is always a child. In the woods, is perpetual youth. Within these plantations of God, a decorum and **sanctity** reign, a **perennial** festival is dressed, and the guest sees not how he should tire of them in a thousand years. In the woods, we return to reason and faith. There I feel that nothing can befall me in life, —no disgrace, no **calamity**, (leaving me my eyes,) which nature cannot repair. Standing on the bare ground, —my head bathed by the **blithe** air, and uplifted into infinite space, —all mean egotism vanishes. I become a **transparent** eye - ball; I am nothing; I see all; the currents of the Universal Being circulate through me; I am part or particle of God. The name of the nearest friend sounds then foreign and accidental: to be brothers, to be acquaintances, —master or servant, is then a trifle and a disturbance. I am the lover of uncontained and immortal beauty. In the wilderness, I find something more dear and **connate** than in streets or villages. In the tranquil landscape, and especially in the distant line of the horizon, man beholds somewhat as beautiful as his own nature.

The greatest delight which the fields and woods minister, is the suggestion of an occult relation between man and the vegetable. I am not alone and unacknowledged. They nod to me, and I to them. The waving of the boughs in the storm, is new to me and old. It takes me by surprise, and yet is not unknown. Its effect is like that of a higher thought or a better emotion coming over me, when I deemed I was thinking justly or doing right.

Yet it is certain that the power to produce this delight, does not reside in nature, but in man, or in a harmony of both. It is necessary to use these pleasures with great temperance. For, nature is not always tricked in holiday attire, but the same scene which yesterday breathed perfume and glittered as for the **frolic** of the **nymphs**, is overspread with **melancholy** today. Nature always wears the colors of the spirit. To a man laboring under calamity, the heat of his own fire hath sadness in it. Then, there is a kind of contempt of the landscape felt by him who has just lost by death a dear friend. The sky is less grand as it shuts down over less worth in the population.

译文

6 大自然(节选)

拉尔夫·沃尔多·爱默生

自然既可是悲剧的,也可以是喜剧的背景。身体康健时,空气就是让人难以置信的补剂甜酿。越过空旷的公地,停留深雪潭边,注目晨昏曦微光芒,在满布乌云的天空下,并非出于特别的当头好运,我享受了完美无缺的欣喜。我欣喜以至于有些胆怯。在树林里也是一样,人们抖落岁月如蛇蜕旧皮,无论身处生命的哪一阶段,都会心如孩童。在森林中,有永恒的青春。在上帝的庄园里,气派和圣洁是主宰,四季的庆典准备就绪,客人们居此千年也不会厌倦。在森林里,我们回归理性和信仰,在那里,任何不幸不会降临于我的生命,没有任何屈辱和灾病——请留下我的双眼——是自然无法平复的。站在空旷大地之上,我的头脑沐浴于欢欣大气并升腾于无限空间,一切卑劣的自高自大和自我中心消失无踪。我变成一个透明的眼球,我化为乌有,我却遍览一切;宇宙精神的湍流环绕激荡着我。我成为上帝的一部分,我是他的微粒。密友的名字听起来陌生而无足轻重,兄弟或朋友,主人或仆从,这一切变得细碎而搅扰。我是不受拘束、永恒不朽自然之美的情人。与街市和村庄相比,在旷野里,我体味到更亲切更可贵的实在。在静谧的风景里,尤其是在那遥远的地平线,我们看到自然美丽,有如美丽自身和本性。

田野和树林带给我们心灵的巨大欢悦,指说着人类和植物的隐秘关联。我并非独在而不受关注,植物向我颔首,我向它们点头。风雨中树枝摇动对我是既新鲜又熟稔。它令我惊异又让我安然。它们对于我的影响,就如同我确信自我思维妥帖所为正当时,全身涌起的超越而高尚的感情。

然而,可以肯定地说,这欢悦的力量不仅源于自然本身,它存在于人,或者说,存在于自然和人的和谐中。要谨慎节制地享有这种欢悦,这很重要。自然并不总悦人以节日盛装,昨日氤氲芬芳晶亮悦目一如为林仙嬉乐而设的同一景致,今天就可能蒙上悲伤的面纱。自然总是折射着观者的精神状态。对于在病痛中挣扎的人,他自身散发的焦虑挣扎就蕴涵着悲伤。当爱友逝去时,人们会对那风景感到些许漠然。当蓝天落幕于社会底层者眼前,它的壮丽也会减色。

(雨树 译)

注释

1. cordial['kɔrdʒəl] *n.* 兴奋剂,兴奋性饮料 *adj.* 热忱的,诚恳的,兴奋的
2. puddle['pʌdl] *n.* 水坑,胶土,污水坑
3. exhilaration[iɡˌziləˈreʃən] *n.* 令人高兴,愉快

4. sanctity['sæŋktiti] *n.* 圣洁
5. perennial[pə'reniəl] *adj.* 四季不断的，终年的，长期的，永久的，(植物)多年生的
6. calamity[kə'læmiti] *n.* 灾难，不幸事件
7. blithe[blaið, blaiθ] *adj.* 愉快的，高兴的
8. transparent[træns'pærənt, -'pær-] *adj.* 透明的，显然的，明晰的
9. connate['kɔneit, kɔ'net] *adj.* 天生的，先天的，同族的
10. frolic['frɔlik] *n.* 嬉闹 *vi.* 嬉戏 *adj.* 嬉戏的，欢乐的
11. nymph[nimf] *n.* [希腊神话][罗马神话]居于山林水泽的仙女，美丽的少女
12. melancholy['melənkɔli] *n.* 忧郁 *adj.* 忧郁的

赏析

拉尔夫·瓦尔多·爱默生 (Ralph Waldo Emerson, 1803—1882)美国散文作家、思想家、文学家、诗人。1803年5月25日出生于马萨诸塞州波士顿附近的康考德村，1882年4月27日在波士顿逝世。他的生命几乎横贯19世纪的美国，他出生时候的美国热闹却混沌，一些人意识到它代表着某种新力量的崛起，却无人能够清晰地表达出来。它此时缺乏统一的政体，更没有相对一致的意识形态。在他去世的时候美国不但因为南北战争而统一，而且它的个性逐渐鲜明起来，除了物质力量引人注目，它的文化也正在竭力走出欧洲的阴影。1837年爱默生以《美国学者》为题发表了一篇著名的演讲词，宣告美国文学已脱离英国文学而独立，告诫美国学者不要让学究习气蔓延，不要盲目地追随传统，不要进行纯粹的模仿。另外，这篇演讲词还抨击了美国社会的拜金主义，强调人的价值。被誉为美国思想文化领域的“独立宣言”。一年之后，爱默生在《神学院献辞》中批评了基督教唯一神教派死气沉沉的局面，竭力推崇人的至高无上，提倡靠直觉认识真理。“相信你自己的思想，相信你内心深处认为对你合适的东西对一切人都适用……”文学批评家劳伦斯·布尔在《爱默生传》所说，爱默生与他的学说，是美国最重要的世俗宗教。

本文节选自爱默生的代表作《论自然》。爱默生被公认为19世纪美国超验主义运动的主要代言人，他在《论自然》中全面深刻地诠释了他的超验主义自然观，被称为“新英格兰超验主义的宣言”。爱默生的超验主义在美国文学史上的地位是独特的，其直接在文学上产生了浪漫主义文学。爱默生认为，自然界是由自然和精神组成的。自然总是披着精神的色彩。自然不仅带给人愉悦，它对人类还有许多实用价值，但它并非为了人类开发利用的目的而存在，它不会成为任何人的财产。爱默生指出，任何企图扰乱自然和它的要素之间的联系的做法都是徒劳与无知的。此外，自然的美是不为人所过度追寻的，也不应将其中的任何个体要素与其整个环境分开来看。否则，自然中内在的美就会丧失。爱默生，一生渴望像自然一样，

不断创造，不断成长，永不停滞。他的每一部作品都在具体层面上表达了他的哲学和他不断蜕变的思想。而他关于人、自然与上帝的关系的哲学思考，成为了他超验主义思想的精髓。

原文

7 Solitude

Henry David Thoreau

I find it wholesome to be alone the greater part of the time. Being in company, even with the best, is soon **wearisome** and **dissipating**. I love to be alone. I have never found a companion that was so companionable as solitude. We are for the most part lonelier when we go abroad among men than when we stay in our chambers. A man thinking or working is always alone, let him be where he will. Solitude is not measured by the miles of space that intervene between a man and his fellows men. The really diligent student in one of the crowed hives of Cambridge College is as solitary as a **dervish** in the desert. The farmer can work alone in the field or the woods all day, hoeing or chopping, and not feel lonesome, because he is employed; but when he comes home at night, he cannot sit down in a room alone, at the mercy of his thoughts, but must be where he can "see the folks" he thinks, **remunerate** himself for his day's solitude; and hence he wonders how the student can sit alone in the house all night and most of the day without ennui and "the blues"; but he does not realize that the student, though in the house, is still at work in his field, and chopping in his woods, as the farmer in his, and in turn seeks the same recreation and society that the latter does, though it may be a more condensed form of it.

Society is commonly too cheap. We meet at very short intervals, not having had time to acquire any new value for each other. We meet at meals three times a day, and give each other a new taste of that old musty cheese that we are. We have had to agree on a certain set of rules, called **etiquette** and politeness, to make this frequent meeting tolerable and that we need not come to open war. We meet at the post - office, and at the sociable, and about the fireside every night; we live thick and are in each other's way, and stumble over one another, and I think that we thus lose some respect for one another. Certainly less frequency would suffice for all important and hearty communications. Consider the girls in a factory - never alone, hardly in their dreams. It would be better if there were but one inhabitant to a square mile, as where I live. The value of a man is not in his skin, that we should touch him.

I have a great deal of company in my house; especially in the morning, when nobody calls. Let me suggest a few comparisons, that some one may convey an idea of my situation. I am no more lonely than the loon in the pond that laughs so loud, or than **Walden Pond** itself. What company has that lonely lake, I pray?

And yet it has not the blue devils, but the blue angels in it, **in the azure tint of its waters**. The sun is alone, except in thick weather, when there sometimes appear to be two, but one is a **mock sun**. God is alone — but the devil, he is far from being alone; he sees a great deal of company; he is **legion**. I am no more lonely than a single **mullein** or **dandelion** in a pasture, or a bean leaf, or sorrel, or a horse-fly, or a bumblebee. I am no more lonely than the **Millbrook**, or a weathercock, or the north star, or the south wind, or an April shower, or a January thaw, or the first spider in a new house.

译文

7 独 居

H. D. 梭罗

我发现人若大部分时间用于独处，将有益身心。与人为伴，即使是挚友，也很快会有厌烦或虚度光阴的感觉。我爱独处，我发现没有比独处更好的伴侣了。出国，身在熙攘人群中，要比退守陋室更让人寂寞。心有所想，身有所系的人总是孤身一人，不论他身处何地。独处与否也不是由人与人之间的距离来确定。在剑桥苦读的学子虽身处蜂巢般拥挤的教室，实际上却和沙漠中的苦行僧一样，是在独处。农人终日耕于田间，伐于山野，此时他虽孤单但并不寂寞，因他专心于工作；但待到他日暮而息，却未必能忍受形影相吊，空有思绪做伴的时光，他必到“可以看见大伙儿”的去处去找乐子，如他所认为的那样以补偿白日里的孤独；因此他无法理解学子如何能竟夜终日独坐而不心生厌倦或倍感凄凉；然而他没意识到，学子虽身在学堂，但心系劳作，但是耕于心田，伐于学林，这正和农人一样，学子在寻求的无非是和他一样的快乐与陪伴，只是形式更简洁罢了。

与人交往通常都因唾手可得而毫无价值，在频繁的相处中，我们无暇从彼此获取新价值。我们每日三餐相聚，反复让彼此重新审视的也是依旧故我，并无新奇之处。为此我们要循规蹈矩，称其为懂礼仪，讲礼貌，以便在这些频繁的接触中相安无事，无须论战而有辱斯文。我们相遇在邮局，邂逅在社交场所，围坐在夜晚的炉火旁，交情甚笃，彼此干扰着，纠缠着；实际上我认为这样我们都或多或少失去了对彼此的尊重。对于所有重要的倾心交流，相见不必过频。想想工厂里的女孩，她们虽从不落单，但也少有梦想。像这样方圆一英里仅一人居住，那情况会更好。人的价值非在肌肤相亲，而在心有灵犀。

我的房子里有很多伙伴，尤其在无人造访的清晨。我把自己和周围事物对比一下，你或许能窥见我生活的一斑。比起那湖中长笑的潜鸟，还有那湖，我并不比它们孤独多少。你看：这孤单的湖又何以为伴呢？

然而它那一湾天蓝的湖水里有的却是天使的纯净，而非魔鬼的忧郁。太阳是孤独的，虽然时而在阴郁的天气里会出现两个太阳，但其中之一为幻日；上帝是孤独的，魔鬼才从不孤单，他永远不乏伙伴，因为从他者甚众。比起牧场上的一朵毛蕊花，一枝蒲公英，一片豆叶，一束酢浆草，一只牛虻或大黄蜂来，我并不孤单多少；比起密尔溪、风标、北极星、南风、四月春雨、正月融雪，或者新房中的第一只蜘蛛，我也并不更加孤单。

注释

1. wearisome[ˈwirisəm] *adj.* 令人疲乏的，令人厌烦的
2. dissipating[ˈdisəˌpetiŋ] *v.* 驱散，消失（dissipate的现在分词）；浪费
3. dervish[ˈdə:viʃ] *n.*（伊斯兰教的）托钵僧，（伊斯兰教的）苦修僧人
4. remunerate[riˈmjunəˌret] *vt.* 酬劳
5. etiquette[ˈetiˌket, -kit] *n.* 礼仪，礼节；规矩；礼数
6. Walden Pond: 马萨诸塞州的康科德城瓦尔登湖
7. in the azure tint of its waters: 一湾天蓝的湖水里
8. mock sun[mɔk sʌn] *n.* 幻日，假日
9. legion[ˈlidʒən] *n.* 大批部队；众多，大量；古罗马军团 *adj.* 众多的；大量的
10. mullein[ˈmʌlən] *n.* 毛蕊花属的植物
11. dandelion[ˈdændilaiən] *n.* ［植］蒲公英
12. Millbrook: ［地名］［爱尔兰、加拿大、美国、英国］米尔布鲁克，此处译为美国的密尔溪。

赏析

H. D. 梭罗（Henry David Thoreau，1817—1862）。19世纪美国最具有世界影响力的作家、哲学家。梭罗在生前只出版过两本书，第一本是他在1849年自费出版的《康科德河和梅里麦克河上的一星期》，第二本就是《瓦尔登湖》了，于1854年出版，150年来风行天下，不知出版了多少个版本。他投入数十载的时间对野生果实、野草及森林演替进行观察研究，写出了《种子的信念》一书，但直到梭罗逝世150多年后，耗费他数十年心血的此书才得以出版。

他的著作都是根据他在大自然中的体验写成的。《独居》选自他的代表作《瓦尔登湖》，该书记录了他在康科德附近瓦尔登湖畔度过的一段隐居生活。在他的笔下，自然、人以及超验主义理想交融汇合。他提倡返璞归真，反对奢华虚荣，反对追求物质享受。他强调亲近自然、学习自然、热爱自然，追求“简单些，再简单些”的质朴生活，提倡短暂人生因思想丰盈而臻于完美。

原文

8 If I Rest, I Rust

Orison Marden

The significant **inscription** found on an old key — "If I rest, I rust" — would be an excellent motto for those who **are afflicted with** the slightest bit of idleness. Even the most **industrious** person might adopt it **with advantage to** serve as a reminder that, if one allows his faculties to rest, like the iron in the unused key, they will soon show signs of rust and, ultimately, cannot do the work required of them.

Those who would attain the heights reached and kept by great men must keep their faculties polished by constant use, so that they may unlock the doors of knowledge, the gate that guard the entrances to the professions, to science, art, literature, agriculture — every department of human endeavor.

Industry keeps bright the key that opens the treasury of achievement. If Hugh Miller, after toiling all day in a quarry, had devoted his evenings to rest and recreation, he would never have become a famous geologist. The **celebrated** mathematician, Edmund Stone, would never have published a mathematical dictionary, never have found the key to science of mathematics, if he had given his spare moments to idleness, had the little Scotch lad, Ferguson, allowed the busy brain to go to sleep while he tended sheep on the hillside instead of calculating the position of the stars by a string of beads, he would never have become a famous astronomer.

Labor **vanquishes** all, — not inconstant, spasmodic, or ill — directed labor; but faithful, **unremitting**, daily effort toward a well-directed purpose. **Just as** truly **as** eternal **vigilance** is the price of liberty, so is eternal industry the price of noble and enduring success.

译文

8 如果我休息，我就会生锈

奥里森·马登

在一把旧钥匙上发现了一则意义深远的铭文——如果我休息，我就会生锈。对于那些懒散而烦恼的人来说，这将是至理名言。甚至最为勤勉的人也以此作为警示：如果一个人有才能而不用，就像废弃钥匙上的铁一样，这些才能就会很快生锈，并最终无法完成安排给自己的工作。

有些人想取得伟人所获得并保持的成就，他们就必须不断运用自身的才能，以便开启知识的大门，即那些通往人类努力探求的各个领域的大门，这些领域包括各种职业：科学、艺术、文学、农业等。

勤奋使开启成功宝库的钥匙保持光亮。如果休·米勒在采石场劳作一天后，晚上的时光用来休息消遣的话，他就不会成为名垂青史的地质学家。著名数学家爱德蒙·斯通如果闲暇时无所事事，就不会出版数学词典，也不会发现开启数学之门的钥匙。如果苏格兰青年弗格森在山坡上放羊时，让他那思维活跃的大脑处于休息状态，而不是借助一串珠子计算星星的位置，他就不会成为著名的天文学家。

劳动征服一切。这里所指的劳动不是断断续续的、间歇性的或方向偏差的劳动，而是坚定的、不懈的、方向正确的每日劳动。正如要想拥有自由就要时刻保持警惕一样，要想取得伟大的、持久的成功，就必须坚持不懈地努力。

注释

1. inscription[in'skripʃən] *n.* the mark of a surface in written words.（作者）题词；献词；碑文
2. be afflicted with: to cause to suffer in body or mind. 折磨，使痛苦
3. industrious[in'dʌstriəs] *adj.* hardworking 勤劳的，勤奋的 ◆industry的同词根词汇。
4. with advantage to: 优点，优势
5. celebrated['seləˌbretid] *adj.* 有名的，著名的
6. vanquish['væŋkwiʃ, 'væn-] *vt.* conquer and defeat. 征服；战胜
7. unremitting[ˌʌnri'mitiŋ] *adj.* never stopping 不懈的；始终不懈；坚持不懈
8. just as...as...: 关联连接词，引起类比句式
9. vigilance['vidʒələns] *n.* 警觉；警惕

赏析

奥里森·马登（Orison Marden ,1848—1924），美国成功学的奠基人和最伟大的成功励志导师，成功学之父。《成功》杂志的创办人，如今《成功》杂志在美国无人不晓，它通过创造性地传播成功学改变了无数美国人的命运，致力于马登尚未完成的事业：把个人成功学传授给每一个想出人头地的年轻人。他撰写了大量鼓舞人心的著作，包括《做最好的自己》（*Be Good To Yourself*）、《获得你想得到的一切》（*How to Get What You Want*）、《正确思考的奇迹》（*The Miracle of:Right Thought*）、《获得杰出的人生》（*Making Life A Masterpiece*）、《给青年人读的故事》（*Stories from Life ;a Book for Young People*）、《性格决定一切》（*Character: The Grandest Thing of All*）、《获得成功的秘诀》（*How to Succeed:*

stepping Stones to Fame & Fortune)等。林语堂先生曾向人们推荐他的书:“对于时代青年所经验的烦闷、消极等等滋味,我亦未曾错过……希望他们从马登的书中,能获得(与我)同样的兴奋影响。”美国第25任总统威廉姆·麦金莱曾说:“马登的书对所有具有高尚和远大抱负的年轻读者都是一个巨大的鼓舞。马登的著作和他所倡导的成功原则改变了世界各地千百万贫苦人民的命运,使他们由一贫如洗变为百万富翁,从无名之辈变为社会名流。”

这是一篇富有哲理的小品文。作者通过一句铭文,告诫世人勤奋可以创造一切。生而为赢(*Born to Win*),是生命赋予我们的一种力量。我们每个人期待生命的华丽转身,我们拒绝平凡的人生过于平庸,我们写下“雨后的铅华是展翅待飞的蝶”,但千万别让生活在疲于奔命中过于匆忙,忽略了美丽的风景和难忘的感动。“生”是前行的状态,平和从容。“赢”是追求的真谛,尽力而为。“生而为赢”不是简单的刻意的名利追逐,它是一种对生命殷实而虔诚的顶礼膜拜。因为生命的内涵是伟大的,真正的成败取决于我们的心态而非外在的表现形式。生而为赢的人生第一条法则:勤奋!

作者善于抓住哲理闪光的瞬间,形诸笔墨,写就内涵丰厚、耐人寻味的美文。时常吟咏这类美文,自然能在潜移默化中受到启迪和熏陶,洗礼和升华,这种内化作用无疑是巨大的。

原文

9 Self-Mastery

Orison Marden

“Ah! Diamond, you little know the mishchief you have wrought,” said Sir Issac Newton, returning from supper to find that his dog had upset a lighted taper upon the laborious calculations of years, which lay in ashes before him. Then he went calmly to work to reproduce them. The man who thus excelled in self-mastery surpassed all his predecessors and contemporaries in mastering the laws of nature.

“The first and best of victories,” says **Plato**, “is for a man to conquer himself; to be conquered by himself is, of all things, the most shameful and vile.”

Self-control is at the root of all the virtues. **Let** a man yield to his impulses and passions, and from that moment he gives up his moral freedom.

Have you a hot, passionate temper? If so, a moment's outbreak, like a rat-hole in a dam, may flood all the work of years. One angry word sometimes raises a storm that time itself cannot **allay**. A single angry word has lost many a friend.

When **Socrates** found in himself any **disposition** to anger, he would check it by speaking low, in opposition to the motions of his displeasure. If you are conscious of being in a passion, keep your mouth shut, lest you increase it. Many a person has dropped dead in a rage. Fits of anger bring fits of disease. "Whom the gods would destroy they first make mad." "Keep cool," says Webster, "anger is not argument." "Be calm in arguing," says **George Herbert**, "for fierceness makes error a fault, and truth discourtesy."

To be angry with a weak man is to prove that you are not strong yourself. "Anger," says **Pythagoras**, "begins with folly and ends with repentance." You must measure the strength of a man by the power of the feelings he subdues, not by the power of those which subdue him.

Did you ever see a man receive a flagrant insult, and only grow a little pale, bite his quivering lip, and then reply quietly? Did you ever see a man in **anguish** stand as if carved out of solid rock, mastering himself? Have you not seen one bearing a hopeless daily trial remain silent and never tell the world what cankered his home peace? That is strength. "He who, with strong passions, remains chaste; he who, keenly sensitive, with manly power of indignation in him, can be provoked, and yet restrain himself and forgive, — these are strong men, the spiritual heroes."

Self-conquest is man's last and greatest victory.

If a man lacks self-control he seems to lack everything. Without it he can have no patience, no power to govern himself; he can have no self-reliance, for he will always be **at the mercy of** his strongest passion. If he lacks self-control, the very backbone, pith, and nervc of character are lacking also.

Many persons are **intemperate** in their feelings; they are emotionally **prodigal**. Passion is intemperance; so is caprice. There is an intemperance even in melancholy and mirth. The temperate man is not mastered by his moods; he will not be driven or enticed into excess; his steadfast will conquers **despondency**, and is not unbalanced by **transient exhilarations**, for **ecstasy** is as fatal as despair. Temper is subjected to reason and conscience. How many people excuse themselves for doing wrong or foolish acts by the plea that they have a quick temper. But he who is king of himself rules his temper, turning its very heat and passion into energy that works good instead of evil. **Stephen Girard**, when he heard of a clerk with a strong temper, was glad to employ him. He believed that such persons, taught self-control, were the best workers. Controlled temper is an element of strength; wisely regulated, it expends itself as energy in work, just as heat in an engine is transmuted into force that drives the wheels of industry.

译文

9 自我克制

奥里森·马登

"啊！金刚钻儿，你一点不知道你闯下的大祸，"艾萨克·牛顿爵士说。他晚饭后回来发现他的狗把点亮着的蜡烛翻倒在他多年艰苦计算的结果上，这些计算已在他面前化为灰烬。接着,他平静地重新着手计算。这位如此擅长自我克制的人在掌握自然法则上超过了所有的前辈和同时代的人。

柏拉图说:“就一个人而论,最重要与最大的胜利是征服自己,最可耻、最卑鄙的莫过于被自己的私欲所征服。”

自制是一切美德之本。假定一个人屈服于冲动和激情,他就是从那一刻起抛弃了道德上的自主。

你有火爆易怒的脾气吗?如果有的话,片刻的发作无异于“千里之堤,溃于蚁穴”,会冲垮长年累月完成的全部工程。有时,一句怒言会掀起一场经久不息的风波。仅只一句怒言就会失掉好多朋友。

苏格拉底发觉自己要发怒时,总是以降低声调来抑制怒火,阻止不愉快情绪的发展。如果你意识到你情绪激动,就保持缄默,免得怒火越烧越旺。不少人盛怒之下一命呜呼。阵阵愤怒招来疾病的频频发作。“神要毁灭谁,先使他疯狂。”韦伯斯特说,“要保持冷静,愤怒不等于争辩。”乔治·赫伯特说:“辩论时要心平气和,因为狂怒使谬误铸成大错,使真理变成无礼。”

对弱者发怒只证明你绝非强者。毕达哥拉斯说:“愤怒始于愚蠢,终于懊悔。”你应该以一个人抑制感情的能力作为衡量一个人力量的尺度,而不要以其感情用事来衡量。

你可曾见过受到公然侮辱,却只是脸色变得稍微苍白,咬紧颤抖的嘴唇,然后安详作答的人吗?你可曾见过精神上极度痛苦,却好像坚石凿出的雕像一样耸立着,控制着自己的人吗?难道你没有见过这样的人:天天忍受着绝望的折磨,仍然保持沉默不语,从不对人说有人毁坏了他的家庭宁静?这就是力量。“他满怀激情却依然洁身自好;他特别敏感,具有男子气概的愤怒力量,若是受人挑衅,也能严于律己,宽以恕人——他们是强者,是精神境界的英雄。”

自我克制是人类最后、最伟大的胜利。

如果一个人缺乏自制,他就似乎缺乏了一切。没有自制就不可能有耐心,就不可能有律己的力量;因为他总是受最强烈激情的摆布,就不可能特立独行。如果他缺乏自制,他也就没有那宝贵的骨气、精力和胆识的品质。

许多人对感情没有节制,他们纵情放荡。热情无节制,任性也无节制,甚至忧郁和欢乐皆无度。有节制的人不为情绪所左右,他不会失之过甚,他坚定的意志战胜沮丧,不为片刻的欢乐使精神失去平衡,因为狂喜与绝望同样是不幸的。脾气应服从理性和良知。有多少人以脾气急躁为借口,原谅自己做了错事或蠢事。但是主宰自己的人控制脾气,把强烈的热情变为做善事而不做恶事的能力。斯蒂芬·吉拉德听说一位办事员脾气大,便乐于雇用他。吉拉德相信只要教育这样的人自制,他们准会成为最好的工作者。控制好了的脾气是力量的要素;予以合理地使用的就会成为工作的能量,正如蒸汽机的热力转变成推动工业车轮的力量一样。

(胡君倩　译)

注释

1. Plato['pleitəu]柏拉图(427BC— 347BC),古希腊哲学家,著有30多篇对话和书信等。

2. let: 假定;假设(用于论述数学或哲学问题的祈使句中。如:Let AB be equal to CD. 设AB等于CD)。

3. allay [ə'lei] *vt.* make less减轻;缓和

4. Socrates: 苏格拉底 (469 BC—399 BC),古希腊哲学家,本人无著作,其学说仅见于他的学生柏拉图和色诺芬的著作。

5. disposition [ˌdispə'ziʃn] *n.* 倾向;性情

6. George Herbert: 乔治·赫伯特(1593—1633),英国玄学派宗教诗人,诗作有《圣殿:圣诗及抒怀》等。

7. Pythagoras: 毕达哥拉斯(580? BC—500? BC),古希腊哲学家、数学家,著作已失传。

8. anguish ['æŋgwiʃ] *n.* (精神上的)极度痛苦;悲痛

9. at the mercy of: under the control of 任凭……的摆布

10. Intemperate [in'tempərit, - prit] *adj.* showing lack of self- control 无节制的;放纵的

11. prodigal ['prɔdigəl] *adj.* extravagant 挥霍的

12. despondency [di'spɔndənsi] *n.* loss of hope 沮丧,失望

13. transient ['trænʃənt, - ʒənt, - ziənt] *adj.* lasting for only a short time 片刻的;瞬间的

14. exhilaration [igˌzilə'reʃn] *n.* 愉快的心情,兴奋;高兴

15. ecstasy ['ekstəsi] *n.* great joy or happiness 狂喜;狂欢

16. Stephen Girard: 斯蒂芬·吉拉德 (1750—1831),美国金融家,慈善家。

赏析

这是一篇能够帮助你充分挖掘自身潜能、推动你开启智慧和勇气之门、引导你踏上快乐和幸福人生之旅的心理励志的文章。成功的资本不是与生俱来的,而是后天修炼而得的。只要用少许的时间学习,积极借鉴成功的经验,了解某些简单的人生法则,你便会受益一生,轻松地达成各种目标。

奥里森·马登认为,习惯每时每刻都在影响着我们的生活,要学会通过自我控制改变不良习惯,一定要养成控制情绪的好习惯,改掉缺乏自制的坏毛病,别让不成功的情绪管理成为你成功路上的绊脚石。积极向上的心态是成功者的一大资本,每一个人都有改变人生的潜在能力,要有效地改变自我,首先必须改变观念,要不断地暗示自己一定会成功,通过积极的自我暗示提升自

我形象。一定要敢于满怀信心地向自己挑战，面对困难要持敢于拼搏的态度，把你的能量放在你所想要得到的事物上。让“稳操胜券的心理”助你成功。

正如文中所说：“自我克制是人类最后、最伟大的胜利。”

原文

10 My Wonderful **Lousy** Poem

Budd Schulberg

When I was eight or nine years old, I wrote my first poem.

At that time my father was head of **Paramount Studios**. My mother was involved in various intellectual projects.

My mother read the little poem and began to cry. “Buddy, you didn’t really write this beautiful, beautiful poem!”

Shyly, proudbursting, I **stammered** that I had. She poured out her praise. Why, this poem was nothing short of genius!

I glowed. “What time will Father be home?”I asked. I could hardly wait to show him.

I spent **the best part of that afternoon** preparing for his arrival. First, I wrote the poem out in my **finest flourish**. Then I **crayoned** an elaborate border around it that would so justice to its brilliant content. As seven o’clock drew near, I confidently placed it on my father’s plate on the dining-room table.

But my father did not return at seven. Seven-fifteen. Seven-thirty. I could hardly stand the **suspense**. I admired my father. He had begun his motion-picture career as a writer. He would be able to appreciate this wonderful poem of mine even more than my mother.

This evening when my father burst in, his mood seemed even more thunderous than usual. An hour late for dinner, he could not sit down but circled the long dining-room table with a drink in his hand, calling down terrible **oaths** on his employees.

He wheeled in his pacing, paused and glared at his plate. There was a suspenseful silence. “What is this? ” He was reaching for my poem.

I kept my face lowered to my plate as he read that poem. It was only ten lines. But it seemed to take hours. I remember wondering why it was taking so long. I could hear my father breathing. Then I could hear him dropping the poem back on the table. Now came the moment of decision.

“I think it’s lousy, ” he said.

I couldn’t look up. My eyes were getting wet.

“Ben, sometimes I don’t understand you,”my mother was saying, “This is just a little boy.

These are the first lines of poetry he's ever written. He needs encouragement."

"I don't know why. "My father **held his ground**."Isn't there enough lousy poetry in the world already? No law says Buddy has to become a poet."

They quarreled over it. I couldn't stand it another second. I ran from the dining room bawling. Up in my room I threw myself on the bed and sobbed.

That may have been the end of the anecdote, but not of its significance for me. Inevitably the family wounds healed.

A few years later I took a second look at that first poem; It was a pretty lousy poem. After a while, I walked up the courage to show him something new, a short story. My father thought it was overwritten but not hopeless. I was learning to rewrite. And my mother was learning that she could criticize me without crushing me. You might say we were all learning. I was going on 12.

But it wasn't until years later that the true meaning of that painful "first poem" experience dawned on me. As I became a professional writer, it became clearer and clearer to me how fortunate I had been. I had a mother who said, "Buddy, did you really write this? I think it's wonderful!" and a father who shook his head no and drove me to hear with "I think it's lousy".

A writer — in fact every one of us in life — needs that loving force from which all creation flows. Yet alone that force is incomplete, even misleading, balance of the force that cautions, "Watch. Listen. Review. Improve."

Sometimes you find these opposing forces in associates friends, loved ones. But finally you must balance these opposites within yourself; first, the confidence to go forward, to do, to become; second, the tempering of self - approval with hard - headed, realistic **self-appraisal**.

译文

10　我美妙而糟糕的诗

巴德·舒尔伯格

八九岁时候，我写出了生平第一首诗。那时，父亲是派拉蒙影片公司的负责人，母亲从事文化工作。母亲读了这首小诗后激动得哭了，"巴德，难道真是你写出这么漂亮的诗？"我结结巴巴承认是我的作品。母亲的赞誉接踵而来："噢，这首诗真是天才的杰作。"

我喜形于色。"爸爸什么时候回家呢？"我已是迫不及待地要给他看。

那天下午大半的时间我都在等父亲回家。我先用自己所能书写的最好的花体字把诗重抄了一遍，然后用蜡笔给它加了些精美的花边，让它配得上精彩的诗句内容。快到七点时，我自信地把它放在餐桌上父亲的餐碟里。

我崇拜父亲，他进入电影行业时是剧本作者，他也许会比母亲更能欣赏我的诗。

那天晚上当父亲冲进门时，脾气比平时要糟。虽然已经过了晚餐时间一小时，可他仍没有坐下来,而是拿着酒杯绕着长餐桌转,嘴里叨念着他的雇员。

突然,他转过脚步,停下来盯着餐碟。我的心悬了起来。"这是什么?"父亲拿起我的诗。他读诗时,我低头对着餐碟,那仅只有十行的诗,可好像花费了几个小时,我奇怪他为什么花了这么长时间。我几乎能听到父亲的呼吸声,然后我听到他把诗放回桌上。这时父亲开始评价了。

"我想这首诗很糟。"他说。

我不敢抬头。我的眼睛湿润了。

"本,我有时真不理解你。"母亲说,"他只是个孩子,这是他写的第一首诗。他需要鼓励。"

"我不知道为什么。"父亲坚持他的立场,"这个世界上难道糟糕的诗还不够多吗?没谁说巴德非得做个诗人。"

他们为此而争吵起来。我一秒钟也待不下去了,哭着冲出厨房,跑进房间,一头埋到床上,蒙头抽泣。

作为我人生中的一件轶事,它就这样结束了,但它对于我的重要意义却未结束。

几年后,我又重拾起当年的第一首诗,它的确很糟。过了些时候,我鼓起勇气,决定给父亲看自己的新作品,一篇短篇小说。父亲认为词语过于堆砌,但并非一无是处。于是我不断修改。我母亲也知道她的批评不会压垮我了。你不妨认为我们全家都在学习,这种情形持续到我12岁。

直到多年后,我才明白那首尴尬处女作的真正意义所在。当我成为一名职业作家时,我越来越庆幸那时我多么幸运。我有一位母亲,她说:"巴德,这真是你写的吗?我认为它棒极了!"还有一位父亲,他摇头说不,"我看它糟透了,"这句话弄得我流泪。

一位作家——实际上我们生活中的每个人——都需要爱的力量,它也是创造的动力所在。但仅有这一力量是不够的,有时会误导;这就需要另一种力量来提醒人们:"观察、倾听、总结、提高。"

有时你会在同事、朋友、爱人中发现这些抵触的力量,但最终得靠自己来平衡:第一,要有前进、去做、去取得成就的信心;第二,用冷静的头脑客观、现实地自我评价,克服自满情绪。

(姚军　译)

注释

1. lousy['lauzi] *adj.* 讨厌的;糟糕的

2. Paramount Studios: 派拉蒙电影公司

3. stammer['stæmə] *vt. & vi.* 结巴地说出;口吃

4. the best part of the afternoon: 意为下午大半的时间,并非下午最美的时间。best还有"大半的、最多的"意思,词性为形容词。

5. finest flourish: 花体字

6. crayon['kreiən, -ən] *vt.* & *vi.*用彩色蜡笔[粉笔]画

7. suspense[sə'spens] *n.* 挂念;悬念

8. oaths[əuθs] *n.* 誓言(oath的名词复数);誓约;咒骂;诅咒语

9. held his ground: 坚持立场

10. self-appraisal[self-ə'prezəl] *n.*自我评估

赏析

巴德·舒尔伯格(Budd Schulberg,1914—2009),美国著名的编剧、畅销书作家。在他68年的写作生涯里,共创作了34部作品,其中13部被拍成电影或搬上舞台。所出版的作品有《在滨水区》《码头风云》《什么使萨米逃走》《醒着的梦》《聪明的糊涂和糊涂的聪明》《我喜欢这个不讨人喜欢的人》等。作为知名的作家,由他担任编剧的好莱坞影片《码头风云》最为人知晓,该片的领衔主演是马龙·白兰度。

巴德·舒尔伯格,1914年3月27日生于美国纽约, 其父亲是派拉蒙影片公司的老板本杰明·斯楚伯格。母亲是左翼作家。他生长在文化气氛浓郁的富有家庭,自小喜欢写诗。他记得,在他八岁那年,写完第一首诗让父母评分时,他父亲却说:"糟糕透了!"母亲则说:"精彩极了!""他们教会了我,不能因为别人的否定而丧失勇气;也不能因为别人的赞扬,而自我陶醉。"这个故事,就以第一人称写在《我美妙而糟糕的诗》里面。"我"以一位成年人的眼光看待孩童时发生的一件小事,岁月荏苒,时光改变了当初他对父亲的看法,并从中得到新的领悟。人生的第一步需要有人正确的引导,父母至关重要。

第二章　名诗精选

原文

1　Sonnet 18

William Shakespeare

Shall I compare thee to a summer's day?
Thou art more lovely and more temperate:
Rough winds do shake the darling **buds of May**,
And summer's **lease** hath all too short a date;
Sometime too hot the **eye of heaven** shines
And often is **his gold complexion dimm'd**;
And every **fair** form **fair** sometimes declines,
By chance or nature's changing course untrimm'd;
But thy **eternal summer** shall not fade,
Nor lose possession of that fair thou **ow'st**;
Nor shall death brag thou wander'st in his shade.
When in eternal lines to time thou grow'st:
So long as men can breathe, or eyes can see,
So long lives this, and this gives life to thee.

译文

1　十四行诗(其十八)

威廉·莎士比亚

我可能把你和夏天相比拟？
你比夏天更可爱更温和：
狂风会把五月的花苞吹落地，

夏天也嫌太短促，匆匆而过：
有时太阳照得太热，
常常又遮暗他的金色的脸；
美的事物总不免要凋落，
偶然的，或是随自然变化而流转。
但是你的永恒之夏不会褪色；
你不会失去你的俊美的仪容；
死神不能夸说你在他的阴影里面走着，
如果你在这不朽的诗句里获得了永生；
只要人们能呼吸，眼睛能看东西，
此诗就会不朽，使你永久生存下去。

（梁实秋 译）

注释

1. rough winds: 狂风、恶风
2. buds of May: 五月的花蕊
3. lease[lis] *n.* 租约；租契；租赁物 ◆此处指期限，与后面的date意思相同。
4. sometime: sometimes, occasionally
5. the eye of heaven: the sun
6. his gold complexion: 太阳神阿波罗的金色面容
7. 第一个fair指beautiful person（美人），第二个fair指beauty（美）
8. eternal summer: 永恒的美
9. ow'st: you own.

赏析

威廉·莎士比亚（William Shakespeare，1564—1616），英国文艺复兴时期杰出的戏剧家和诗人，代表作有四大悲剧《哈姆雷特》《奥赛罗》《李尔王》《麦克白》，喜剧《威尼斯商人》《无事生非》等。还写过154首十四行诗，3首或4首长诗。他是“英国戏剧之父”，英国文艺复兴时期伟大的戏剧家和诗人。

*Sonnet 18*是莎士比亚献给William Herbert的。William Herbert，是一位英俊的贵族青年，莎士比亚对他的喜爱超出了一般同性之间的友谊。在这首诗里，莎士比亚把友人Herbert比作夏天，用夏天的美好、短暂比喻年轻、美貌会随时间而逝，而友人Herbert的美却与诗长存，走向永恒。由此可

见,莎士比亚对Herbert的感情非同一般。莎士比亚的英语不同于现代英语,他所使用的某些单词、语法现在已不再使用，如: thee, thou相当于you, thy相当于your,thine相当于your (yours),art相当于are,hath相当于has, doth相当于does,I know not相当于I don't know, more better相当于better。

原文

2 Sonnet 73

William Shakespeare

That time of year thou mayst in me behold
When yellow leaves, or none, or few, do hang
Upon those boughs which shake against the cold,
Bare ruin'd choirs, where late the sweet birds sang.
In me thou sees the twilight of such day
As after sunset **fadeth** in the west,
Which by and by **black night** doth take away?
Death's second self, that seals up all in rest.
In me **thou see'st** the glowing of such fire
That on the ashes of his youth **doth** lie,
As the death-bed whereon it must expire
Consumed with that which it was nourish'd by.
This thou perceive, which makes thy love more strong,
To love that well, which thou must leave **ere long**.

译文

2 十四行诗(其七十三)

威廉·莎士比亚

你在我身上会看到这样的时候,
那时零落的黄叶会残挂枝头,
三两片在寒风中索索发抖,

荒凉的歌坛上不再有甜蜜的歌喉。
你在我身上会看到黄昏时候
落霞消残，渐沉入西方的天际，
夜幕迅速将它们通通带走，
恰如死神的替身将一切锁进牢囚。
你在我身上会看到这样的火焰，
它在青春的灰烬上闪烁摇头，
如安卧于临终之榻，待与
供养火种的燃料一同烧尽烧透。
看到了这一切，你的爱会更加坚贞，
爱我吧，我在世的日子已不会太久。

（辜正坤　译）

注释

1. that time of year: 深秋或初冬
2. bare ruin'd choirs: 教堂的残留物
3. fadeth:（古，第三人称单数）= fades
4. black night: 比喻死亡。
5. death's second self: 承上文时，即指black night, 这里指sleep，也　就是"死亡"。
6. thou see'st:（古，第二人称单数）= you see.
7. doth = does
8. ere long = before long 不久

赏析

这首十四行诗讲述了由于诗人的过度劳累以及身体健康状况不佳使他感觉自己的生命快接近尽头，表达了诗人对爱友之深情，同时，诗人希望年轻友人意识到他的衰老，从而加深对诗人的爱，这就是这首诗要表达的主题思想。诗中的"我"感到自己到了"老年"，不久就要和"爱友""永别"了，因此希望在"我"离开人世之前，爱友能好好地、强烈地爱着"我"。诗人首先没有直抒胸臆，而是寓情于物，借物抒情，让可见、可感的外景来表达内心的情感。此外，本诗充满了诙谐与幽默以及鲜明而不乏浪漫的意味，让读者在诗的境界里读到诗人自然流溢的今昔之感，从而得到浓厚的美的感受。

原文

3 Sonnet 138

William Shakespeare

When my love swears that she is **made of truth**
I **do believe her** though I know she lies,
That she might think me some untutor'd youth,
Unlearned in the world's **false subtleties**
Thus vainly thinking that she thinks me young
Although she knows my days are past the best,
Simply I credit her false-speaking tongue:
On both sides thus is simple truth **suppress'd.**
But wherefore says she not she is unjust?
And wherefore say not I that I am old?
O! love's best habit is in seeming trust,
And age in love, loves not to have years told:
Therefore I lie with her, and she with me,
And in our faults by **lies** we flatter'd be.

译文

3 十四行诗(其一百三十八)

威廉·莎士比亚

我爱人赌咒说她浑身是忠实，
我相信她(虽然明知她在撒谎)，
让她认为我是个无知的孩子，
不懂得世间种种骗人的勾当。
于是我就妄想她当我还年轻，
虽然明知我盛年已一去不复返；
她的油嘴滑舌我天真地信任：
这样，纯朴的真话双方都隐瞒。
但是为什么她不承认说假话？

为什么我又不承认我已经衰老？
爱的习惯是连信任也成欺诈，
老年谈恋爱最怕把年龄提到。
因此，我既欺骗她，她也欺骗我，
咱俩的爱情就在欺骗中作乐。

（辜正坤　译）

注释

1. made of truth: 即“浑身是忠实”,“made”:“maid”谐音,“made of truth”亦可理解为“maid of truth(“诚实的姑娘”)。
2. I do believe her: do为强调。
3. Simply I credit her: simply为强调。
4. false subtleties: “假精明”之意，译为“小聪明”。
5. suppress[sə'pres] *vt.* 镇压，压制
6. lie是双关语，两个意思：“撒谎”和“躺，睡”。

赏析

爱情需要信任。这首诗意味深长，诗人笔下的这对恋人各有隐痛，为了不伤害对方的感情才没有揭露真相，并努力维护现在的恋情，使其不受伤害，并得以健康顺利地发展。诗人以结尾的对偶句中使用的双关语来表明现存的欺骗是他俩爱情的体现。这样的结尾加深了意义上的回环曲折，留下了耐人寻味的余味。对于本诗，诗中注重于调侃、自嘲或淡淡的幽默。

原文

4　She Walks in Beauty

George Gordon Byron

She **walks in beauty**, like the night
Of cloudless **climes** and **starry** skies;
And all **that's best of dark and bright**
Meet in her aspect and her eyes:
Thus **mellow'd** to that tender light

Which heaven to **gaudy** day **denies**.
One shade the more, one ray the less,
Had half impair'd the nameless grace
Which waves in every **raven** tress,
Or softly **lightens** o'er her face;
Where thoughts **serenely** sweet express
How pure, how dear their dwelling-place.
And on that cheek, and o'er that brow,
So soft, so calm, yet eloquent,
The smiles that win. the tints that glow,
But tell of days in goodness spent,
A mind at peace with all below,
A heart whose love is innocent!

译文

4 她走在美的光彩中

乔治·戈登·拜伦

她走在美的光彩中,像夜晚
皎洁无云而且繁星漫天;
明与暗的最美妙的色泽
在她的仪容和秋波里呈现:
耀目的白天只嫌光太强,
它比那光亮柔和而幽暗。
增加或减少一份明与暗
就会损害这难言的美。
美波动在她乌黑的发上,
或者散布淡淡的光辉,
在那脸庞,恬静的思绪,
指明它的来处纯洁而珍贵。
呵,那额际,那鲜艳的面颊,
如此温和,平静,而又脉脉含情,
那迷人的微笑,那容颜的光彩,
都在说明一个善良的生命:
她的头脑安于世间的一切,

她的心充溢着真纯的爱情!

（查良铮 译）

注释

1. walks in beauty: 表示“步态优美”或“舞姿翩翩”。

2. clime[klaim] *n.*气候，地方，地域

3. starry['stɑ:ri] *adj.* 布满星星的

4. that's best of dark and bright: 这是一个定语从句，that's即that is。mellow'd=mellowed, mellow'd是古英语拼法，原意为“成熟”，此处为“柔和”之意。

5. mellow['meləu] *adj.* 柔和、柔软的、甜蜜的；芳醇的 ◆mellowed (to)表示“变得柔和”。

6. gaudy['ɡɔdi] *adj.* 花哨的，俗气的；华而不实的 ◆贬义

7. deny[di'nai] *vi.* 否认，拒绝，不给予

8. raven['reivən] *adj.* 乌黑的

9. lighten['laitən] [古语]闪烁；闪光；明亮

10. serenely[sə'ri:nli] *adv.* 沉着地，宁静地，安详地

赏析

乔治·戈登·拜伦(George Gordon Byron 1788—1824)，英国19世纪初期伟大的浪漫主义诗人。其代表作品有《恰尔德·哈罗德游记》《唐璜》等。在他的诗歌里塑造了一批“拜伦式英雄”。拜伦不仅是一位伟大的诗人，还是一个为理想战斗一生的勇士；他积极而勇敢地投身革命，参加了希腊民族解放运动，并成为领导人之一。

《她走在美的光彩中》是一首歌颂女性美的抒情诗，诗中的“她”是诗人表妹威尔莫特夫人(Mrs Wilmot)。诗人在一次舞会上遇到这位表妹，倾其美貌，遂成此诗。诗人在诗中极尽赞美之词，仰慕之情跃然笔端。其诗诗文流动，明快而轻柔，字字牵制着诗人和读者的感受，随着“她”的身姿倩影而移动，颇有神韵。在诗篇的末尾，诗人笔锋一转，由渲染“她”外表的美丽转向颂扬其心灵美，由表及里，深化了主题。

原文

5 When We Two Parted

George Gordon Byron

When we two parted
In silence and tears,
Half broken-hearted
To sever for years,
Pale grew thy cheek and cold,
Colder **thy** kiss;
Truly that hour foretold
Sorrow to this!
The **dew** of the morning
Sunk **chill** on my brow—
It felt like the warning
Of what I feel now.
Thy vows are all broken,
And light is thy fame:
I hear thy name spoken,
And share in its shame.
They name **thee** before me,
A **knell** to mine ear;
A **shudder** comes o'er me —
Why wert thou so dear?
They know not I knew thee
Who knew thee too well:
Long, long shall I **rue** thee,
Too deeply to tell.
In secret we met —
In silence I **grieve**,
That thy heart could forget,
Thy spirit deceive.
If I should meet thee
After long years,

How should I greet thee?
With silence and tears.

译文

5 昔日依依别

乔治·戈登·拜伦

昔日依依别，
泪流默无言；
离恨肝肠断，
此别又几年。
冷颊何惨然，
一吻寒更添；
日后伤心事，
此刻已预言。
朝起寒露重，
凛冽凝眉间——
彼时已预告：
悲伤在今天。
山盟今安在？
汝名何轻贱！
吾闻汝名传，
羞愧在人前。
闻汝名声恶，
犹如听丧钟。
不禁心怵惕——
往昔情太浓。
谁知旧日情，
斯人知太深。
绵绵长怀恨，
尽在不言中，
昔日喜幽会，
今朝恨无声。
旧情汝已忘，
疾心遇薄幸。
多年离别后，

抑或再相逢，
相逢何所语？
泪流默无声。

（隐锡麟 译）

注释

1. thy: your的古用法
2. dew[du:,dju:] *n.* 露（水）
3. chill[tʃil] *n.* 寒意、寒心
4. thee: you的古用法
5. knell[nel] *n.* 丧钟
6. shudder['ʃʌdə] *n.* 战栗、发抖
7. rue[ru:] *v.* 懊悔、悲伤
8. grieve[gri:v] *v.* 悲痛、伤心

赏析

拜伦的这首抒情诗，回忆了与爱人分别的情景和感受以及后来的心情。诗中，诗人情感真挚，毫不矫揉造作，真挚动人。整首诗读来有一种郁结之感，还有那心头久久不能散去的缱绻迷离之感，这种凄迷之情都汇聚于这首短小淡然的诗歌之中。这是拜伦在20多岁写出的最引人注目的抒情诗之一，诗中虽没有孤傲叛逆和特立独行的精神气质，却能触摸到读者心底最脆弱的部位，代表着无数颗纯真心灵的逼真写照。诗中“In silence and tears”的重复，不仅使全诗前后照应，浑然一体，而且强化了过去和将来都不会更改的情感；另一方面，诗人运用了较短的诗节和众多断开的句子，暗示出他难以压抑的、无法平静的痛苦心境。

原文

6 When You Are Old

William Butler Yeats

When you are old and **grey** and full of sleep,
And **nodding** by the fire, **take down** this book,
And slowly read, and dream of **the soft look**
Your eyes had once, and of their shadows deep;
How many loved your moments of glad grace,
And loved your beauty with love false or true,
But one man loved the **pilgrim** Soul in you,
And loved the sorrows of your changing face;
And **bending down** beside the **glowing bars**,
Murmur, a little sadly, how Love fled
And **paced** upon the mountains overhead
And hid his face **amid** a crowd of stars.

译文

6 当你年老时

威廉·巴特勒·叶芝

当你年老，鬓斑，睡意昏沉，
在炉旁打盹时，取下这本书，
慢慢诵读，梦忆从前你双眸
神色柔和，眼波中倒影深深；
多少人爱你风韵妩媚的时光，
爱你的美丽出自假意或真情，
但唯有一人爱你灵魂的至诚，
爱你渐衰的脸上愁苦的风霜；
弯下身子，在炽红的壁炉边，
忧伤地低诉，爱神如何逃走，
在头顶上的群山巅漫步闲游，

把他的面孔隐没在繁星中间。

（傅浩　译）

注释

1. gray[grei] *adj.* 灰色，指头发灰白
2. nod[nɔd] *v.* 打瞌睡，点头
3. take down: 拿下
4. the soft look: 柔和的眼神
5. pilgrim['pilgrim] *n.* 朝圣者，追寻者
6. bend down: 弯腰
7. glow[glo] *v.* 灼热，发红光
8. bar[bɑr] *n.* 炉栅
9. murmur['mə:mə] *v.* 喃喃低语
10. pace[pes] *v.* 踱步
11. amid[ə'mid] *prep.* 在……中

赏析

威廉·巴特勒·叶芝(William Butler Yeats, 1869—1939)是20世纪英国最伟大的诗人。获得1923年诺贝尔文学奖。他创作了许多反映爱尔兰民族精神的诗歌，也创作了不少爱情诗，《当你老了》就是其中比较著名的一首。

这首诗选自叶芝1893年的诗集《玫瑰》，是叶芝早期的代表作之一，写给他心中的女神，也是他一生中最重要的女人：茉德·冈。第一节，诗人设想茉德·冈已经头发斑白，老态龙钟，坐在炉火旁打盹，诗人请她打开诗集，感受诗人对她炽热的情感，勾起对美妙往昔的回忆。第二节，诗人希望茉德·冈能体会到诗人对她的一往情深。在这里诗人把自己对她的爱情同其他人的爱情作了对比，以表达自己始终如一的爱慕。其他人对她的爱出自于对她的美貌的倾慕，而他的爱则不仅如此。第三节，诗人又重新回到自己在第一节的设想。他想象茉德·冈回忆之后会流露出一丝惆怅，哀叹爱情再次渐渐远离意识领域，而遁入潜意识和无意识之中。这一节意境深远，很值得品味。这首诗境深远，语言朴实生动，表达的感情深沉真挚，不愧为名家名作。

原文

7 I'm Nobody!

Emily Dickinson

I'm nobody! Who are you?
Are you nobody, too?
Then there's a pair of us — don't tell!
They'd **banish** us, you know!

How **dreary** to be **somebody**!
How public, like a frog
To tell your name the **livelong day**
To an admiring **bog**!

译文

7 我是无名之辈

艾米莉·狄金森

我是无名之辈，你是谁？
你，也是，无名之辈？
这就凑成一双，别声张！
你知道，他们会大肆张扬！

做个，显要人物，好不无聊！
像个青蛙，向仰慕的泥沼——
在整个六月，把个人的姓名
聒噪——何等招摇！

注释

1. banish['bæniʃ] *vt.* 放逐，驱逐；消除，排除
2. dreary['driəri] *adj.* 沉寂的；阴沉的；令人厌烦的；枯燥的
3. somebody: a person of importance. 重要人物，有名气的人

4. livelong day: 终日，整天整日

5. bog[bɔg] *n.* 沼泽，泥塘；沼泽地区：底面为酸性和湿软的地带，主要由灌木、草类及一些树的水藓泥沼和泥煤构成。

赏析

艾米莉·狄金森 (Emily Dickinson，1830—1886)，19世纪美国杰出的女诗人，生于美国马萨诸塞州。她被认为是美国隐士式的女诗人。她生前写过1700多首令人耳目一新的短诗。她深居简出，终生未婚，过着孤独的生活。题材多限于个人的内心生活，善于以奇特的意象表现平常的生活事物，并把深邃的思想融入简短的诗句中。她的诗歌言简意赅，寓意深远，善用警句概括出人生哲理。她诗风独特，以文字细腻、观察敏锐、意象突出而著称。

读狄金森的诗，“隐蔽”是一个关键词，暗示着她向往“无名”的世界。这首诗也许就是她一生的写照吧，她不喜欢那种浮躁的贵族式交际，放弃了显赫的家族荣耀，过着孤独却丰富的隐居生活。很简单很警世的一首小诗，一如狄金森自身的真实写照：“多无聊——身为赫赫显要！”确实，做一个小人物，过平淡的生活，拥有平常的幸福，又有什么不好的呢？某种意义上，一首诗完成后她愿意退至幕后。你必须仔细地去体会，去沉浸，才能对她的诗有所领悟。这领悟哪怕是短暂的，也许因为“青蛙的聒噪”是讳莫如深。唯其短暂，才有了诗人抽身回去，给读者以无限遐想的空间，她的“隐蔽”成就了她的一首诗歌。

原文

8 Because I Could Not Stop for Death

Emily Dickinson

Because I could not stop for Death,
He kindly stopped for me;
The carriage held but just ourselves
And **immortality**.
We slowly drove, he knew no haste,
And I had put away

My labour, and my leisure too,
For his **civility**.
We passed the school where children played,
Their lessons scarcely done;
We passed the fields of gazing grain,
We passed the setting sun.
We paused before a house that seemed
A **swelling** of the ground
The roof was scarcely visible,
The **cornice** but a mound.
Since then '**tis** centuries; but each
Feels shorter than the day
I first surmised the horses' heads
Were toward eternity.

译文

8　因我不能停候死神

艾米莉·狄金森

因我不能停候死神
死神好意地停候我
马车仅乘载他与我
外加上永生

马车缓缓地而行
死神知悉不赶忙
只因他殷勤好礼
吾将作息置一旁

我们经过了学校
学童下课操场奔
我们经过伫立的稻田
我们经过落日
宁说落日经过我们
露水带来了寒意

只因吾衣服单薄
围巾只是柔丝绸

我们停于一屋前
犹如凸起之地面
屋顶几乎看不见
隐藏于地下飞檐

自该程后已数百年
感觉不比当日长久
当初推测马车头
朝永恒方向迈进

(余光中 译)

注释

1. immortality[ˌimɔ:'tæliti] *n.* 不朽,不朽的声名
2. civility[si'viləti] *n.* 礼貌;客气;礼仪;客套
3. swelling['sweliŋ] *n.* 肿胀;膨胀;增大;隆起
4. cornice['kɔ:nis] *n.* 檐口;门楣
5. tis: 即it is

赏析

此诗大约写于1863年,发表于1890年,编号第712首。它以死亡为题材,行文极其洒脱,反映了迪金森视死如归的人生态度。她认为死是一种特殊的光荣,意味着悠闲、庄严和永生。表面上全诗在描绘一次传统的送葬仪式,记述死者一路到达墓地的情形,语调平静,节奏沉稳,随着马车徐徐向前。实际上诗中隐藏着一个象征性的框架。作者利用有代表性的、具体可感的意象,打动读者的感官和心灵,对人生历程做了一番巡视:学校令人联想到人的童年;稻田暗指青壮年时期;落日象征晚年;夜露和薄衣暗示尸骨之寒;隆出地面的矮屋代表坟墓;马车就是灵车。现实生活中迪金森的死亡观正如该诗中描写的那样。在1886年5月15日新英格兰(New England)那个明媚的初夏黄昏,迪金森异常平静地撒手人寰,临终前留给自己两个小表妹的遗言只有两个字:"唤归(Called back)"。

原文

9 I Wandered Lonely as a Cloud

William Wordsworth

I wandered lonely as a cloud
That floats on high o'er **vales** and hills,
When all at once I saw a crowd,
A host, of golden **daffodils**;
Beside the lake, beneath the trees,
Fluttering and dancing in the breeze.

Continuous as the stars that shine
And twinkle on **the milky way**,
They stretched in never-ending line
Along the margin of a bay:
Ten thousand saw I at a glance,
Tossing their heads in **sprightly** dance.

The waves beside them danced; but they
Outdid the sparkling waves in **glee**;
A poet could not but be gay,
In such a **jocund** company;
I gazed — and gazed — but little thought
What wealth the show to me had brought:

For **oft**, when on my couch I lie
In vacant or in **pensive** mood,
They flash upon that inward eye
Which is the **bliss** of **solitude**;
And then my heart with pleasure fills,
And dances with the daffodils.

译文

9 我好似一朵孤独的流云

威廉·华兹华斯

我好似一朵孤独的流云，
高高地飘游在山谷之上，
突然我看到一大片鲜花，
是金色的水仙遍地开放。
它们开在湖畔，开在树下，
它们随风嬉舞，随风飘荡。

它们密集如银河的星星，
像群星在闪烁一片晶莹；
它们沿着海湾向前伸展，
通往远方仿佛无穷无尽；
一眼看去就有千朵万朵，
万花摇首舞得多么高兴。

粼粼湖波也在近旁欢跳，
却不如这水仙舞得轻俏；
诗人遇见这快乐的旅伴，
又怎能不感到欢欣雀跃；
我久久凝视——却未领悟
这景象所给的精神至宝。

后来多少次我郁郁独卧，
感到百无聊赖心灵空漠；
这景象便在脑海中闪现，
多少次安慰过我的寂寞；
我的心又随水仙跳起舞来，
我的心又重新充满了欢乐。

（顾子欣 译）

注释

1. vale[veil] *n.* (平缓而低的)谷,山谷
2. daffodil['dæfədil] *n.* 水仙花 *adj.* 水仙花色的
3. the Milky Way: 银河
4. sprightly['spraitli] *adj.* 轻快的
5. glee[gli:] *n.* 欢乐, 高兴
6. jocund['dʒɔkənd] *adj.* 欢乐的, 高兴的
7. oft=often, *adv.* 经常, 常常
8. pensive['pensiv] *adj.* 沉思的
9. bliss[blis] *n.* 无上幸福;极乐
10. solitude ['sɔlitju:d] *n.* 孤独

赏析

威廉·华兹华斯 (William Wordsworth,1770—1850),英国诗人,生于英格兰西北部昆布兰郡科克茅斯的一个律师之家,被称为"湖畔派"的代表诗人,是英国早期浪漫主义的代表。他反对古典主义传统,向往唯情论,歌颂大自然。19世纪30年代起,华兹华斯开始受到评论界的一致称赞。1843年他被授予英格兰"桂冠诗人"的称号。

《我好似一朵孤独的流云》,创作于1804年,是英国诗歌史上最著名的杰作之一。 这首诗运用了拟人、比喻等手法将大自然的美妙景象表现得生动逼真,似乎将读者置身于湖畔上连绵的水仙花随风舞动的风景当中。可以看得出来,华兹华斯回归自然,在自然中找到心灵的慰藉,如同孩子被不公的势力欺负后跑到母亲的怀抱。另外,我们从中了解到诗人经历了社会生活的方方面面:邪恶的、粗俗的、自私的、虚情假意的,所有的一切令诗人大失所望,所以他那向往自然的一面就不奇怪了。自然是美好的、柔弱的、神秘的,令诗人充满遐想,比如在这首诗中,"流云"和"金色的水仙" 相互辉映而又交织融合,让诗人的心"又重新充满了快乐"。该诗行文流畅,措辞简洁,给人精神上的洗礼。

原文

10 A Red, Red Rose

Robert Burns

O my **Luve's** like a red, red rose,
That's newly **sprung** in June;
O my Luve's like the **melodie**,
That's sweetly played in tune.
As fair **thou art**, my **bonnie** lass,
So deep in luve am I;
And I will luve **thee** still, my dear,
Till a' the seas **gang** dry:
Till a' the seas gang dry, my dear,
And the rocks melt **wi'** the sun;
I will luve thee still, my dear,
While the **sands o'** life shall run.
And fare thee **weel**, my only Luve,
And fare thee weel a while!
And I will come again, my Luve,
Tho' it ware ten thousand mile.

译文

10 一朵红红的玫瑰

罗伯特·彭斯

啊,我的爱人像一朵红红的玫瑰,
它在六月里初开,
啊,我的爱人像一支乐曲,
美妙地演奏起来。

你是那么美,漂亮的姑娘,
我爱你那么深切;

亲爱的，我会永远爱你，
一直到四海枯竭。

亲爱的，直到四海枯竭，
到太阳把岩石烧裂！
我会永远爱你，亲爱的
只要是生命不绝。

我唯一的爱人，我向你告别，
我和你小别片刻；
我要回来的，亲爱的，
即使万里相隔！

（袁可嘉 译）

注释

1. luve= love 苏格兰方言
2. sprung: spring 的过去分词，意为“生长，出现”。
3. melodie: melody的变体，意为“旋律，曲调；美妙的音乐；歌曲”。
4. thou=you
5. art=are旧语
6. bonnie=bonny 健康的；活泼的；愉快的
7. thee=you
8. till a'=till all
9. gang=go 苏格兰方言
10. wi'=with
11. sands o'=sands of
12. weel: well的方言
13. Tho': though

赏析

罗伯特·彭斯（Robert Burns，1759—1796），苏格兰农民诗人；他的诗歌富有音乐性，可以歌唱。他的诗歌充满了激进的民主、自由的思想。他的诗歌主要歌颂了故乡的秀美，抒写了劳动者淳朴的友谊和爱情。著名的情诗还包括：《玛丽·莫里逊》《天风来自四面八方》《约翰·安特森，我的爱人》《一次亲吻》《高原的玛丽》《走过麦田来》等等，可以说，诗人前期的创作基本上是围绕着爱情这条主线，这条线索甚至几乎贯穿了诗人的创作生涯。

这首《我的爱人像朵红红的玫瑰》，是Burns的抒情诗里的名作，表现人类共通的感情—爱情。这首诗出自诗人的《主要用苏格兰方言写的诗集》，是诗集中流传最广的一首。这是诗人写给他的恋人琪恩的一首诗。诗人歌颂了恋人的美丽，表达了诗人对恋人的炽热感情和对爱情的坚定决心。诗人用流畅悦耳的音调、质朴无华的词语和热烈真挚的情感打动了千百万恋人的心，也使得这首诗在问世之后成为人们传唱不衰的经典。

原文

11 The Furthest **Distance** in the World

Tagore

The furthest **distance** in the world
Is not between life and death.
But when I stand in front of you,
Yet you don't know that I love you.
The furthest distance in the world,
Is not when I stand in front of you,
Yet you can't see my love.
But when **undoubtedly** knowing the love from both,
Yet cannot be together.
The furthest distance in the world,
Is not being **apart** while being in love.
But when **plainly** cannot **resist** the **yearning**,
Yet **pretending** you have never been in my heart.
The furthest distance in the world,
Is not but using one's **indifferent** heart,
To dig an uncrossible river,
For the one who loves you.

译文

11　世界上最遥远的距离

泰戈尔

世界上最遥远的距离，
不是生与死之间的距离；
而是我站在你面前，
你却不知道我爱你；
世界上最遥远的距离，
不是我站在你面前，
你却看不到我对你的爱；
而是感受到对方坚定的爱意，
却不能在一起。
世界上最遥远的距离，
不是相爱的人不能在一起；
而是明明不能停止思念，
却装作对方从未走进自己心间。
世界上最遥远的距离，
是用冷漠的心，
为爱你的人，
挖掘一条无法穿越的鸿沟。

（郑振铎　译）

注释

1. distance[ˈdistəns] *n.* 距离
2. undoubtedly[ʌnˈdautidli] *adv.* 真正地
3. apart[əˈpɑːt] *adv.* 相隔
4. plainly[ˈpleinli] *adv.* 清楚地
5. resist[riˈzist] *vt.* 抵抗
6. yearning[ˈjəːniŋ] *n.* 思慕
7. pretend [priˈtend] *vi.* 假装，装作
8. indifferent[inˈdifərənt] *adj.* 冷淡的

赏析

拉宾德拉纳特·泰戈尔（Rabindranath Tagore, 1861—1941），印度著名诗人、文学家、作家、艺术家、社会活动家、哲学家和印度民族主义者，生于加尔各答市一个有深厚文化教养的贵族家庭，属于婆罗门种姓。1913年他成为第一位获得诺贝尔文学奖的亚洲人。他的诗中含有深刻的宗教和哲学的见解，对泰戈尔来说，他的诗是他奉献给神的礼物，而他本人是神的求婚者。泰戈尔的诗在印度享有史诗的地位，代表作《吉檀迦利》《飞鸟集》。

印度诗人泰戈尔的《世界上最遥远的距离》令许多人潸然泪下。人世间有一种比生与死更遥远的距离，不是时间上的跨古今，也非空间上的囊括宇宙，而是一种最难逾越的距离，心与心的距离。全诗以爱为主线，诗人敏感的字里行间，流露着痛苦而无奈的情感，不能不令人从容。诗歌简短而整齐，读至最后令人恍然大悟时——世界上最遥远的距离实际上是心与心的距离，早已泪眼模糊。诗人层层深入把读者带到了那种痛苦的最遥远的距离；世界上最远的距离是心与心的距离，但归根结底还是梦想和现实的距离，是理智与情感的距离，是相爱不能相守的两颗心咫尺天涯的距离！

原文

12 Stray Birds

Tagore

Life, thin and light- off time and time again
Frivolous tireless
One
I heard the **echo**, from the valleys and the heart
Open to the lonely soul of sickle harvesting
Repeat outrightly, but also repeat the well- being of
Eventually swaying in the desert oasis

I believe I am
Born as the bright summer flowers

Do not withered undefeated fiery demon rule
Heart rate and breathing to bear the load of the **cumbersome**
Bored

Two

I heard the music, from the moon and carcass
Auxiliary extreme **aestheticism** bait to capture **misty**
Filling the intense life, but also filling the pure
There are always memories throughout the earth

I believe I am
Died as the quiet beauty of autumn leaves
Sheng is not chaos, smoke gesture
Even wilt also retained bone proudly Qing Feng muscle
Occult

Three

I hear love, I believe in love
Love is a pool of struggling blue-green algae
As desolate micro-burst of wind
Bleeding through my veins
Years stationed in the belief

Four

I believe that all can hear
Even **anticipate discrete**, I met the other their own
Some can not grasp the moment
Left to the East to go West, the dead must not return to nowhere

See, I wear Zan Flowers on my head, in full bloom along the way all the way
Frequently missed some, but also deeply moved by wind, frost, snow or rain

Five

Prajna Paramita, soon as soon as
life be beautiful like summer flowers and death like autumn leaves
Also care about what has

译文

12 生如夏花

泰戈尔

生命，一次又一次轻薄过
轻狂不知疲倦

——题记

1
我听见回声，来自山谷和心间
以寂寞的镰刀收割空旷的灵魂
不断地重复决绝，又重复幸福
终有绿洲摇曳在沙漠

我相信自己
生来如同璀璨的夏日之花
不凋不败，妖冶如火
承受心跳的负荷和呼吸的累赘
乐此不疲
2
我听见音乐，来自月光和胴体
辅极端的诱饵捕获缥缈的唯美
一生充盈着激烈，又充盈着纯然
总有回忆贯穿于世间

我相信自己
死时如同静美的秋日落叶
不盛不乱，姿态如烟
即便枯萎也保留丰肌清骨的傲然
玄之又玄
3
我听见爱情，我相信爱情
爱情是一潭挣扎的蓝藻
如同一阵凄微的风
穿过我失血的静脉

驻守岁月的信念

4

我相信一切能够听见
甚至预见离散，遇见另一个自己
而有些瞬间无法把握

任凭东走西顾，逝去的必然不返
请看我头置簪花，一路走来一路盛开
频频遗漏一些，又深陷风霜雨雪的感动

5

般若波罗蜜，一声一声
生如夏花，死如秋叶
还在乎拥有什么

（郑振铎 译）

注释

1. frivolous['frivələs] *adj.* 无价值的，毫无意义的
2. echo['ekəu] *n.* 回声，共鸣；（言语、作风、思想等的）重复
3. cumbersome['kʌmbəsəm] *adj.* 笨重的；累赘的，难以携带的；冗长的
4. auxiliary[ɔg'ziljəri, -'ziləri] *adj.* 辅助的；备用的，补充的；附加的
5. aestheticism[i:s'θetisizəm] *n.* 唯美主义
6. misty['misti] *adj.* 多雾的，被雾笼罩的；模糊的
7. anticipate[æn'tisipeit] *vt.* 预感；预见；预料；先于……行动
8. discrete[di'skri:t] *adj.* 分离的，不相关联的；分立式的；非连续
9. Prajna[ˌprudʒnə] *n.* 般若，智慧（大乘佛教修习的主要内容之一，超越世俗达到佛的境界的六 种方法之一）
10. Paramita 波罗蜜

赏析

泰戈尔的诗是优美的画，无声无息，水乳交融。他的每一首诗，都闪耀着炽热的火花，照亮了读者的心，使他们的心灵日臻超脱，得以净化。

这首《生如夏花》带给了我们“生如夏花之灿烂，死如秋叶之静美”的意境。泰戈尔的文字，于沉凝、淳朴与华美之间透露出一种超脱世俗、朦胧缥缈、清正淡雅、超然物外之美。“生如夏花”揭示了生命的短暂匆忙，青春如诗，岁月如歌，当过去的甜美成了回忆，人们无法挽留生命趋向衰落，正如人们无法阻止花儿的凋谢。诚然，人的一生漫长而又短暂，我们要时时刻刻珍惜身边的每一个人。因为生是如此的绚烂，死也如此的静美！

原文

13 **Ode** to the West Wind

Percy Bysshe Shelley

One

O wild West Wind, thou breath of Autumn's being,
Thou, from whose unseen **presence** the leaves dead
Are driven, like ghosts from an enchanter fleeing,

Yellow, and black, and pale, and hectic red,
Pestilence-stricken multitudes: O thou,
Who chariotest to their dark wintry bed

The wingéd seeds, where they lie cold and low,
Each like a corpse within its **grave**, until
Thine **azure sister of the Spring** shall blow

Her clarion o'er the dreaming earth, and fill
(Driving sweet buds like flocks to feed in air)
With living hues and odors plain and hill:

Wild Spirit, which art moving everywhere;
Destroyer and preserver; hear, oh, hear!

Two

Thou on whose **stream**, 'mid the **steep** sky's **commotion,**
Loose clouds like earth's decaying leaves are **shed,**
Shook from the **tangled** boughs of Heaven and Ocean,

Angels of rain and lightning: there are spread

On the blue surface of thine aery **surge**,
Like the bright hair uplifted from the head

Of some fierce Maenad, even from the **dim** verge
Of the horizon to the **zenith's** height,
The locks of the approaching storm. Thou dirge

Of the dying year, to which this closing night
Will be the **dome** of a vast sepulcher,
Vaulted with all thy congregated might

Of vapors, from whose solid atmosphere
Black rain, and fire, and hail will **burst**: oh, hear!

Three
Thou who didst waken from his summer dreams
The blue Mediterranean, where he lay,
Lulled by the coil of his crystalline streams,

Beside a pumice isle in Baiae's bay,
And saw in sleep old palaces and towers
Quivering within the wave's intenser day,

All overgrown with azure moss and flowers
So sweet, the sense faints picturing them! Thou
For whose path the Atlantic's level powers

Cleave themselves into chasms, while far below
The sea-blooms and the oozy woods which wear
The sapless foliage of the ocean, know

Thy voice, and suddenly grow gray with fear,
And tremble and despoil themselves: oh, hear!

Four
If I were a dead leaf thou mightest bear;
If I were a **swift** cloud to fly with thee;

A wave to pant beneath thy power, and share

The **impulse** of thy strength, only less free
Than thou, O **uncontrollable**! If even
I were as in my boyhood, and could be

The comrade of thy wanderings over Heaven,
As then, when to **outstrip** thy skyey speed
Scarce seemed a vision; I would ne'er have striven

As thus with thee in prayer in my sore need.
Oh, lift me as a wave, a leaf, a cloud!
I fall upon the thorns of life! I bleed!

A heavy weight of hours has chained and bowed
One too like thee: tameless, and swift, and proud.

Five

Make me thy lyre, even as the forest is:
What if my leaves are falling like its own!
The tumult of thy mighty harmonies

Will take from both a deep, autumnal tone,
Sweet though in sadness. Be thou, Spirit fierce,
My spirit! Be thou me, **impetuous** one!

Drive my dead thoughts over the universe
Like **withered** leaves to quicken a new birth!
And, by the **incantation** of this verse,

Scatter, as from an **unextinguished** hearth
Ashes and sparks, my words among mankind!
Be through my lips to unawakened earth

The **trumpet** of a **prophecy**! O Wind,
If Winter comes, can Spring be far behind?

译文

13　西风颂

珀西·比西·雪莱

1
呵,狂野的西风,你把秋气猛吹,
不露脸便将落叶一扫而空,
犹如法师赶走了群鬼,
赶走那黄绿红黑紫的一群,
那些染上了瘟疫的魔怪——
呵,你让种子长翅腾空,
又落在冰冷的土壤里深埋,
像尸体躺在坟墓,但一朝
你那青色的东风妹妹回来,
为沉睡的大地吹响银号,
驱使羊群般的蓓蕾把大气猛喝,
就吹出遍野嫩色,处处香飘。
狂野的精灵!你吹遍大地山河,
破坏者、保护者,听吧——听我的歌!

2
你激荡长空,乱云飞坠
如落叶;你摇撼天和海,
不准它们像老树缠在一堆;
你把雨和电赶了下来,
只见蓝空上你驰骋之处
忽有万丈金发披开,
像是酒神的女祭司勃然大怒,
楞把她的长发遮住了半个天,
将暴风雨的来临宣布。
你唱着挽歌送别残年,
今夜这天空宛如圆形的大墓,
罩住了混沌的云雾一片,
却挡不住电火和冰雹的突破,

更有暴雨倾盆而下！呵，听我的歌！

3
你惊扰了地中海的夏日梦，
它在清澈的碧水里静躺，
听着波浪的催眠曲，睡意正浓，
朦胧里它看见南国港外石岛旁，
烈日下古老的宫殿和楼台
把影子投在海水里晃荡，
它们的墙上长满花朵和藓苔，
那香气光想想也叫人醉倒！
你的来临叫大西洋也惊骇，
它忙把海水劈成两半，为你开道，
海底下有琼枝玉树安卧，
尽管深潜万丈，一听你的怒号
就闻声而变色，只见一个个
战栗、畏缩——呵，听我的歌！

4
如果我能是一片落叶随你飘腾，
如果我能是一朵流云伴你飞行，
或是一个浪头在你的威力下翻滚，
如果我能有你的锐势和冲动，
即使比不上你那不羁的奔放，
但只要能拾回我当年的童心，
我就能陪着你遨游天上，
那时候追上你未必是梦呓，
又何至沦落到这等颓丧，
祈求你来救我之急！
呵，卷走我吧，像卷走落叶，波浪，流云！
我跌在人生的棘树上，我血流遍体！
向你苦苦祈求。哦，快把我扬起，
就像你扬起的波浪、浮云、落叶！
我倾覆于人生的荆棘！我在流血！
岁月沉重如铁链，压着的灵魂
原本同你一样：高傲、飘逸、不驯。
岁月的重负压制着的这一个太像你，

像你一样，骄傲、不驯，而且敏捷。

5
让我做你的竖琴吧，就同森林一般，
纵然我们都落叶纷纷，又有何妨！
我们身上的秋色斑斓，
好给你那狂飙曲添上深沉的回响，
甜美而带苍凉。给我你迅猛的劲头！
豪迈的精灵，化成我吧，借你的锋芒，
把我的腐朽思想扫出宇宙，
扫走了枯叶好把新生来激发；
凭着我这诗韵做符咒，
请把我枯萎的思绪播送宇宙，
就像你驱遣落叶催促新的生命，
请凭借我这韵文写就的符咒，
犹如从未灭的炉火照出火花，
把我的话散布在人群之中
对那沉睡的大地，拿我的嘴当喇叭，
吹响一个预言！呵，西风，
如果冬天已到，难道春天还用久等？

（王佐良　译）

注释

1. ode[od] *n.* 颂诗，颂歌
2. thou:古英语you; thine=your; o'er=over
3. presence['prezəns] *n.* 存在；出席；参加；风度；仪态
4. grave[greiv] *n.* 墓穴，坟墓；死亡
5. azure sister of the Spring: 据说出自拉丁神话，指的是春风。意思是种子被西风吹落。
6. stream[stri:m] *n.* 溪流；流动；潮流；光线
7. steep[sti:p] *n.* 峭壁；浸渍
8. commotion[kə'məuʃən] *n.* 骚动；暴乱
9. shed[ʃed] *vt.* 流出；摆脱；散发；倾吐
10. tangled['tæŋgld] *adj.* 紊乱的；纠缠的；缠结的；复杂的
11. surge[sə:dʒ] *n.* 大浪；汹涌澎湃　*vt.* 使颠簸
12. dim[dim] *adj.* 暗淡的，昏暗的　*n.* [美俚]笨蛋，傻子
13. zenith['zeniθ,'zi:-] *n.* 顶峰；顶点；最高点

14. dome[dəum] *n.* 圆屋顶
15. burst[bə:st] *vi.* 爆发,突发;爆炸　*vt.* 爆发,突发;爆炸
16. swift[swift] *n.* 褐雨燕　*adj.* 快的;迅速的;敏捷的;立刻的
17. impulse[ˈimpʌls] *n.* 冲动;脉冲;刺激;神经冲动;推动力
18. uncontrollable[ʌnkənˈtrəuləbl] *adj.* 无法控制的;无法管束的;难以驾驭的
19. outstrip[autˈstrip] *vt.* 超过;胜过;比……跑得快
20. impetuous[imˈpetjuəs] *adj.* 冲动的;鲁莽的;猛烈的
21. wither[ˈwiðə] *vt.* 使凋谢;使畏缩;使衰弱
22. incantation[ˌinkænˈteʃən] *n.*咒语,符咒
23. unextinguished: extinguished 的反义词,这里指未灭的。
24. trumpet[ˈtrʌmpit] *n.* 喇叭;喇叭声
25. prophecy[ˈprɔfisi] *n.* 预言;[宗]预言书;预言能力

赏析

珀西·比西·雪莱 (Percy Bysshe Shelley, 1792—1822),生于英国萨塞克斯郡。1816年前往瑞士,之后与拜伦结为好友。1822年与友人驾帆船出海,遇暴风,舟沉身亡。作品包括长诗《仙后麦布》(*Queen Mab*)、《阿多尼斯》(*Adonais*)等。

《西风颂》是欧洲诗歌史上的艺术珍品。全诗共五节,由五首十四行诗组成。诗文结构严谨,层次清晰,主题集中,这是本诗一个突出的艺术特点。《西风颂》采用了象征手法,从头至尾环绕着秋天的西风作诗, 但诗人实质上是通过歌唱西风来歌唱革命。诗中的西风、残叶、流云、暴雨雷电、大海波涛、海底花树等等,都富有象征性,它们有着深刻的寓意:大自然风云激荡的动人景色,乃是人间蓬勃发展的革命斗争的象征性反映。因此, 《西风颂》不是风景诗,而是政治抒情诗,它虽然没有一句直接描写革命,但整首诗都是在反映革命,尤其是结尾脍炙人口的诗句,既概括了自然现象,也深刻地揭示了人类社会的历史规律,指出了革命斗争经过艰难曲折走向胜利的光明前景。其寓意深远,余味无穷,一百多年来成了人们广泛传诵的名言警句。在这首颂歌中,诗人愿借西风之力,荡涤自己心中的沉暮之气,以激发自己的灵感,并将自己的诗名传播四方,唤醒昏昏然的芸芸众生。

原文

14 If

Rudyard Kipling

IF you can keep your head when all about you
Are losing theirs and blaming it on you,
If you can trust yourself when all men doubt you,
But make **allowance** for their doubting too;
If you can wait and not be tired by waiting,
Or being lied about, don't deal in lies,
Or being hated, don't give way to hating,
And yet don't look too good, nor talk too wise:

If you can dream — and not make dreams your master;
If you can think— and not make thoughts your aim;
If you can meet with Triumph and Disaster
And treat those two **impostors** just the same;
If you can bear to hear the truth you've spoken
Twisted by **knaves** to make a trap for fools,
Or watch the things you gave your life to, broken,
And **stoop** and build 'em up with worn-out tools:

If you can make one heap of all your winnings
And risk it on one turn of **pitch-and-toss**,
And lose, and start again at your beginnings
And never breathe a word about your loss;
If you can force your heart and **nerve** and **sinew**
To **serve your turn** long after they are gone,
And so hold on when there is nothing in you
Except the Will which says to them: "Hold on! "

If you can talk with crowds and keep your virtue,
'Or walk with Kings — nor lose the common touch,
if neither foes nor loving friends can hurt you,

If all men count with you, but none too much;
If you can fill the unforgiving minute
With sixty seconds' worth of distance run,
Yours is the Earth and everything that's in it,
And — which is more — you'll be a Man, my son!

译文

14 如果

拉迪亚德·吉卜林

如果周围的人毫无理性地向你发难,你仍能镇定自若保持冷静;
如果众人对你心存猜忌,你仍能自信如常并认为他们的猜忌情有可原;
如果你肯耐心等待不急不躁,
或遭人诽谤却不以牙还牙,
或遭人憎恨却不以恶报恶;
既不装腔作势,亦不气盛趾高;
如果你有梦想,而又不为梦主宰;
如果你有神思,而又不走火入魔;
如果你坦然面对胜利和灾难,对虚渺的胜负荣辱胸怀旷荡;
如果你能忍受有这样的无赖,歪曲你的口吐真言蒙骗笨汉,
或看着心血铸就的事业崩溃,仍能忍辱负重脚踏实地重新攀登;
如果你敢把取得的一切胜利,为了更崇高的目标孤注一掷,
面临失去,决心从头再来而绝口不提自己的损失;
如果人们早已离你而去,你仍能坚守阵地奋力前驱,
身上已一无所有,唯存意志在高喊"顶住";
如果你跟平民交谈而不变谦虚之态,
抑或与王侯散步而不露谄媚之颜;
如果敌友都无法对你造成伤害;
如果众人对你信赖有加却不过分依赖;
如果你能惜时如金利用每一分钟不可追回的光阴;
那么,你的修为就会如天地般博大,并拥有了属于自己的世界,
更重要的是:孩子,你成为了真正顶天立地之人!

注释

1. allowance[ə'lauəns] *n.* 宽容,体谅, 原谅
2. impostor[im'pɔstə] *n.* 冒名顶替者,骗子
3. knave[neiv] *n.* 恶棍,无赖;(纸牌中的)杰克 流氓、无赖、恶棍
4. stoop[stu:p] *n.* 门廊; 弯腰
5. pitch-and-toss 掷硬币游戏(瞄准目标投掷钱币的游戏)
6. nerve[nə:v] *n.* 神经;勇气,胆量
7. sinew['sinju:] *n.* 肌肉、精力、体力
8. serve one's (own) turn 满足某人的需要,(紧急时)能起作用

赏析

拉迪亚德·吉卜林 (Rudyard Kipling,1865—1936),英国小说家、诗人。吉卜林的作品风格清新自然,生动展现了印度的风土人情,曾使当时英国读者耳目一新。

吉卜林的《如果》是一首写给儿子的相当励志的诗,勉励他要勇于接受挑战,战胜困难。青少年常以此勉励自己,激发前进动力,诗人在诗中展示了成功背后,包含多少辛酸,经历多少磨难,忍受多少痛楚。诗人在诗中假设了任何一个人在一生中可能遇到的十四个如果,涵盖了人格、意志、奋斗、为人、处事、修养等方面。对于每个如果,诗人都给出了自己理想的抉择。吉卜林确实给这个世界留下了一部伟大的人生鸡汤,所有的人,都需要这些假如,都需要这些抉择。

原文

15 The Sleeping Beauty

Samuel Rogers

Sleep on, and dream of Heaven awhile —
Tho' shut so close **thy** laughing eyes,
Thy rosy lips still wear a smile
And move and breathe delicious sighs!
Ah, now soft **blushes** tinge her cheeks
And **mantle o'er** her neck of snow;

Ah, now she murmurs, now she speaks
What most I wish——and fear to know!
She starts, she trembles, and she weeps!
Her fair hands folded on her breast;
——And now, how like a saint she sleeps!
A **seraph** in the realms of rest!
Sleep on secure! A bove control
Thy thoughts belong to Heaven and **thee**;
And may the secret of thy soul
Remain within its **sanctuary**!

译文

15 睡美人

塞缪尔·罗杰斯

睡不停,梦见天堂有一阵——
纵使笑眼闭得紧,
红唇依旧绽笑纹,
唇动叹息也可人!

羞涩浅红染两颊,
雪白玉颈相掩映;
细细语,低低吟,
尤喜尤恐知其声!

梦惊,颤栗,泪几行!
纤纤素手覆胸上;
睡稳又似高者卧!
仿佛天使眠安详!

睡不停,睡安然!
思绪带你到天堂;
愿你心中隐秘事,
留在灵魂庇护殿!

(若寒 译)

注释

1. 古英语单词: tho'=though;thy=your; o'er=over, thee=you(宾格)
2. blush[blʌʃ] *n.* 红晕(因为害羞)
3. mantle['mæntl] *vt.* & *vi.*覆盖
4. seraph['serəf] *n.* 六翼天使(相传为最高天使)
5. sanctuary['sæŋktʃu'əri] *n.* 圣殿,庇护所

赏析

塞缪尔·罗杰斯(Samuel Rogers,1763—1855),英国银行家兼诗人。其著名作品有诗集《记忆中的欢乐》(*Pleasures of Memory*)。诗人喜欢写一些怪诞的作品,他的长诗《意大利》是所有作品当中最成功的一部。这部巨著让他成为一位与拜伦、华兹华斯等齐名的英国浪漫主义诗人。

《睡美人》写美女的梦境,梦到快乐的事笑,梦到委屈的事哭。因为人美,所以笑也美,哭也美。诗中有一个悬念:美人说梦话了,诗人最想知道又最怕知道内容。最后一段写了诗人只有怕而不想知道了。

原文

16 Break, Break, Break

Alfred, Lord Tennyson

Break, break, break,
On thy cold grey stones, O Sea!
And I would that my tongue could utter
The thoughts that arise in me.
O well for the fisherman's boy
That he shouts with his sister at play!
O well for the sailor lad
That he sings in boat on the bay!
And the stately ships go on
To their **haven** under the hill.
But O for the touch of a **vanished** hand,
And the sound of a voice that is still!

Break, Break, Break,
At the foot of thy **crags**, O Sea !
But the **tender** grace of a day that is dead
Will never come back to me.

译文

16 渤泙声声

阿尔弗雷德·丁尼生

渤泙声声似哭泣,
澥波湍注冲苍砦!
口张舌举述衷肠,
思绪如潮万千阕。
渔家男童今何在,
昔日呼妹嬉海潮!
船家水手何处觅,
歌声悠扬海湾飘!
江船肃穆归纷纷,
夜泊山村凹口渡。
但愿重执子之手,
不闻君声在何处!
渤泙声声似哭泣,
苍岩脚下作坟地!
柔情岁月渐行远,
盼君归来竟成忆。

(颜林海 译)

注释

1. break[brek] *vt.& vi.* 打破;折断;弄坏 ◆这里指浪花不停地冲到岩石上,浪花飞溅
2. haven['hevən] *n.* 港口,安全地方;避难所,安息所
3. vanished['væniʃ] *vi.* 消失;突然不见;消亡,消灭 *vt.* 使消失,使不见
4. crags[kræg] *n.* 悬崖,峭壁
5. tender['tendə] *adj.* 纤弱的;脆弱的;难对付的;温柔的,慈悲的

赏析

阿尔弗雷德·丁尼生(Alfred Tennyson,1809—1892),维多利亚时期代表诗人，是英国维多利亚时代最受欢迎及最具特色的诗人。他的诗歌准确地反映了他那个时代占主导地位的看法及兴趣,这是任何时代的英国诗人都无法比拟的。代表作品为组诗《悼念》。丁尼生晚年对英国社会风尚的败坏日益感到失望和不满,作品中流露出愤世嫉俗的心情。

《渤泙声声》是诗人悼念好友阿瑟·海拉姆(Arthur Hallam)而作。原诗题目:“Break,Break,Break”,具有多层含义,第一,为象声词,模拟大海波涛撞击海岸的声音;第二,预示大海波涛吞没了诗人好友;第三,表示诗人因好友坠水而亡,心痛如绞。

《渤泙声声》是一首触景抒情诗,表现了诗人的怀旧情结。诗人看到波涛拍岸,按抑不住内心世界的潮起潮落。眼前井然悠然欣欣然的人和景物,与诗人心境形成对比。诗人胸中的惆怅思绪和哀伤,难以用语言表达。这是丁尼生感觉自己人微言轻,借眼前景物表达诗人独特的意识。过去比现在和将来更容易使他涔然而泪下。整首诗读来舒缓徘徊,节奏较慢,这与诗的郁郁沉思的内容是和谐的。此外,诗人语言简练,含蓄隽永。

原文

17 Paradise lost（Extract）

John Milton

Of Mans First Disobedience, and the **Fruit**
Of that **Forbidden** Tree, whose mortal tast
Brought Death into the World, and all our **woe,**
With loss of EDEN, till one greater Man
Restore us, and regain the blissful Seat,
Sing **Heav'nly** Muse, that on the secret top
Of OREB, or of SINAI, didst inspire
That **Shepherd**, who first taught the chosen Seed,
In the Beginning how the Heav'ns and Earth
Rose out of CHAOS: Or if SION Hill
Delight thee more, and SILOA'S Brook that **flow'd**
Fast by the Oracle of God; I thence

Invoke thy aid to my adventrous Song,
That with no middle flight intends to soar
Above th' AONIAN Mount, while it pursues
Things unattempted yet in Prose or Rhime.
And chiefly Thou O Spirit, that dost prefer
Before all Temples th' upright heart and pure,
Instruct me, for Thou know'st; Thou from the first
Wast present, and with mighty wings outspread
Dove-like satst brooding on the vast Abyss
And mad'st it pregnant: What in me is dark
Illumine, what is low raise and support;
That to the highth of this great Argument
I may assert th' Eternal Providence,
And justifie the wayes of God to men.
Say first, for Heav'n hides nothing from thy view
Nor the deep Tract of Hell, say first what cause
Mov'd our Grand Parents in that happy State,
Favour'd of Heav'n so highly, to fall off
From their Creator, and transgress his Will
For one restraint, Lords of the World besides?
Who first seduc'd them to that fowl revolt?
Th' infernal Serpent; he it was, whose guile
Stird up with Envy and Revenge, deceiv'd
The Mother of Mankinde, what time his Pride
Had cast him out from Heav'n, with all his Host
Of Rebel Angels, by whose aid aspiring
To set himself in Glory above his Peers,
He trusted to have equal'd the most High,
If he oppos'd; and with ambitious aim
Against the Throne and Monarchy of God
Rais'd impious War in Heav'n and Battel proud
With vain attempt. Him the Almighty Power
Hurld headlong flaming from th' Ethereal Skie
With hideous ruine and combustion down
To bottomless perdition, there to dwell
In Adamantine Chains and penal Fire,
Who durst defie th' **Omnipotent** to Arms.

Nine times the Space that measures Day and Night
To mortal men, he with his horrid crew
Lay vanquisht, rowling in the fiery Gulfe
Confounded though immortal: But his doom
Reserv'd him to more wrath; for now the thought
Both of lost happiness and lasting pain
Torments him; round he throws his baleful eyes
That witness'd huge **affliction** and **dismay**
Mixt with obdurate pride and stedfast hate:
At once as far as Angels kenn he views
The dismal Situation waste and wilde,
A Dungeon horrible, on all sides round
As one great Furnace flam'd, yet from those flames
No light, but rather darkness visible
Serv'd only to discover sights of woe,
Regions of sorrow, doleful shades, where peace
And rest can never dwell, hope never comes
That comes to all; but **torture** without end
Still urges, and a fiery Deluge, fed
With ever-burning Sulphur unconsum'd:
Such place Eternal Justice had prepar'd
For those rebellious, here their Prison ordain'd
In utter darkness, and their portion set
As far remov'd from God and light of Heav'n
As from the Center thrice to th' utmost Pole.
O how unlike the place from whence they fell!
There the companions of his fall, o'rewhelm'd
With Floods and Whirlwinds of **tempestuous** fire,
He soon discerns, and weltring by his side
One next himself in power, and next in crime,
Long after known in PALESTINE, and nam'd
BEELZEBUB. To whom th' Arch-Enemy,
And thence in Heav'n call'd Satan, with bold words
Breaking the horrid silence thus began.

译文

17 失乐园(节选)

约翰·弥尔顿

人类最初的违抗,还有那禁果
它那必死的味道
将死亡带到世上,连同我们所有的悲哀
自伊甸园失去,到更伟大的人
修复我们,让我们重回福地
唱天堂般的音乐,在神秘的欧瑞伯山顶
和西耐山顶,真正赋予那牧者灵感
第一个教晓那些被选出的种子
最初天堂与大地是如何
在一片混沌中出现;或假如锡安山
更喜爱你,那地底的溪流
恰带来神谕;我从此
让你助我完成那冒险之歌
平庸者所不敢飞越的高度
翻越阿诺安山,追逐着
诗歌与散文里未曾尝试之事
你,灵魂做主,更爱
在所有庙宇之前,以正直纯粹之心
指引我,因你知道;你自最初
即已在此,伸开有力的双翼
鸽子般安坐在巨大的深渊前沉思
看穿我内心的黑暗
照亮那卑微,唤起并支持着我
直到这伟大的辩论
我可断言永恒的天意
证明神对世人的方式
预言,因天对人无所隐藏
地狱亦是如此,言明何因
令我们的祖先自那欢乐境界
先得天宠,因违背其意

从他们的创造者那里堕落
世界的主宰们竟然失去耐性
引他们发动家禽般的反抗
邪恶的魔鬼,他的诡计
因嫉妒和复仇而起,欺骗了
人类的母亲,当他的自尊
将他自天堂抛弃,以他为首的
叛逆天使,因他们的热情
赋予他高于同类的光荣
相信他具有与最高者同等的地位
他野心勃勃
反抗神的王座和权力
徒然在天堂骄傲的发起不敬的战争
全能的力量
自天上投射熊熊烈火
可怕的毁灭和燃烧降临
无尽的毁灭,若无休止
坚硬的锁链和惩罚之火
加于敢对全能之神挑战者
九倍于凡人以日夜计算的时间
他和他可怕的队伍
被击溃,倒在烈火的深渊
虽不死却充满困惑;但他的厄运
使他更加愤怒;想起
失去的快乐和永恒的痛苦折磨
他以邪恶的眼神望向四周
只看到巨大的痛苦和沮丧
混合着冷酷的骄傲和笃实的憎恨
旋以天使之眼看到
荒芜凄惨的境遇
四周皆是恐怖的地牢
如巨大的洪炉,那火焰之中
没有光,只有看得见的黑暗
只为让你看见悲哀的景象
悲痛的领域,阴沉的影子,
永无和平与休息,人人都有的希望在这里
永不来临,只有无穷的折磨

仍在以燃烧不尽的硫黄，
持续那烈火的狂潮
这样的地方是永恒的正义
为反叛者所准备，这里注定是他们的监狱
在绝对的黑暗中，他们的身体
被置于离神和天堂的光明玄远之地
三倍于天堂的中心到最远支柱的距离
与他们坠落的地方多么的不同
那和他一起坠落的，是无法抗拒的
有如洪水旋风般的狂暴的火焰
他很快辨认出，在他之旁
和他一样具有权力和罪行的
那以后很久才在巴勒斯坦被名以
别卜西以及他们头号敌人的
当时在天堂被称作撒旦的，
以大胆言词打破恐怖的沉默的魔王。

（朱维之　译）

注释

1. paradise[ˈpærəˌdais, -ˌdaiz] *n.*天堂；伊甸园；乐园
2. forbidden fruit[fəˈbidn fruːt] 禁果(由于被禁止而更想得到的东西)
3. woe[wəu] *n.* 悲哀；悲伤；灾难，灾殃；苦恼
4. Heav'nly: Heavenly　Heav'ns: Heavy's
5. flow'd: flowed
6. shepherd[ˈʃepəd] *n.* 牧羊人，羊倌；牧师；指导者
7. illumine[iˈluːmin] *vt.* 照亮，照明；启发
8. Omnipotent[ɔmˈnipətənt] *adj.* 全能的，权力无限的
9. affliction[əˈflikʃən] *n.* 苦恼，痛苦；灾难；哀伤
10. dismay[disˈmei] *vt.* 使惊愕，使焦虑，使气馁　*n.* 惊愕，气馁
11. torture[ˈtɔːtʃə] *n.* 拷问；折磨；痛苦；折磨　*vt.* 使痛苦；使苦恼；使焦急；曲解
12. tempestuous[temˈpestʃuəs] *adj.* 暴风雨的；暴风雪的；剧烈的；狂暴的

赏析

约翰·弥尔顿(John Milton,1608—1674)，英国诗人、政论家，民主斗士。代表作《失乐园》和《荷马史诗》《神曲》并称为西方三大诗歌。弥尔顿是一位清教徒文学的代表，他的一生都

在为资产阶级民主运动而奋斗。他用史诗的形式，通过他个人的体会，把他所处的英国革命时代反映进人类的悲剧。

弥尔顿诗作《失乐园》(*Paradise Lost*,1667)是弥尔顿的巨著，是文学上的最高成就之一，被视为英国文学史上的一座丰碑，堪与荷马的《伊利亚特》、但丁的《神曲》相媲美。《失乐园》以圣经传说为原本，记述了撒旦率领三分之一的天军反叛天国，被打败后落入地面成为魔鬼。撒旦化身为一条蛇进入伊甸园，欺骗夏娃吃下智慧果，成为诱惑人类的始祖。亚当和夏娃被天主赶出了伊甸园，他们被迫在荒凉的大地上，擦干眼泪，开始新的生活。撒旦人物形象是文学史上创造最成功的形象之一。诗中主人公撒旦形象的复杂性是多年来评论界关注的焦点，他的形象的复杂性激发人们尝试从不同角度、不同方面去诠释。撒旦与诗人的经历存在着某种程度的相似点，唤起了他内心深处的无意识，引起了他心灵的共鸣，为诗人倾吐自己和英国广大人民的苦闷和对自由的不懈追求找到了很好的寄托。

在撒旦这形象中，应当看到一个英雄主义的面貌，他认为自己个人是“衡量万物的标准”，是整个宇宙的中心。《失乐园》是一首英雄史诗，作者虽没有亲身参加过当代的斗争，但是他善于在长篇史诗的范围内尽量写出了战争的威力，作者不仅仅是描述英雄们的宏伟的战斗场面，同时他还歌颂了同时代人的英勇无畏的精神。诗人写这首诗的目的在于说明人类不幸的根源。诗人通过对夏娃、亚当、撒旦的堕落的遭遇，暗示英国资产阶级革命也是由于道德堕落、骄奢淫逸而惨遭失败。

原文

18 The Tiger

William Blake

Tiger, tiger, burning bright
In the forests of the night,
What **immortal** hand or eye
Could **frame** thy **fearful symmetry**?

In what **distant deeps or skies**
Burnt the fire of thine eyes?
On what wings dare he **aspire**

What the hand **dare seize the fire**?

And what **shoulder** and what art
Could twist the sinews of thy heart?
And **when thy heart began to beat**,
What dread hand and what dread feet?

What the **hammer**? What the **chain**?
In what **furnace** was thy brain?
What the **anvil**? What dread grasp
Dare its deadly terrors clasp?

When the stars threw down their spears,
And water'd heaven with their tears,
Did He smile His work to see?
Did He who made the lamb make thee?

Tiger, tiger, burning bright
In the forests of the night,
What immortal hand or eye
Dare frame thy fearful symmetry?

译文

18 老 虎

威廉·布莱克

老虎！老虎！火一样辉煌，
烧穿了黑夜的森林和草莽，
什么样非凡的手和眼睛
能塑造你一身惊人的匀称？

什么样遥远的海底、天边
烧出了做你眼睛的火焰？
跨什么翅膀它胆敢去凌空？
凭什么铁掌抓一把火种？

什么样功夫，什么样胳膊
拗得成你五脏六腑的筋络？
等到你的心一开始蹦跳，
什么样惊心动魄的手、脚？

什么样铁链？什么样铁锤？
什么样熔炉里炼你的脑髓？
什么样铁砧？什么样猛劲
一下子掐住了骇人的雷霆？

到临了，星星扔下了金枪，
千万滴银泪洒遍了苍穹，
完工了再看看，他可会笑笑？
不就是造羊的把你也造了？

老虎！老虎！火一样辉煌，
烧穿了黑夜的森林和草莽，
什么样非凡的手和眼睛
能塑造你一身惊人的匀称？

（卞之琳　译）

注释

1. immortal[i'mɔ:tl] *n.*神仙，上帝

2. frame[freim] *vt.* 创造，造就

3. fearful symmetry: 表示老虎既凶猛恐怖，又有漂亮的外观。

4. distant deeps or skies: 暗示修辞法，指天堂和地狱。

5. aspire[ə'spaiə]（古）上升，飞上高空，翱翔 ◆On what wings dare he aspire? 这句有可能暗指希腊神话中的伊卡洛斯，他曾创造翅膀，振翅高飞，以此摆脱迷宫的困扰。

6. dare seize the fire: 擒住火焰的人，有可能暗指希腊神话中的普罗米修斯，他从宙斯那里偷到火，并把它赐予了凡人。“被缚的普罗米修斯”说的就是此后宙斯为惩罚他，把他绑在一块岩石上，每天让鹰来啄吃他的肝，等第二天长出一点，再受啄食之苦。

7. shoulder: 提喻修辞法，以局部的胳膊代表整个身体、体力。

8. when thy heart began to beat: 当你有了生命；上帝造物，先赋予身体外形，然后再赋予生命。

9. hammer, chain, furnace, anvil：锤子、铁链、熔炉、铁钻，都是希腊神话中的火神赫菲斯托斯(Hephaestus)常用的工具。

赏析

威廉·布莱克(William Blake,1757—1827),英国第一位重要的浪漫主义诗人、版画家。1789年,他出版了诗集《纯真之歌》(*Songs of Innocence*),其中有一首《羔羊》(*The Lamb*)是这部诗集中最著名的。《老虎》一诗,发表在1794年出版的《经验之歌》(*Songs of Experience*),后来成为布雷克最著名的诗歌,并被视作《羔羊》的姊妹篇,与《羔羊》形成对比。布莱克的诗歌具有明显的宗教性、预言性、哲理性和艺术性等几大特点。他对英国诗歌,特别是浪漫主义诗歌做出了巨大的贡献。

前期的诗作简洁明快,语言简单易懂,且以短诗为主,音节也较短,题材内容则以生活中的所见所闻为主;而后期的诗作篇幅明显增长,趋向玄妙深沉,充满神秘的色彩,有时长达数百乃至上千行,内容也明显地晦涩起来,以神秘、宗教,以及象征为主要特征。布莱克的诗中透出一种天真,诗人借这种天真想象进行创作,布莱克借神秘与梦幻经验而表达了一种皈依与信仰,这或许是布莱克为后人留下的最重要的经验与价值。

威廉·布莱克的这首《老虎》,广泛地受到读者的喜爱,是被阐释、解读、赏析得最多的诗篇之一。众多的文学评论家、文学赏析人士把这首诗分拆成段,从作者的写作状态到老虎的精神倾向性,逐一研究,进而对个别的字词都深入探讨,利用他们天才的笔表达了对这位18世纪最伟大诗人的认同与赞美。

原文

19 The Darkling Thrush

Thomas Hardy

I leant upon a **coppice** gate
When Frost was spectre-gray,
And Winter's **dregs** made **desolate**
The weakening eye of day.
The tangled bine-stems scored the sky
Like strings of broken lyres,

And all mankind that haunted nigh
Had sought their household fires.
The land's sharp features seemed to be
The Century's corpse outleant,
His crypt the cloudy canopy,
The wind his death-lament.
The ancient pulse of germ and birth
Was shrunken hard and dry,
And every spirit upon earth
Seemed fervourless as I.
At once a voice arose among
The bleak twigs overhead
In a full-hearted evensong
Of joy illimited;
An aged thrush, frail, gaunt, and small,
In blast-beruffled **plume,**
Had chosen thus to fling his soul
Upon the growing gloom.
So little cause for carolings
Of such ecstatic sound
Was written on **terrestrial** things
Afar or nigh around,
That I could think there trembled through
His happy good-night air
Some blessèd Hope, whereof he knew
And I was unaware.

译文

19 黑暗中的鸫鸟

托马斯·哈代

我倚在以树丛作篱的门边，
寒霜像幽灵般发灰，
冬的沉渣使那白日之眼
在苍白中更添憔悴。

纠缠的藤蔓在天上画线，
宛如断了的琴弦，
而出没附近的一切人类
都已退到家中火边。

陆地轮廓分明，望去恰似
斜卧着世纪的尸体，
阴沉的天穹是他的墓室，
风在为他哀悼哭泣。
自古以来萌芽生长的冲动
已收缩得又干又硬，
大地上每个灵魂与我一同
似乎都已丧失热情。
突然间，头顶上有个声音
在细枝萧瑟间升起，
一曲黄昏之歌满腔热情
唱出了无限欣喜，
这是一只鸫鸟，瘦弱、老衰，
羽毛被阵风吹乱，
却决心把它的心灵敞开，
倾泻向浓浓的黑暗。

远远近近，任你四处寻找，
在地面的万物上
值得欢唱的原因是那么少，
是什么使它欣喜若狂？
这使我觉得：它颤音的歌词，
它欢乐的晚安曲调
含有某种幸福希望——为它所知
而不为我所晓。

（飞白　译）

注释

1. thrush[θrʌʃ] *n.* 画眉鸟
2. coppice[ˈkɔpis] *n.* 矮林
3. dregs[dregz] *n.* 渣滓，糟粕

4. desolate['desəlit] *adj.* 荒凉的，无人烟的
5. plume[plu:m] *n.* 羽毛
6. terrestrial[tə'restriəl] *adj.* 世俗的

赏析

托马斯·哈代(Thomas Hardy,1840—1928)，英国诗人、小说家。他是横跨两个世纪的作家，早期和中期的创作以小说为主，继承和发扬了维多利亚时代的文学传统；从小生长在英国西南部的偏远乡村，他的作品以英格兰西南部地区为背景，富有浓重的地方色彩，注重传统与自然。晚年以其出色的诗歌开拓了英国20世纪的文学，成为英国19世纪后期的代表作家。

《黑暗中的鸫鸟》(*The Darkling Thrush*)是哈代的一首著名的抒情诗，诗人通过这首诗向维多利亚时代的旧有习俗观念和制度提出了严正的挑战，在当时遭到非议。哈代的诗冷峻、深刻；诗文细腻、优美，言简意赅，具有现代意识。该诗创作于19世纪最后一天，诗人在诗中表达了他那百感交集的心情，是世纪末的深沉反思，原先被诗人命名为《世纪临终之时》。哈代是一个善于用环境来烘托人物性格、反映现实的诗人。诗中运用比喻与白描结合的手法，勾画了冬天傍晚落日时分的萧条景象。全诗以"我"在残冬日落时刻的感受以及由此引起的感情起伏作为线索，以写实的笔触融情于景，展现出阴冷、灰暗、衰败的景象，抒发了诗人心头的诸多惆怅与不安，衬托了诗人内心说不尽的悲情。诗中还大量运用拟人的手法，弥漫着宿命论的气息，让人绝望到窒息，仿佛大地上的一切都被莫名的力量主宰着，人类社会的各种悲剧不可避免。新世纪即将到来，在诗人眼里却毫无希冀，漫长的死寂终于被一只瘦弱老衰的鸫鸟的鸣叫打破了。

哈代的《黑暗中的鸫鸟》有预言新世纪的味道。这首诗是20世纪最早的诗歌之一，以感官体验为中心展开描绘，穿插了哈代式的奇妙修辞，充分表达了对人类社会不可逆转的灾难的现实思考，是形意俱佳、流传久远的一首欧美经典诗歌。

第三章 哲理故事

原文

1 Prometheus and Man

In the conflict between Cronus and Jupiter, Prometheus had adopted the cause of the Olympian **deities**. To him and his brother Epimetheus was now committed the office of making man and providing him and all other animals with the **faculties** necessary for their preservation. Epimetheus proceeded to **bestow** upon the different animals the various gifts of courage, strength, swiftness, and **sagacity**. Taking some earth and kneading it with water. Prometheus made man in the image of the gods. He gave him an upright stature. Then since Epimetheus had been so **prodigal** of his gifts to other animals that no blessing was left worth conferring upon the noblest of creatures, Prometheus ascended to heaven, lighted his torch at the **chariot** of the sun, and brought down fire. But it was only rather **grudgingly** that Jupiter granted mortals the use of fire.

Then there came the occasion that when gods and men were in dispute at Sicyon concerning the **prerogatives** of each, Prometheus, by an **ingenious** trick, attempted to settle the question in favor of man. Dividing into two portions a sacrificial bull, he wrapped all the eatable parts in the skin, cunningly surmounted with uninviting **entrails**; but the bones he **garnished** with a **plausible** mass of fat. He then offered Jupiter his choice. The king of Heaven, although he perceived the intended fraud, took the heap of bones and fat, and forthwith availing himself of this insult as an excuse for punishing mankind, deprived the race of fire. But Prometheus regained the treasure, stealing it from heaven in a hollow tube.

By Jove's order Prometheus was chained to a rock on Mount Caucasus, and subjected to the attack of an eagle which, for ages, **preyed upon** his liver, yet succeeded not in consuming it.

In his steadfastness to withstand the torment the Titan was supported by the knowledge that in the thirteenth generation there should arrive a hero, — sprung from Jove himself, — to release him. And in fullness of time the hero did arrive: none other than the mighty Hercules. No higher service, thinks this radiant and masterful personage, remains to be performed than to free the champion of mankind. Hercules utters these words to the Titan:

The soul of man can never be enslaved —

Save by its own **infirmities**, nor freed —
Save by its very strength and own resolve
And constant vision and supreme endeavor!
You will be free? Then, courage, O my brother!
O let the soul stand in the open door
Of life and death and knowledge and desire
And see the peaks of thought kindle with sunrise!
Then shall the soul return to rest no more,
Nor harvest dreams in the dark field of sleep —
Rather the soul shall go with great resolve
To dwell at last upon the shining mountains
In liberal converse with the eternal stars.
Thereupon he kills the eagle; and sets Jove's victim free.

(From *100 Myths of Greece and Rome*)

译文

1 普罗米修斯与人类

在克洛诺斯反对朱庇特的斗争中，普罗米修斯站到了奥林波斯山诸神的一边。后来塑造人和赋予人和其他所有动物以生存本领的任务就交给了他和他的弟弟厄庇墨透斯。厄庇墨透斯将勇敢、力气、快速、伶俐等天赋分别赐予各种动物。普罗米修斯则用土和水揉成了泥，照着神的模样捏出了人；他使人呈站立的姿势。厄庇墨透斯把各种天资都慷慨地赠予了其他动物，竟没有剩下什么像样的天赋能赐给最崇高的被造物了。于是普罗米修斯升到天上，在太阳马车那里点燃了一只火把，将火送到地上来。可是，朱庇特却是不大乐意允准人们用火的。

有一次，神和人对各自在西锡安的权限争执不休，普罗米修斯要了一个聪明的计谋，企图使问题的解决对人类有利。他把一头献祭用的牛分为两份，把所有可食用的部分包在牛皮里，并狡猾地在上面摆满不招人喜欢的内脏；把骨头用一层肥脂裹起来，看上去像是好肉。然后他让朱庇特挑选。天国之王看穿了他的阴谋诡计，但还是挑了那堆骨头和肥膘，从而利用这一侮辱为借口剥夺人类使用火的权利。但是普罗米修斯用一根空心管子从天府偷盗火种，再次取得了宝贵的天火。

为此，朱庇特命令将普罗米修斯锁在高加索山上的一块绝岩峭壁上，成年累月地受着一头老鹰的折磨，它天天啄食他的肝脏却总不能把它吃光。这位提坦巨人坚忍不拔地忍受着煎熬，因为他知道在第十三代时就会有一个英雄—— 朱庇特的亲儿子——来解救他。果然不爽，时候一到，英雄真的来了。他不是别人，就是那个力大无穷的海格立斯。这个奋焕英伟的人物认为他需要做的最大贡献莫过于解救这个人类的卫士。海格立斯向提坦巨人说：

人的灵魂永远不能被征服——
除非自身变得脆弱；也永远不能得解放——
除非自身充满决心和力量，以及
不稍亏的目光和无以复加的努力！
想自由吗？那就鼓起勇气，我的兄弟！
啊！让灵魂站在生与死，知与欲
敞开的门扉前，
见到旭日点燃思想的顶峰！
那时灵魂再不会依然故态，
或在黑色的睡乡中收获梦幻——
灵魂将迈着坚定的步伐
直上光芒万丈的山巅
和不落的群星自由交谈。
然后他杀死了老鹰解放了朱庇特的囚徒。

（李淑言　译）

（选自《希腊罗马神话100篇》）

注释

1. deity['deiiti] *n.* 神
2. faculty['fækltі] *n.* 能力
3. bestow[bi'stəu] *vt.* 授予
4. sagacity[sə'gæsəti] *n.* 聪敏；有远见
5. prodigal['prɔdigl] *adj.* 十分慷慨的
6. chariot['tʃæriət] *n.* 战车
7. grudging['ɡrʌdʒiŋ] *adj.* 勉强的
8. prerogative[pri'rɔgətiv] *n.* 特权
9. ingenious[in'dʒiniəs] *adj.* 机灵的
10. entrails['entrelz] *n.* 内脏
11. garnish['gɑ:niʃ] *vt.* 装饰
12. plausible['plɔ:zibl] *adj.* 貌似真实的
13. prey upon: 掠夺，折磨；捕食
14. infirmity[in'fə:məti] *n.* 衰弱

赏析

希腊神话体系中的神有老一代与新生代之分。读者们比较熟悉的生活在奥林匹斯山上,由主神宙斯与天后赫拉统领的这一代属于新生代。他们之前有第一代苍穹之神乌拉诺斯 (Uranus) 与大地女神该亚(Gaea),他们生下的六男六女被称为十二提坦 (Titans);十二提坦中最年轻的克洛诺斯(Cronus)设计推翻了父亲的统治,解救出所有被父亲困在母亲该亚体内的其他提坦巨神,成为第二代神;克洛诺斯与妹妹瑞亚(Rhea) 所生的孩子都被因担心被子女推翻的克洛诺斯吞入体内,唯有小儿子宙斯(Zeus)被母亲藏匿起来。宙斯成人后打败克洛诺斯,解救出众兄弟姐妹,并被推举为主神,成为第三代神。

在宙斯率领众兄弟姐妹对克洛诺斯和其他提坦巨神发动的战争中,只有普罗米修斯和俄克拉俄斯站在宙斯一边。因此,当宙斯最终打败了克洛诺斯和其支持者,将他们关在冥界的最深处塔尔塔洛斯受尽苦难与折磨时,普罗米修斯和俄克拉俄斯却受到众神和人类的尊重。

本文选自《希腊罗马神话100篇》中的第一篇。讲述普罗米修斯创造了人类,盗取天火供他们使用并竭力保护人类使他们免受神祇的迫害。这使宙斯(朱庇特)大为恼火,于是他下令将普罗米修斯锁在高耸入云的高加索山脉之巅的岩石上,派鹰每天啄食他的肝脏。肝脏每夜复原以供再次啄食,使得普罗米修斯的痛苦绵绵不绝。数百年过后,大英雄海格立斯路过此地,才将普罗米修斯拯救出来。

普罗米修斯的故事为此后众多的文学作品提供了素材。希腊著名的三大悲剧家之一的埃斯库罗斯被恩格斯称为“悲剧之父”,他最重要的作品《普罗米修斯三部曲》中的第一部《被缚的普罗米修斯》就取材于这段神话,这出剧中的普罗米修斯被塑造成了人类的保护神和一个悲剧英雄,以普罗米修斯被打进深渊结束。第二部《被释放的普罗米修斯》和第三部《带火的普罗米修斯》虽已失传,但据传以宙斯和普罗米修斯和解结尾。18世纪末德国伟大作家歌德创作了诗歌《普罗米修斯》,剧中的普罗米修斯否认宙斯的权利,反对宙斯的专横跋扈,并且要创造和他一样蔑视宙斯的新人类,歌德把维特身上所缺乏的那种坚韧的性格,在这个神话人物身上充分体现了出来。19世纪英国浪漫主义诗人雪莱沿用了埃斯库罗斯的情节,创作了诗剧《解放了的普罗米修斯》,但改变了前者妥协的结局。在他的诗歌里,普罗米修斯不仅得到了解放,而且宙斯 (朱庇特)的统治也被推翻。

原文

2 The Different Ages of Man

In the Age of Gold, the world was first furnished with inhabitants. This was an age of innocence and happiness. Truth and right prevailed, thought not enforced by law, nor was there any in authority to threaten or to punish. The earth brought forth all things necessary for man, without his labor in plowing or sowing. **Perpetual** spring reigned, flowers sprang up without seed, the rivers flowed with milk and wine, and yellow honey distilled from the oaks.

The Silver Age came next, inferior to the golden. Jupiter shortened the spring, and divided the year into seasons. Then, first, men suffered the extremes of heat and cold, and houses became necessary. Crops would no longer grow without planting. This was a race of manly men, but **insolent** and **impious**.

Next to the Age of Silver came that of brass, more savage of temper and readier for the strife of arms, yet not altogether wicked.

Last came the hardest age and worst - of iron. Crime burst in like a flood; modesty, truth, and honor fled. The gifts of the earth were put only to **nefarious** uses. Fraud, violence, war at home and abroad were rife.

Jupiter, observing the condition of things, burned with anger, He summoned the gods to council. Jupiter set forth to the assembly the frightful condition of the earth, and announced his intention of destroying its inhabitants, and providing a new race, unlike the present, which should be worthier of life and more **reverent** toward the gods. Fearing lest a **conflagration** might set Heaven itself on fire, he proceeded to drown the world. Speedily the race of men and their possessions, were swept away by the **deluge**.

Parnassus alone, of the mountains, overtopped the waves, and there Deucalion, son the Prometheus, and his wife Pyrrha, daughter of Epimetheus, found refuge - he a just man and she a faithful worshiper of the gods. Jupiter, remembering the harmless lives and pious **demeanor** of this pair, caused the waters to recede. Then Deucalion and Pyrrha, entering a temple defaced with slime, approached the enkindled altar and, falling **prostrate**, prayed for guidance and aid. The oracle answered, "Depart from the temple with head veiled and garments unbound, and cast behind you the bones of your mother." They heard the words with astonishment. Pyrrha first broke silence: "We cannot obey; we dare not **profane** the remains of our parents." They sought the woods. and revolved the oracle in their minds. At last Deucalion spoke:"Either my wit fails me or the command is one we may obey without impiety. The earth is the great parent of all; the stones are her bones; these we may cast behind us; this, I think, the oracle means. They veiled their faces, unbound their garments, and , picking up stones, cast them behind them. The stones began to grow soft and to assume shape. By degrees they put on a rude resemblance to the human form . Those thrown by Deucalion became men; those by Pyrrha, women.

(From *100 Myths of Greece and Rome*)

译文

2 人类的各个时代

黄金时代,地球上最初有了居民。这是一个天真无邪和幸福的时代。真理和正义主宰一切,但不是靠法律的约束,也没有什么权贵的恫吓和惩处。人们不用耕种,一切生活必需全可仰给于大地。春天永在,不用种子,地里也长出鲜花来;河里流的是奶和酒,以及从橡树蒸馏而来的黄澄澄的蜜糖。

接下来的是逊于黄金时代的白银时代。朱庇特缩短春天,把一年分为四季。于是人们首先尝到了酷暑严寒之苦,不得不找一个蔽身之所。要吃谷物就得耕作。这时的人类雄伟刚毅,但却骄横不虔。

白银时代之后就是青铜时代。人们的禀性更加粗野,动辄就要大兴干戈,但是还没有达到十恶不赦的地步。

最后到了最棘手和最糟糕的时代——黑铁时代。罪恶像洪水一样泛滥成灾,谦虚、真理和尊严逃得无影无踪。大地的赐予全被用去造孽。欺诈、暴力、对内对外的战争四处猖獗。

朱庇特见到这种情况怒不可遏。他召集众神商讨对策。在神祇大会上,朱庇特陈述了地球上不堪容忍的情况,并宣布了他要毁灭地上现在居民的意向,表示要另置新人。这种新人不同于现有的人,他们将更有生存的价值,对神祇也更加敬重。朱庇特唯恐用火烧会危及天宫本身,就决定用洪水淹没地球,转瞬间洪水就把地球上的人和他们的财物席卷而去。

在所有的山峰中唯有帕尔纳索斯没有被洪水的浪涛所淹没, 普罗米修斯的独生子丢卡利翁和他的妻子皮拉——厄庇墨透斯的女儿——就躲到这个山峰上去。丢卡利翁为人正直,他的妻子则虔诚敬神。朱庇特怜惜他们夫妻一生清白,品行端正,就斥令洪水退去。这时丢卡利翁和皮拉走进了一个溅满了泥浆的神庙里,在香火未燃的祭坛前,他俩伏身在地祈求神祇的指引和帮助。神谕指出说:“裹起头,松开衣带,出庙去,一路走一路将你们母亲的尸骨丢在身后。”这话使他们惊愕不已。皮拉首先打破了沉寂:“我们不能照着这个神谕办事;我们不敢亵渎父母的尸骨。”他们躲进树林,苦苦思索着神谕的含义。最后丢卡利翁说:“要不就是我发了昏,要不就是我们不犯逆忤罪也能执行神谕。大地是万物之母,石头就是她的尸骨。我们可以往身后扔石头,我想神谕说的就是这个意思。”他俩蒙住颜面,松开衣带,捡起石头朝身后扔去。这些石头开始变软,呈现形状,渐渐地带上了略似于人的状貌。丢卡利翁扔的石头变成了男人,皮拉扔的则成了女人。

(李淑言 译)

(选自《希腊罗马神话100篇》)

注释

1. perpetual[pə'petʃuəl] *adj.* 永久的
2. insolent['insələnt] *adj.* 无礼的;傲慢的
3. impious['impaiəs] *adj.* 不虔诚的
4. nefarious[ni'feəriəs] *adj.* 邪恶的
5. reverent['revərənt] *adj.* 恭敬的;尊敬的
6. conflagration[ˌkɔnflə'ɡreiʃən] *n.* 大火
7. deluge['delju:dʒ] *n.* 洪水
8. demeanor[di'mi:nə] *n.* 行为
9. prostrate['prɔstret] *vt.* 使……俯伏
10. profane[prə'fen] *vt.* 亵渎

赏析

每个民族的神话传说都能体现本民族童年的天真淳朴、活泼浪漫,以及渴望征服自然的顽强意志和美好理想。没有神话传说的民族和文化是没有血肉、没有活力的,神话传说是艺术的宝库,也是为其提供养分的土壤。这点在希腊罗马神话中显得尤其突出,正因如此,它才能和希伯来文明一起并称西方文明的源头。

希腊罗马神话是希腊神话与罗马神话的混合体。在罗马人与希腊文化接触并融合的过程中,罗马人以前所秉持的带有宗教信仰性质的神话逐渐被"神人合一"的希腊神话所同化。希腊神话是主体,罗马神话的独创成分很少,基本是对希腊神话的复制。但各自有不同的称谓,如罗马神话中的朱庇特是最高神,相当于希腊神话里的大神宙斯,朱诺等同于赫拉,马尔斯相当于阿波罗,弥涅瓦等同于雅典娜等。

希腊罗马神话有神的故事和英雄传说两大部分,是世界各民族神话中发展特别完美,且有鲜明特色,较少受宗教影响的神话体系。与其他古老民族的神话传说一样,希腊罗马神话的内容包括了世界的由来、众神的诞生、人类的起源及众神的生活等。希腊罗马神话的显著特色就是人本主义色彩浓厚,神与人是同形同性的,即"神人合一"。神话中的神有着与人一致的七情六欲、烦恼纷争。不同的是，众神永生不死，比人更高大，更有力量，而且主宰着人间的祸福与命运。英雄传说中的英雄都是神与凡间女子所生的半人半神。希腊罗马神话有生动的形象和优美的意境，在艺术手法上把浪漫的夸张与现实的描写完美结合了起来，表现了希腊人丰富的想象力和极大的创造力。

本文选自《希腊罗马神话100篇》中的第二篇。讲述继普罗米修斯创造人类后，人类所经历的各个时代。从黄金时代到白银时代到青铜时代再到黑铁时代，人类不断堕落，罪恶不断滋生，直到神忍无可忍决定用洪水毁灭地上的人类，但不至于让人类彻底灭绝。读到这里，读者自然会联想到《圣经·旧约》中的诺亚方舟，的确，有类似大洪水情节的神话还不止这两处，如印度神话、巴比伦神话。显然，这处神话是受到比希腊文明发展更早的巴比伦神话和希伯来神话的影响。

原文

3 Genesis 2:18 – 3:19

And the Lord God said, "It is not good for the man to be by himself: I will make one like himself as a help to him." And from the earth the Lord God made every **beast** of the field and every bird of the air, and took them to the man to see what names he would give them: and whatever name he gave to any living thing, that was its name. And the man gave names to all **cattle** and to the birds of the air and to every beast of the field; but Adam had no one like himself as a help.

And the Lord God sent a deep sleep on the man, and took one of the bones from his side while he was sleeping, joining up the **flesh** again in its place: And the bone which the Lord God had taken from the man he made into a woman, and took her to the man. And the man said, "This is now bone of my bone and flesh of my flesh: let her name be Woman because she was taken out of Man." For this cause will a man go away from his father and his mother and be joined to his wife; and they will be one flesh.

And the man and his wife were without clothing, and they had no sense of shame.

Now the snake was wiser than any beast of the field which the Lord God had made. And he s aid to the woman, "Has God truly said that you may not take of the fruit of any tree in the garden?" And the woman said, "We may take of the fruit of the trees in the garden: But of the fruit of the tree in the middle of the garden," God has said, "If you take of it or put your hands on it, death will come to you." And the snake said, "Death will not certainly come to you: for God sees that on the day when you take of its fruit, your eyes will be open, and you will be as gods, having knowledge of good and evil."

And when the woman saw that the tree was good for food, and a delight to the eyes, and to be desired to make one wise, she took of its fruit, and gave it to her husband. And their eyes were open and they were **conscious** that they had no clothing and they made themselves coats of leaves **stitched** together.

And there came to them the sound of the Lord God walking in the garden in the evening wind: and the man and his wife went to a secret place among the trees of the garden, away from the eyes of the Lord God. And the voice of the Lord God came to the man, saying, "Where are you?" And he said, "Hearing your voice in the garden I was full of fear, because I was without clothing: and I kept myself from your eyes." And he said, "Who gave you the knowledge that you were without clothing? Have you taken of the fruit of the tree which I said you were not to take?" And the man said, "The woman whom you gave to be with me, she gave me the fruit of the tree and I took it." And the Lord God said to the woman, "What have you done?" And the woman said, "I was **tricked** by the **deceit** of the snake and I took it."

And the Lord God said to the snake, "Because you have done this, you are **cursed** more than all cattle and every beast of the field; you will go flat on the earth, and **dust** will be your food all the days of your life: and there will be war between you and the woman and between your seed and her seed: by him will your head be **crushed** and by you his foot will be wounded." To the woman he said, "Great will be your pain in childbirth; in sorrow will your children come to birth; still your desire will be for your husband, but he will be your master." And to Adam he said, "Because you gave ear to the voice of your wife and took of the fruit of the tree which I said you were not to take, the earth is cursed on your account; in pain you will get your food from it all your life. **Thorns** and waste plants will come up, and the plants of the field will be your food; With the hard work of your hands you will get your bread till you go back to the earth from which you were taken: for dust you are and to the dust you will go back."

译文

3 《创世纪》第2章第18节—第3章第19节

耶和华神说："那人独居不好，我要为他造一个配偶帮助他。"耶和华神用土所造成的野地各样走兽和空中各样飞鸟都带到那人面前，看他叫什么。那人怎样叫各样的活物，那就是它的名字。那人便给一切牲畜和空中飞鸟，野地走兽都起了名。只是那人没有遇见配偶帮助他。

耶和华神使他沉睡，他就睡了。于是取下他的一条肋骨，又把肉合起来。耶和华神就用那人身上所取的肋骨，造成一个女人，领她到那人跟前。那人说："这是我骨中的骨，肉中的肉，可以称她为女人，因为她是从男人身上取出来的。"因此，人要离开父母与妻子结合，二人成为一体。

当时夫妻二人赤身露体,并没有羞耻之感。

耶和华神所造的,唯有蛇比田野一切的活物更狡猾。蛇对女人说:“神岂是真说,不许你们吃园中所有树上的果子吗?”女人对蛇说:“园中树上的果子我们可以吃,唯有园当中那棵树上的果子,神曾说:‘你们不可吃,也不可摸,免得你们死。’”蛇对女人说:“你们不一定死,因为神知道,从你们吃过果子的那天起,你们的眼睛就明亮了,你们便如神能知道善恶。”

于是女人见那棵树的果子可作食物,也悦人的眼目,且是可喜爱的,能使人有智慧,就摘下果子来吃了。又给她丈夫,她丈夫也吃了。他们二人的眼睛就明亮了,才知道自己是赤身露体,便拿无花果树的叶子,为自己编作裙子。

天起了凉风,耶和华神在园中行走。那人和他妻子听见神的声音,就藏在园里的树木中,躲避耶和华神的面。耶和华神呼唤那人,对他说:“你在哪里。”他说:“我在园中听见你的声音,我就害怕。因为我赤身露体,我便藏了。”耶和华说:“谁告诉你赤身露体呢?莫非你吃了我吩咐你不可吃的那树上的果子吗?”那人说:“你所赐给我的、与我同居的女人,她把那树上的果子给我,我就吃了。”耶和华神对女人说:“你做的是什么事呢?”女人说:“那蛇引诱我,我就吃了。”

耶和华神对蛇说:“你既做了这事,就必受诅咒,比一切的牲畜野兽更甚。你必用肚子行走,终身吃土。我又要叫你和女人彼此为仇。你的后裔和女人的后裔也彼此为仇。女人的后裔要伤你的头,你要伤他的脚跟。”又对女人说:“我必多多加增你怀胎的苦楚,你生产儿女必多受苦楚。你必恋慕你丈夫,你丈夫必管辖你。”又对亚当说:“你既听从妻子的话,吃了我所吩咐你不可吃的那树上的果子,地必为你的缘故受诅咒。你必终身劳苦,才能从地里得吃的。地必给你长出荆棘和蒺藜来,你也要吃田间的菜蔬。你必汗流满面才得糊口,直到你归了土,因为你是从土而出的。你本是尘土,仍要归于尘土。”

(《圣经·旧约》和合本)

注释

1. beast[bi:st] *n.* 野兽
2. cattle['kætl] *n.* [总称]牲畜
3. flesh[fleʃ] *n.* 肉体
4. conscious['kɔnʃəs] *adj.* 意识到的
5. stitch[stitʃ] *vt.* 缝合
6. trick[trik] *vt.* 哄骗
7. deceit[di'si:t] *n.* 谎言
8. curse[kə:s] *vt.* 诅咒
9. dust[dʌst] *n.* 尘埃
10. crush[krʌʃ] *vt.* 压碎
11. thorns[θɔ:nz] *n.* 荆棘

赏析

基督教《圣经》又称《新旧约全书》，是世界上最幽邃神奇而富有魅力的书。《圣经》作为西方两希文明（希腊—罗马文明与希伯来文明）的源头之一，不仅对人类的宗教和信仰体系有着突出贡献，而且对信仰以外的哲学、科学、文学、艺术等诸多领域都产生了久远且深刻的影响。《圣经·旧约》约形成于公元前1300年至公元前100年间，汇集了古希伯来民族的神话、传说、历史、人物、诗歌等内容，共有39卷，分为4部分：创世纪与摩西律法、以色列历史、智慧书与诗歌、先知书。

本文选自《圣经·旧约》《创世纪》第2章第18节到第3章第19节，讲述上帝创造了人类始祖亚当和夏娃，二人受到引诱犯罪后被逐出伊甸园，从此将宗教中的"原罪"一代代传下来。英国著名作家弥尔顿就曾以这段文字为原型创作了英国文学史上著名的史诗《失乐园》。整篇文字简洁、清新但又不失宗教的威严与深刻的哲理。从世俗角度分析，这段文字蕴含的哲理充斥在生活的方方面面：任何人都难免受到各种诱惑，当需要为抵制不住诱惑付出代价且承担责任时，总会首先将责任推至诱惑本身。既然人人难于幸免于诱惑，就要为此付出代价，这就是绝对的公平。

原文

4 Exodus 20:1-21（Extract）

And God said all these words: I am the Lord your God who took you out of the land of Egypt, out of the prison-house.

You are to have no other gods but me.

You are not to make an image or picture of anything in heaven or on the earth or in the waters under the earth: You may not go down on your faces before them or give them **worship**: for I, the Lord your God, am a God who will not give his honour to another; and I will send punishment on the children for the wrongdoing of their fathers, to the third and fourth generation of my **haters**; And I will have **mercy** through a thousand generations on those who have love for me and keep my laws.

You are not to make use of the name of the Lord your God for an **evil** purpose; whoever takes the Lord's name on his lips for an evil purpose will be judged a **sinner** by the Lord.

Keep in memory the **Sabbath** and let it be a holy day. On six days do all your work: But the seventh day is a Sabbath to the Lord your God; on that day you are to do no work, you or your son or your daughter, your man-servant or your woman-servant, your cattle or the man from a strange country who is living among you: for in six days the Lord made heaven and earth, and the sea, and everything in them, and he took his rest on the seventh day: for this reason the Lord has given his **blessing** to the seventh day and made it holy.

Give honour to your father and to your mother, so that your life may be long in the land which the Lord your God is giving you.

Do not put anyone to death without cause.

Do not be false to the married relation.

Do not take the **property** of another.

Do not give false **witness** against your neighbour.

Let not your desire be turned to your neighbor's house, or his wife or his man-servant or his woman-servant or his ox or his ass or anything which is his.

And all the people were watching the **thunderings** and the **flames** and the sound of the **horn** and the mountain smoking; and when they saw it, they kept far off, shaking with fear. And they said to Moses, "To your words we will give ear, but let not the voice of God come to our ears, for fear death may come on us." And Moses said to the people, "Have no fear: for God has come to put you to the test, so that fearing him you may be kept from sin." And the people kept their places far off, but Moses went near to the dark cloud where God was.

(From *The Old Testament. Holy Bible*)

译文

4 《出埃及记》第20章第1—21节(节选)

神吩咐这一切的话说:"我是耶和华你的神,曾将你从埃及之地为奴之家领出来。"

"除了我以外,你不可有别的神。"

"不可为自己雕刻偶像,也不可做什么形象仿佛天上、地面上、地底下、水中的百物。不可跪拜那些偶像,也不可侍奉它,因为我耶和华你的神是忌邪的神。恨我的,我必追讨他的罪,自父及子,直到三四代;爱我、守我诫命的,我必向他们发慈爱,直到千代。"

"不可妄称耶和华你神的名,因为妄称耶和华名的,耶和华必不以他为无罪。"

"当记念安息日,守为圣日。六日要劳碌做你一切的工作,但第七日是向耶和华你神当守的安息日。这一日你和你的儿女、仆婢、牲畜,并你城里寄居的客旅,无论何工都不可做,因为六日之内,耶和华造天、地、海和其中的万物,第七日便安息,所以耶和华赐福予安息日,定为圣日。"

"当孝敬父母,使你的日子在耶和华你神所赐你的地上得以长久。"

"不可杀人。"

"不可奸淫。"

"不可偷盗。"

"不可作假见证陷害人。"

"不可贪恋人的房屋,也不可贪恋人的妻子、仆婢、牛驴、并他一切所有的。"

众百姓见雷轰、闪电、角声,山上冒烟,就都发颤,远远地站立。对摩西说:"求你和我们说话,我们必听,不要让神和我们说话,以免我们死亡。"摩西对百姓说:"不要惧怕,因为神降临是要试验你们,叫你们时常敬畏他,不致犯罪。"于是百姓远远地站立,摩西就挨近神所在的幽暗之中。

(《圣经·旧约》和合本)

注释

1. worship[ˈwəːʃip] *n.* 崇拜
2. hater[ˈheitə] *n.* 怀恨者
3. mercy[ˈməːsi] *n.* 仁慈,宽容
4. evil[ˈiːvəl] *adj.* 邪恶的
5. sinner[ˈsinə] *n.* 罪人
6. Sabbath[ˈsæbəθ] *n.* 安息日,是犹太人的宗教节日。即每六天后的一天——第七天。由第六天的日落起至第七天的日落止,在这一天应停止做一切的工作。在安息日这一天,不但以色列子民,而且连他们的奴隶,以及住在他们家里的外侨,甚至牲畜(如驴牛),都要停止工作。
7. blessing[ˈblesiŋ] *n.* 祝福;赐福
8. property[ˈprɔpəti] *n.* 财产
9. witness[ˈwitnis] *n.* 证据
10. thundering[ˈθʌnd(ə)riŋ] *n.* 打雷
11. flame[fleim] *n.* 火焰
12. horn[hɔːn] *n.* 号角

赏析

《出埃及记》是《圣经·旧约》中摩西五经的第二卷,共40章,据传为摩西所作。《出埃及记》叙述了以色列人民沦为埃及境内的奴隶,在他们的民族英雄摩西带领下,冲破法老设置的重重障碍,过红海前往西乃山的过程。据圣经记载,摩西带领他的族人在西奈山下祈祷,请求耶

和华为他的族人指一条道路。一只看不见的手——上帝之手在西奈山的峭壁上刻出十条戒律。此卷的中心内容是上帝通过摩西带领以色列人民摆脱埃及人的奴役,并与摩西和以色列民众立约,称为"摩西十诫"。

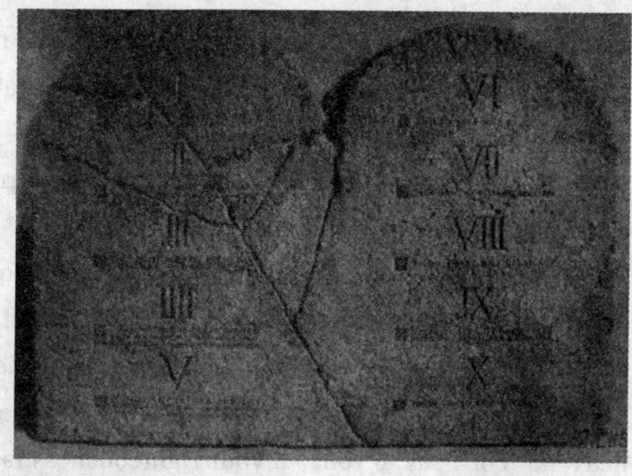

本篇选自《出埃及记》第20章第1节至第21节，系上帝在西奈山上向摩西授予十诫。"摩西十诫" 在旧约部分的地位与作用相当重要,被视为希伯来最古老的宗教与民事法典。这十诫也是上帝与以色列民众所立之"约",与耶稣诞生之后所立之"约"形成对照,故前者称旧约,后者称新约。这段文字铿锵坚定,处处显露着上帝的威严与律例的不容违背性。

原文

5 The Beatitudes(Extract)

And seeing great **masses** of people he went up into the mountain; and when he was seated his **disciples** came to him. And with these words he gave them teaching, saying:

Happy are the poor in spirit: for the kingdom of heaven is theirs.

Happy are those who are sad: for they will be **comforted**.

Happy are the gentle: for the earth will be their **heritage**.

Happy are those whose heart's desire is for **righteousness**: for they will have their desire.

Happy are those who have **mercy**: for they will be given mercy.

Happy are the clean in heart: for they will see God.

Happy are the peacemakers: for they will be named sons of God.

Happy are those who are attacked **on account of** righteousness: for the kingdom of heaven will be theirs.

Happy are you when men give you a bad name, and are cruel to you, and say all evil things against you falsely, because of me. Be glad and full of joy; for great is your reward in heaven: for so were the **prophets** attacked who were before you.

You are the salt of the earth; but if its taste goes from the salt, how will you make it salt again? it is then good for nothing but to be put out and crushed under foot by men.

You are the light of the world. A town put on a hill may be seen by all. And a burning light is not put under a vessel, but on its table; so that its rays may be shining on all who are in the house. Even so let your light be shining before men, so that they may see your good works and give glory to your Father in heaven.

Let there be no thought that I have come to put an end to the law or the prophets. I have not come for destruction, but to make complete.

Truly I say to you, "Till heaven and earth come to an end, not the smallest letter or part of a letter will in any way be taken from the law, till all things are done. Whoever then goes against the smallest of these laws, teaching men to do the same, will be named least in the kingdom of heaven; but he who keeps the laws, teaching others to keep them, will be named great in the kingdom of heaven." For I say to you, "If your righteousness is not greater than the righteousness of the scribes and Pharisees, you will never go into the kingdom of heaven."

(From *Matthew 5:1-12, The New Testament. Holy Bible*)

译文

5 八福(节选)

耶稣看见这许多的人,就上了山,既已坐下,门徒到他跟前来。他就开口教训他们说:

虚心的人有福了,因为天国是他们的。

哀恸的人有福了,因为他们必得安慰。

温柔的人有福了,因为他们必承受土地。

渴慕正义的人有福了,因为他们必得饱足。

怜恤人的人有福了,因为他们必蒙怜恤。

清心的人有福了,因为他们必得见神。

使人和睦的人有福了,因为他们必称为神的儿子。

为义受逼迫的人有福了,因为天国是他们的。

人若因我辱骂你们,逼迫你们,捏造各样坏话毁谤你们,你们就有福了。 应当欢喜快乐,因为你们在天上的赏赐是大的。在你们以前的先知,人也是这样逼迫他们。

你们是世上的盐。盐若失了味,怎能叫他再咸呢?以后无用,不过丢在外面,被人践踏了。

你们是世上的光。城造在山上,是不能隐藏的。人点灯,不放在斗底下,是放在灯台上,就照亮一家的人。你们的光也当这样照在人前,叫他们看见你们的好行为,便将荣耀归给你们在天上的父。

莫想我来要废掉律法和先知。我来不是要废掉,乃是要成全。我实在告诉你们,直到天地都废去了,律法的一点一画也不能废去,都要成全。 所以无论何人废掉这诫命中最小的一条，又教训人这样做，他在天国要称为最小的。但无论何人遵行这诫命，又教训人遵行，他在天国要称为大的。我告诉你们，你们的义，若不胜于文士和法利赛人的义，断不能进天国。

（选自《圣经·新约·马太福音》和合本第5章第1—20节）

注释

1. mass[mæs] *n.* 大量，众多

2. disciple[di'saipl] *n.* 门徒 ◆耶稣有十二门徒，其中为利出卖耶稣的叫犹大。达·芬奇的名画《最后的晚餐》表现的即是耶稣受难前与十二门徒共进晚餐。画中的耶稣泰然自若，其余门徒镇定祥和，唯有犹大手持钱袋、内心难以平静。

3. comfort['kʌmfət] *vt.* 安慰

4. heritage['heritidʒ] *n.* 遗产

5. righteousness['raitʃəsnis] *n.* 正义

6. mercy['mə:si] *n.* 怜悯

7. on account of: 由于，为了……的缘故

8. prophet['prɔfit] *n.* 先知

赏析

《圣经·新约》共有27卷，约于公元4世纪成型。主要讲述耶稣基督的生平言行及其门徒传播福音的过程。“新约”的内容分为三部分：四福音书、使徒行传、启示录。基督教教义称：“旧约”是上帝的诺言，突出强调“律法”“公义”，并预言基督降生；“新约”是诺言的实践，强调“救赎”，是预言的完成。

本文选自四福音书之首的《马太福音》第五章第一至二十节，是著名的“登山宝训”片段。这里耶稣向包括门徒在内的众人教导什么类型的人可以享受地上乃至永生天国里的福气，句句饱含深刻的宗教、人生和处世哲学，为基督教许多重要观点的出处。此处语言平实，展现的是一个和蔼可亲、平易近人的耶稣，与旧约中威严、不可亲近的上帝形象形成了鲜明的对比。

原文

6 Chapter IV Loneliness(Extract)

E. B. White

For a while he stood gloomily indoors. Then he walked to the door and looked out. Drops of rain struck his face. His yard was cold and wet. His **trough** had an inch of rainwater in it. Templeton was nowhere to be seen.

"Are you out there, Templeton?" called Wilbur. There was no answer. Suddenly Wilbur felt lonely and friendless.

"One day just like another," he groaned. "I'm very young, I have no real friend here in the barn, it's going to rain all morning and all afternoon, and Fern won't come in such bad weather. Oh, honestly!" And Wilbur was crying again, for the second time in two days.

At six - thirty Wilbur heard the banging of a **pail**. Lurvy was standing outside in the rain, stirring up breakfast.

"C'mon, pig!" said Lurvv.

Wilbur did not **budge**. Lurvy dumped the **slops**, scraped the pail, and walked away. He noticed that something was wrong with the pig.

Wilbur didn't want food, he wanted love. He wanted a friend — someone who would play with him. He mentioned this to the goose, who was sitting quietly in a corner of the sheepfold.

"Will you come over and play with me?" he asked.

"Sorry, sonny, sorry," said the goose, "I'm sitting — sitting on my eggs. Eight of them. Got to keep them toasty — oasty — oasty warm. I have to stay right here, I'm no flibberty — ibberty — gibbet. I do not play when there are eggs to hatch. I'm expecting goslings."

"Well, I didn't think you were expecting wood-peckers," said Wilbur, bitterly.

Wilbur next tried one of the lambs.

"Will you please play with me?" he asked.

"Certainly not," said the lamb. "In the first place, I cannot get into your pen, as I am not old enough to jump over the fence. In the second place, I am not interested in pigs. Pigs mean less than nothing to me."

"What do you mean, less than nothing?" replied Wilbur. "I don't think there is any such thing as less than nothing. Nothing is absolutely the limit of nothingness. It's the lowest you can go. It's the end of the line. How can something be less than nothing? If there were something that was less than nothing, then nothing would not be nothing, it would be something — even though it's just a very little bit of something. But if nothing is nothing, then nothing has nothing that is less than it is."

"Oh, be quiet! " said the lamb. "Go play by yourself! I don't play with pigs."

Sadly, Wilbur lay down and listened to the rain. Soon he saw the rat climbing down a slanting board that he used as a stairway.

"Will you play with me, Templeton?" asked Wilbur.

"Play?" said Templeton, **twirling** his **whiskers**. "Play? I hardly know the meaning of the word."

"Well," said Wilbur, "it means to have fun, to frolic, to run and skip and make merry."

"I never do those things if I can avoid them," replied the rat, sourly. "I prefer to spend my time eating, gnawing, spying, and hiding. I am a **glutton** but not a merry-maker. Right now I am on my way to your trough to eat your breakfast, since you haven't got sense enough to eat it yourself." And Templeton, the rat, crept stealthily along the wall and disappeared into a private tunnel that he had dug between the door and the trough in Wilbur's yard. Templeton was a **crafty** rat, and he had things pretty much his own way. The tunnel was an example of his skill and cunning. The tunnel enabled him to get from the bam to his hiding place under the pig trough without coming out into the open. He had tunnels and runways all over Mr. Zuckeman's farm and could get from one place to another without being seen. Usually he slept during the daytime and was abroad only after dark.

Wilbur watched him disappear into his tunnel. In a moment he saw the rat's sharp nose **poke** out from underneath the wooden trough. Cautiously Templeton pulled himself up over the edge of : trough. This was almost more than Wilbur could stand: on this dreary, rainy day to see his breakfast being eaten by somebody else. He knew Templeton was getting soaked, out there in the pouring rain, but even that didn't comfort him. Friendless, dejected, and hungry, he threw himself down in the **manure** and sobbed.

Late that afternoon, Lurvy went to Mr. Zuckemlan. "I think there's something wrong with that pig of yours. He hasn't touched his food."

"Give him two spoonfuls of **sulphur** and a little **molasses**," said Mr. Zuckerman.

Wilbur couldn't believe what was happening to him when Lurvy caught him and forced the medicine down his throat. This was certainly the worst day of his life. He didn't know whether he could endure the awful loneliness any more.

Darkness settled over everything. Soon there were only shadows and the noises of the sheep chewing their cuds, and occasionally the rattle of a cow-chain up overhead. You can imagine Wilbur's surprise when, out of the darkness, came a small voice he had ever heard before. It sounded rather thin, but pleasant. "Do you want a friend, Wilbur?" it said. "I'll be a friend to you. I've watched you all day and I like you."

"But I can't see you," said Wilbur, jumping to his feet. "Where are you? And who are you?"

"I'm right up here," said the voice. "Go to sleep. You'll see me in the morning."

(From *Charlotte's Web*)

译文

6 第4章 孤独(节选)

E. B. 怀特

它在圈里扫兴地站了好一会儿,接着它走到门口,望出去。雨点打在它脸上。它的猪栏又冷又湿嗒嗒。它的食槽里面积了一英寸的水。坦普尔顿连个影子也见不着。

"你在外面吗,坦普尔顿?"威尔伯叫道。没有回答。威尔伯一下子感到孤独了,一个朋友也没有。

"天天一个样,"它抱怨说,"我太小,在谷仓这儿我没有真正的朋友,雨要下一整个上午一整个下午,天气这么坏,弗恩不会来了。噢,天啊!"威尔伯又哭了,两天当中这是第二回了。

六点半,威尔伯听到桶子砰砰响。勒维正站在外面顶着雨搅拌它的早饭。

"来吧,小猪!"勒维叫它。

威尔伯一动不动。勒维倒下泔脚,刮干净桶子,走了。他注意到这小猪有点不对头。

威尔伯不要食物,它要爱。它要一个朋友——一个肯和它一起玩的朋友。它对静静地坐在羊栏角落的母鹅讲话。

"你肯过来和我一起玩吗?"它问道

"对不起——对不起——对不起,"母鹅说,"我在孵——孵——孵我的蛋。一共八个蛋。我得让它们热乎乎——热乎乎——热乎乎的。我得蹲在这里不动,我是个负责任——负责任——负责任的鹅妈妈。有蛋要孵我连玩也不玩。我在等着着小鹅出世。"

"当然,我不会以为你在等着啄木鸟出世。"威尔伯挖苦说。

威尔伯接下来试着问一只小羊羔。

"你能跟我玩吗?"它问道。

"当然不能,"那小羊羔说,"第一,我没法到你的圈里去,我还没大到能跳过围栏。第二,我对猪没兴趣。对我来说,猪的价值比零还要少。"

"比零还要少,你这话是什么意思?"威尔伯应道,"我不认为有什么东西会比零还要少。零就是零,什么也没有,这已经到了极限,少到了极限,怎么能有东西比零还要少呢?如果有什么东西比零还要少,那么这零就不能是零,一定要有些东西——哪怕只是一丁点东西。如果零就是零,那就没有什么东西比它还要少。"

"噢,别说了!"小羊羔说,"你自个儿去玩吧!反正我不跟猪玩。"

威尔伯很难过,只好躺下来,听雨声。很快它看到那只老鼠从一块斜板上爬下来,它把它当楼梯使。

"你肯跟我一起玩吗?坦普尔顿?"威尔伯问它。"玩?"坦普尔顿捻捻它的小胡子,"玩?我简直不知道'玩'这个字是什么意思。"

“玩嘛，”威尔伯说：“它的意思是游戏、耍、又跑又跳、取乐儿。”

“这种事我从来能不干就不干，”老鼠尖刻地回答说，“我情愿把时间花在吃啊，啃啊，窥探啊，躲藏啊这些上头。我是个大食鬼而不是个寻欢作乐者。这会儿我正要上你的食槽去吃你的早饭，既然你自己不想吃。”坦普尔顿这老鼠说着偷偷地顺着墙爬，钻进了它在门和猪栏的食槽之间挖的地道。坦普尔顿是只诡计多端的机灵老鼠，它办法多多。这条地道就是它的技巧和狡猾的一个例子，让它不用上地面就能从谷仓到达它在食槽底下的藏身处。它的地道和通路遍布朱克曼先生的整个农场，能够从一个地方到另一个地方而不被人看见。白天它通常睡觉，天黑了才外出活动。

威尔伯看着它钻进地道不见了，转眼就见它的尖鼻子从食槽底下伸出来。坦普尔顿小心翼翼地爬过食槽的边进了食槽。在这可怕的下雨天，眼睁睁地看着自己的早饭被别人吃掉，这简直叫威尔伯无法容忍。就算它知道，瓢泼大雨中，坦普尔顿在那儿浑身都湿透了，也不能让它心里好过些。没有朋友，情绪低落，饿着肚子，它不由得扑倒在肥料上抽抽搭搭哭起来。

那天下午后半晌，勒维去对朱克曼先生说：“我觉得你那只小猪有点不对头。吃的东西它连碰也不碰。”

“给它两匙羹硫黄和一点蜂蜜吧。”朱克曼先生说。

当勒维抓住威尔伯，把药硬灌进它的喉咙时，威尔伯简直不能相信会碰到这种事。这真是它一生中最糟糕的一天。这种可怕的孤独，它真不知道是不是还能再忍耐下去。

黑暗笼罩了一切。很快就只有影子和羊嚼草的声音了，偶尔还有头顶上牛链子的格格声。因此，当黑暗中传来一个威尔伯从没听到过的细小声音时，它有多么吃惊，你们也就可想而知了。这声音听上去很细，可是很好听。“你要一个朋友吗，威尔伯？”那声音说，“我可以做你的朋友。我观察你一整天了，我喜欢你。”

“可我看不见你，”威尔伯跳起来说，“你在哪里？你是谁？”

“我就在上面这儿，”那声音说，“睡觉吧。明天早晨你就看见我了。”

（任溶溶　译）

（选自《夏洛的网》）

注释

1. trough[trɔf] *n.*饲料槽
2. pail[peil] *n.* 桶
3. budge[bʌdʒ] *vi.* 挪动；微微移动
4. slop[slɔp] *n.*流体食物
5. twirl[twə:l] *vt.* 捻弄
6. whisker[hwiskə] *n.* 胡须
7. glutton['glʌtn] *n.* 贪吃的
8. crafty['kræfti] *adj.* 灵巧的
9. poke[pəuk] *vi.* 伸出

10. manure[mə'njuə] *n.* 肥料
11. sulphur['sʌlfə] *n.* 硫黄
12. molasses[mə'læsiz] *n.* 糖蜜

赏析

E. B. 怀特(1899—1985),美国当代著名散文家、儿童文学作家、评论家。以散文名世,“其文风冷峻清丽,辛辣幽默,自成一格”。虽然他一生只写过三部儿童文学作品:《斯图尔特鼠小弟》(又译《精灵鼠小弟》)、《夏洛的网》与《吹小号的天鹅》,但其在世界范围内的影响绝不亚于其散文成就,其中《夏洛的网》位居“美国十佳儿童文学名著”中的首位,可见它受欢迎的程度。怀特生于纽约蒙特弗农,毕业于康奈尔大学。他作为《纽约客》的主要撰稿人,一手奠定了影响深远的“《纽约客》文风”。由于怀特在散文创作等方面取得的突出成绩,他在生前曾获得美国“国家文学奖章”“普利策特别文艺奖”等多项殊荣。

《夏洛的网》是一部童话,故事生动,情节有趣,充满悬念。在朱克曼家的谷仓里,快乐地生活着一群动物,其中小猪威尔伯和蜘蛛夏洛建立了最真挚的友谊。然而,一个最丑恶的消息打破了谷仓的平静:威尔伯未来的命运竟是成为熏肉火腿。作为一只小猪,悲痛绝望的威尔伯似乎只能接受任人宰割的命运了,然而,看似渺小的夏洛却说:“我救你。”于是,夏洛用自己的丝在猪栏上织出了被人类视为奇迹的网上文字,彻底逆转了威尔伯的命运,终于让它在集市的大赛中赢得特别奖和一个安享天命的未来。但这时,蜘蛛夏洛的生命却走到了尽头……这本书里强调:不管是人还是动物的生命,都是一样平等的生命,都有着自己的生存权利。所以一头相对庞大的小猪威尔伯和渺小的蜘蛛可以成为朋友,所以作为人类成员之一的弗恩可以和威尔伯交流感情。本书故事生动,情节有趣,充满悬念,虽然是儿童文学作品,但E. B. 怀特这位散文大师用他幽默的文笔,深入浅出地讲了些很有意义的哲理,关于爱,关于友情,关于生死……正因为这个缘故,这本书也受到成人读者的喜爱。

本文选自小说第四章。小猪威尔伯在百无聊赖的阴雨天找不到一个愿意和自己玩、给他做朋友的人。孤独的小猪“情绪低落,饿着肚子”,还要任主人把他的短见强加在自己身上,这似乎是威尔伯一生中最糟糕的日子了。难道他的一生就要在孤独中消逝?往往希望的曙光就在这时出现,有人喜欢他,要和他做朋友。威尔伯满怀希望地期待黎明降临,迫不及待地一识朋友的真面目。这段文字简洁、细腻,把小猪威尔伯对无聊生活的厌烦、对友谊的渴望刻画得惟妙惟肖,跃然于纸上。

原文

7 Chapter Ⅲ Come Away, Come Away!（Extract）

James Matthew Barrie

Then Wendy saw the shadow on the floor, looking so **draggled**, and she was frightfully sorry for Peter. "How awful! " she said, but she could not help smiling when she saw that he had been trying to stick it on with soap. How exactly like a boy!

Fortunately she knew at once what to do. "It must be sewn on," she said, just a little **patronisingly**.

"What's sewn?" he asked.

"You're dreadfully ignorant."

"No, I'm not."

But she was exulting in his ignorance. "I shall sew it on for you, my little man," she said, though he was as tall as herself; and she got out her housewife, and sewed the shadow on to Peter's foot.

"I dare say it will hurt a little," she warned him.

"Oh, I shan't cry," said Peter, who was already of opinion that he had never cried in his life. And he clenched his teeth and did not cry; and soon his shadow was behaving properly, though still a little **creased.** "Perhaps I should have ironed it," Wendy said thoughtfully; but Peter, boylike, was indifferent to appearances, and he was now jumping about in the wildest glee. Alas, he had already forgotten that he owed his bliss to Wendy. He thought he had attached the shadow himself. "How clever I am," he crowed **rapturously**, "oh, the cleverness of me! "

It is humiliating to have to confess that this conceit of Peter was one of his most fascinating qualities. To put it with brutal frankness, there never was a cockier boy.

But for the moment Wendy was shocked. "You conceit," she exclaimed, with frightful **sarcasm**; "of course I did nothing! "

"You did a little," Peter said carelessly, and continued to dance.

"A little! " she replied with hauteur, "if I am no use I can at least withdraw"; and she sprang in the most dignified way into bed and covered her face with the blankets.

To induce her to look up he pretended to be going away, and when this failed he sat on the end of the bed and tapped her gently with his foot. "Wendy," he said, "don't withdraw. I can't help crowing, Wendy, when I'm pleased with myself." Still she would not look up, though she was listening eagerly. "Wendy," he continued, in a voice that no woman has ever yet been able to resist, "Wendy, one girl is more use than twenty boys."

Now Wendy was every inch a woman, though there were not very many inches, and she peeped out of the bedclothes.

"Do you really think so, Peter?"

"Yes, I do."

"I think it's perfectly sweet of you," she declared, "and I'll get up again"; and she sat with him on the side of the bed. She also said she would give him a kiss if he liked, but Peter did not know what she meant, and he held out his hand expectantly.

"Surely you know what a kiss is?" she asked, **aghast**.

"I shall know when you give it to me," he replied stiffly; and not to hurt his feelings she gave him a **thimble**.

"Now," said he, "shall I give you a kiss?" and she replied with a slight primness, "If you please." She made herself rather cheap by inclining her face toward him, but he merely dropped an acorn button into her hand; so she slowly returned her face to where it had been before, and said nicely that she would wear his kiss on the chain round her neck. It was lucky that she did put it on that chain, for it was afterwards to save her life.

When people in our set are introduced, it is customary for them to ask each other's age, and so Wendy, who always liked to do the correct thing, asked Peter how old he was. It was not really a happy question to ask him; it was like an examination paper that asks grammar, when what you want to be asked is Kings of England.

"I don't know," he replied uneasily, "but I am quite young." He really knew nothing about it; he had merely suspicions, but he said at a venture, "Wendy, I ran away the day I was born."

Wendy was quite surprised, but interested; and she indicated in the charming drawing-room manner, by a touch on her night-gown, that he could sit nearer her.

"It was because I heard father and mother," he explained in a low voice, "talking about what I was to be when I became a man." He was extraordinarily **agitated** now. "I don't want ever to be a man," he said with passion. "I want always to be a little boy and to have fun. So I ran away to Kensington Gardens and lived a long long time among the fairies."

She gave him a look of the most intense admiration, and he thought it was because he had run away, but it was really because he knew fairies. Wendy had lived such a home life that to know fairies struck her as quite delightful. She poured out questions about them, to his surprise, for they were rather a **nuisance** to him, getting in his way and so on, and indeed he sometimes had to give them a hiding. Still, he liked them on the whole, and he told her about the beginning of fairies.

"You see, Wendy, when the first baby laughed for the first time, its laugh broke into a thousand pieces, and they all went skipping about, and that was the beginning of fairies."

Tedious talk this, but being a stay-at-home she liked it.

"And so," he went on good-naturedly, "there ought to be one fairy for every boy and girl."

"Ought to be? Isn't there?"

"No. You see children know such a lot now, they soon don't believe in fairies, and every time a child says," I don't believe in fairies, "there is a fairy somewhere that falls down dead."

Really, he thought they had now talked enough about fairies, and it struck him that Tinker Bell was keeping very quiet. "I can't think where she has gone to," he said, rising, and he called Tink by name. Wendy's heart went flutter with a sudden thrill.

"Peter," she cried, clutching him, "you don't mean to tell me that there is a fairy in this room! "

(from *Peter and Wendy*)

译文

7 第3章 走了,走了(节选)

詹姆斯·马修·巴利

这时候,温迪瞅见了地板上的影子,拖得挺脏的样子,她很替彼得难过。"真糟糕!"她说。 可是,当她看到彼得试着用肥皂去粘,又禁不住笑了起来。真是不折不扣像个小子干的事!

幸好她一下子就想到该怎么办。"得用针线缝上才行。"她说,带点保护人的口气。

"什么叫缝?"彼得问。

"你真笨得要命。"

"不,我不笨。"

不过,温迪喜欢他的正是笨。"我的小家伙,我来给你缝上。"她说,虽然彼得和她一样高。于是,她拿出针线盒来,把影子往彼得的脚上缝。

"怕是要有点儿疼的。"她警告说。

"啊,我一定不哭。"彼得说,他刚哭过,马上就以为他这辈子从来没哭过。他果然咬牙没哭。不一会儿,影子就弄妥了,不过还有点皱。

"也许我应该把它熨熨平。"温迪考虑得很周到;可是,彼得就像个男孩一样,一点也不在乎外表,他这时欢喜得发狂,满屋子乱跳。他早已忘记,他的快乐是温迪赐给的。他以为影子是他自己粘上的。"我多聪明啊,"他开心地大叫,"啊,我多机灵啊!"

说起来,彼得的骄傲自大,正是他招人喜欢的地方,承认这一点,是够叫人难堪的。说句老实话,从来没有一个孩子像彼得这样爱翘尾巴。

不过,当时温迪可惊骇极了。"你这个自大狂,"她讥诮地惊叫说,"当然啰,我什么也没干!"

"你也干了一点点。"彼得漫不经心地说,继续跳着舞。

"一点点!"温迪高傲地说,"既然我没有用,我起码可以退出吧。"她神气十足地跳上了床,用毯子蒙上了脸。

彼得假装要离开的样子,来引温迪抬头,可是没用。于是他坐在床尾那头,用脚轻轻地踢她。“温迪,”他说,“别退出呀,温迪,我一高兴,就禁不住要翘尾巴。”温迪还是不抬头,虽然她是在认真地听着。“温迪,”彼得继续说,他说话的那种声调,是没有一个女孩子能抗拒的,“温迪,一个女孩比二十个男孩都顶用。”

原来温迪从头到脚每一寸都是个女娃,虽说她身高总共也不过几寸。她忍不住从床单底下探出头来。

“你真的这么想吗,彼得?”

“是的,我真的这么想。”

“你实在太可爱了,”温迪说,“我要再起来了。”于是她和彼得并排坐在床沿上。她还说,如果他愿意的话,她想给他一个吻;可是彼得不明白她的意思,就伸出手来,期待地等着。

“你当然知道什么叫吻喽?”温迪吃惊地问。

“你把吻给我,我就会知道。”彼得倔犟地回答。温迪不愿伤他的心,给了他一只顶针。

“现在,”彼得说,“要不要我也给你一个吻?”温迪回答,神情有点拘谨,“那就请吧。”她把脸颊向他凑过去,显得怪贱的。可是彼得只把一粒橡子放在她手里;于是温迪又把脸慢慢地退回原处,并且亲切地说,她要把他的吻拴在项链上,戴在脖子上。幸好,她果真把橡子挂在了项链上,因为后来,这东西救了她的命。

一伙人在彼此介绍以后,照例总是要互问年龄,所以,做事从来正确无误的温迪,这时就问彼得,他多大年纪。这话问得可真不恰当,这就好像是,你希望人家问你英国的国王时,考试题上却问起语法来。

“我不知道,”彼得不安地回答,“可是我还小着呐。”他真的不知道;他只是有一些猜想,于是他揣摩着说:“温迪,我生下来的那天就逃跑了。”

温迪很惊讶,可是又挺感兴趣。她用优美的待客礼貌碰了碰睡衣,表示他可以坐得离她近些。

“因为我听见父亲母亲在谈论,”彼得低声解释说,“我将来长大要做一个什么样的人。”说到这里,他大大激动起来。“我永远也不愿长成大人,”他激愤地说,“我要老是做个小孩,老是玩。所以我就逃到了肯辛顿公园,和仙子们住在一起,很久很久了。”

温迪非常羡慕地瞅了他一眼,彼得以为,这是因为他从家里逃跑了,其实是因为,他认识仙子。

温迪的家庭生活太平淡了,所以在她看来,和仙子们结识,一定有趣极了。她提出一连串关于仙子的问话,这使彼得很惊异,因为,在他看来,仙子们多少是个累赘,她们常常碍他的事,等等。说实在的,他有时还得躲开她们。不过,他大体上还是喜欢她们的,他告诉温迪仙子们的由来。

“你瞧,温迪,第一个婴孩第一次笑出声的时候,那一声笑就裂成了一千块,这些笑到处蹦来蹦去,仙子们就是那么来的。”这话多无聊,不过,温迪是一个很少出家门的孩子,所以也就喜欢听。

“所以,”彼得和气地接着说下去,“每一个男孩和女孩都应该有一个仙子。”

“应该?真的有吗?”

"不,你瞧,孩子们现在懂得太多了,他们很快就不信仙子了,每次有一个孩子说'我不信仙子',就有一个仙子在什么地方落下来死掉了。"

真的,彼得觉得他们谈仙子已经谈得够多了,又想起小叮当已经好半晌没出声了。"不知道她上哪儿去了。"彼得说着,站了起来,叫着小叮当的名字。温迪的心突然喜得猛跳起来。

"彼得,"她紧紧抓住他,"你该不是说这屋里有个仙子吧!"

(选自《彼得和温迪》)

注释

1. draggle['drægl] *vt.* 拖脏
2. patronise['petrənaiz] *vt.* 保护
3. crease[kris] *vt.* 弄皱
4. rapturously['ræptʃərəsli] *adv.* 狂喜地,兴高采烈地
5. sarcasm['sɑ:kæzəm] *n.* 讽刺
6. aghast[ə'ɡæst] *adj.* 吃惊的
7. thimble['θimbl] *n.* 顶针
8. agitate['ædʒiitet] *vt.* 使……激动
9. nuisance['nju:səns] *n.* 麻烦事

赏析

詹姆斯·马修·巴利(1860—1937),英国小说家、剧作家。一生创作中最著名、影响最大的是儿童剧《彼得·潘》。他生于英国东部苏格兰(现安格斯郡)农村一个织布工人之家,自幼酷爱读书写作。1882年在爱丁堡大学毕业后,在诺丁从事新闻工作两年。1885年移居伦敦,当自由投稿的新闻记者,开始创作反映苏格兰人生活的小说和剧本。巴利以他在伦敦肯辛顿公园碰到的一群男孩为原型创作了儿童剧《彼得·潘:不会长大的男孩》(1904)。该剧一经演出就大受欢迎,并于1911年改编为小说《彼得和温迪》。二者皆讲述了彼得·潘,一个会飞的拒绝长大的顽皮男孩在永无岛与温迪以及她的弟弟们所遭遇到的各种历险故事。

《彼得与温迪》是一部幻想作品,创造了一个十分诱人的童话境界——永无岛。作家极力渲染永无岛上儿童式的欢乐,讴歌了美好纯真的童心。巴利正是通过奇妙的永无岛和不肯长大的男孩彼得·潘这样的童话形象深情地告诉人们:童年是人生中最美的乐章,珍惜可贵的童年时代,让孩子们尽情地享受那仅仅属于他们的欢乐。

本文节选自小说第三章。彼得回到温迪弟弟们的育婴房来寻找丢失的影子,被吵醒的温迪帮彼得缝好影子并惊喜地见到了仙女小叮当。整段文字通俗易懂,把彼得的单纯、顽皮、自负与温迪的善解人意、温情、母性等特点充分展示在读者面前。透过这段文字可以让很多为人父母的成人去反思:自己是否也像彼得的父母一样在为孩子"设计"人生?每个孩子纯真无邪的第一次笑声会幻化成众多仙子,可每当一个孩子拒绝相信仙子,就有仙子死掉,这是否是成人化的悲剧呢?香港鬼才导演林奕华曾说:"贾宝玉这个人物,在英国就是哈利·波特,在法国就是小王子,在美国就是彼得·潘,他是个代表性的人物,是我们心里面的永远长不大的小孩子。"

原文

8 Blue Wednesday (Extract)

Jean Webster

The first Wednesday in every month was a Perfectly Awful Day— a day to be awaited with **dread**, endured with courage and forgotten with **haste**. Every floor must be spotless, every chair dustless, and every bed without a wrinkle. Ninety - seven **squirmig** little orphans must be **scrubbed** and combed and buttoned into freshly **starched** ginghams; and all ninety - seven reminded of their manners, and told to say, "Yes, sir," "No, sir" whenever a **trustee** spoke.

It was a distressing time; and poor Jerusha Abbott, being the oldest orphan, had to bear the **brunt** of it. But this particular first Wednesday, like its predecessors, finally dragged itself to a close. Jerusha escaped from the **pantry** where she had been making sandwiches for the **asylum's** guests, and turned upstairs to accomplish her regular work. Her special care was room F, where eleven little tots, from four to seven, occupied eleven little tots set in a row. Jerusha assembled her charges, straightened their **rumpled** frocks, wiped their noses, and started them in an orderly and willing line towards the dining - room to engage themselves for a blessed half hour with bread and milk and prune pudding.

Then she dropped down on the window seat and leaned **throbbing** temples against the cool glass. She had been on her feet since five that morning, doing everybody's bidding, scolded and hurried by a nervous matron. Mrs. Lippett, behind the scenes, did not always maintain that calm and **pompous** dignity with which she faced an audience of trustees and lady visitors. Jerusha gazed out across a broad stretch of frozen lawn, beyond the tall iron paling that marked the confines of the asylum, down **undulating** ridges sprinkled with country estates, to the spires of the village rising from the midst of bare trees.

The day was ended — quite successfully, so far as she knew. The trustees and the visiting committee had made their rounds, and read their reports, and drunk their tea, and now were hurrying home to their own cheerful firesides, to forget their bothersome little charges for another month. Jerusha leaned forward watching with curiosity — and a touch of wistfulness — the stream of carriages and automobiles that rolled out of the asylum gates. In imagination she followed first one equipage then another, to the big houses dotted along the hillside. She pictured herself in a fur coat and a **velvet** hat trimmed with feathers leaning back in the seat and nonchalantly murmuring "Home" to the driver. But on the doorsill her home the picture grew blurred.

Jerusha had an imagination — an imagination, Mrs. Lippett told her that would get her into trouble if she didn't take care — but keen as it was, it could not carry her beyond the front porch of the houses she would enter. Poor, eager, adventurous little Jerusha, in all her seventeen years, had never stepped inside an ordinary house; she could not picture the daily routine of those other human beings who carried on their lives undiscommonded by orphans.

译文

8 蓝色星期三(节选)

简·韦伯斯特

每个月的第一个星期三是个糟糕的日子——它是一个在忧虑中等待,勇敢地忍耐,然后在忙碌中忘记的日子。这一天,每层楼的地板都必须纤尘不染,每张椅子都要光洁照人,全部床单都不能有半条皱褶。还要把97个活蹦乱跳的小孤儿梳洗一遍,给他们穿上浆洗过的格子衬衫,嘱咐他们要注意礼貌,回答理事们的问话时要说:"是的,先生。"或者"不是的,先生。"

这个日子真是令人沮丧,可怜的乔若莎·艾伯特,作为孤儿院里年纪最大的孤儿当然更加倒霉。不过,这个特别的星期三,像平时一样,终于到头了。乔若莎逃离厨房,她刚在这里为来客们做了三明治,又跑回楼上完成她每天的例行工作。她负责第6室,那里有11个4岁到7岁的小家伙和11张排成一列的小床。乔若莎好不容易把他们叫过来,帮他们整理好皱巴巴的衣服,擦干净鼻涕,排成一行,然后带领他们去餐室,在那里他们可以尽情地享受半小时的好时光,喝牛奶,吃面包和梅子布丁。

她疲惫地跌坐在窗台的椅子上,把涨得发疼的太阳穴贴在冰冷的玻璃上。从早晨5点钟开始,她的手脚就不停地忙碌着,听从所有人的命令,还不时被神经兮兮的女监事骂得晕头转向。私底下的李皮太太可不是像她面对理事们和来访的女士时那样冷静、庄重。乔若莎的眼神掠过孤儿院高高的铁栏杆外一片上了冻的开阔草地,看到远处起伏的山峰,山上散落着一座座村舍,光秃秃的树丛中露出了房屋的尖顶。

这一天就算过去了——据她所知,应该是圆满落幕,没有出现任何差错。理事们和来访团已经巡视过一遍,听取了汇报,也喝了茶,现在正忙着赶回自家温暖的炉火边,起码要再过一个月才会想起这些需要他们照管的磨人的小家伙。乔若莎倚着窗台,好奇地看着一连串的马车、汽车穿过孤儿院的大门。她不禁产生了幻想。她想象自己跟着一辆又一辆车,来到坐落在山脚下的密密麻麻的大房子前。她看见自己穿着一件貂皮大衣,并带着天鹅绒装饰的丝织帽子靠在车座上,漫不经心地对司机说:"回家!"不过,当她回到家门口,整个想象就变得模糊不清了。

乔若莎喜欢幻想——李皮太太说,如果不小心,幻想就会让她惹上麻烦。但是,不管她的想象力多么丰富,都无法带领她走进那些渴望进入的大门,她只能待在门廊上。可怜的充满冒险精神的小乔若莎,在她17年的岁月里,从未进入任何一个家庭。她完全无法想象,没有孤儿干扰的其他人会有怎样的日常生活。

(杜静斐　译)

(选自《长腿叔叔》)

注释

1. dread[dred] *n.* 恐惧
2. haste[hest] *n.* 匆忙
3. squirm[skwə:m] *vi.* 蠕动
4. scrub[skrʌb] *vt.* 用力擦洗
5. starch[stɑ:tʃ] *vt.* 给……上浆
6. trustee[trʌ'sti] *n.* 托管人
7. brunt[brʌnt] *n.* 冲击
8. pantry['pæntri] *n.* 食品室
9. asylum[ə'sailəm] *n.*救济院
10. rumple['rʌmpl] *vt.* 弄皱
11. throb[θrɔb] *vi.* 悸动
12. pompous['pɔmpəs] *adj.* 自大的
13. undulating['ʌndjəˌletiŋ] *adj.* 波状的
14. velvet['velvit] *n.* 天鹅绒

赏析

简·韦伯斯特(1876—1916),美国著名小说家。出生于纽约州,其父亲从事出版业,母亲是美国著名作家马克·吐温的侄女。家庭浓厚的文学氛围为简以后的文学成就奠定了相当的基础。简一生共写了8部小说和无数未能出版的故事和剧本。分别于1912和1915年出版的《长腿叔叔》和《长腿叔叔续集》是她最受欢迎的作品之一,出版后不久便被改编成了舞台剧。她的作品一向以朴实、清新、机智的风格而著称。不幸的是,这颗文学新星于《长腿叔叔续集》出版后的第二年就因分娩而陨落。

简有过在孤儿院生活的经历，故其著作多以孤儿作为主人公。被媒体评价为“一本百年难得一见的好书，内容胜过路易莎·奥尔科特的《小妇人》”的就是《长腿叔叔》。这部作品以书信体的形式讲述了孤儿乔若莎因出色的作文而得到孤儿院一位董事的资助进入大学学习。为了尽她向董事汇报学业的义务，并表达自己发自内心的感激，乔若莎通过84封信向这位“长腿叔叔”理事倾诉着她的大学生活、感情体验，以及理想抱负，故事以乔若莎最终收获了真挚的爱情结束。整部书情节引人入胜，语言清新、细腻，情感真实而充沛，成为众多读者书架上的必备读物。

本文选自小说的第一部分，描述了主人公乔若莎在孤儿院的日子。正常家庭生活的缺失与孤儿院忙碌、繁琐的劳动让这位正值青春、阳光花季的少女内心充满忧虑。能让她得到些许慰藉的事就是结束一天劳动后的沉思、幻想。她对正常生活的渴望让我们看到我们确实拥有太多太多了。但故事的美好结局又让我们由衷地为这位单纯、乐观、积极、热爱生活的少女感到高兴。

原文

9 A Tree Grows in Brooklyn (Extract)

Betty Smith

Serene was a word you could put to Brooklyn, New York. Especially in the summer of 1912. **Somber**, as a word, was better. But it did not apply to Williamsburg, Brooklyn. Prairie was lovely and Shenandoah had a beautiful sound, but you couldn't fit those words into Brooklyn. Serene was the only word for it; especially on a Saturday afternoon in summer.

Late in the afternoon the sun **slanted** down into the **mossy** yard belonging to Francie Nolan's house, and warmed the worn wooden fence. Looking at the shafted sun, Francie had that same fine feeling that came when she recalled the poem they recited in school.

*This is the forest **primeval**.*
*The murmuring pines and the **hemlocks**,*
Bearded with moss, and in garments green,
Indistinct in the twilight,
Stand like Druids of eld.

The one tree in Francie's yard was neither a pine nor a hemlock. It had pointed leaves which grew along green switches which **radiated** from the **bough** and made a tree which looked like a lot of opened green umbrellas. Some people called it the Tree of Heaven. No matter where its seed fell, it made a tree which struggled to reach the sky. It grew in boarded-up lots and out of neglected rubbish heaps and it was the only tree that grew out of cement. It grew lushly, but only in the **tenements** districts.

You took a walk on a Sunday afternoon and came to a nice neighborhood, very refined. You saw a small one of these trees through the iron gate leading to someone's yard and you knew that soon that section of Brooklyn would get to be a tenement district. The tree knew. It came there first. Afterwards, poor foreigners seeped in and the quiet old brownstone houses were **hacked up** into flats, feather beds were pushed out on the window sills to air and the Tree of Heaven flourished. That was the kind of tree it was. It liked poor people.

That was the kind of tree in Francie's yard. Its umbrellas curled over, around and under her third-floor fire escape. An eleven-year-old girl sitting on this fire-escape could imagine that she was living in a tree. That's what Francie imagined every Saturday afternoon in summer.

Oh, what a wonderful day was Saturday in Brooklyn. Oh, how wonderful anywhere! People were paid on Saturday and it was a holiday without the rigidness of a Sunday. People had money to go out and buy things. They ate well for once, got drunk, had dates, made love and stayed up until all hours; singing, playing music, fighting and dancing because the **morrow** was their own free day. They could sleep late — until late **mass** anyhow.

On Sunday, most people crowded into the eleven o'clock mass. Well, some people, a few, went to early six o'clock mass. They were given credit for this but they deserved none for they were the ones who had stayed out so late that it was morning when they got home. So they went to this early mass, got it over with and went home and slept all day with a free conscience.

For Francie, Saturday started with the trip to the **junkie**. She and her brother, Neeley, like other Brooklyn kids, collected rags, paper, metal, rubber, and other junk and **hoarded** it in locked cellar bins or in boxes hidden under the bed. All week Francie walked home slowly from school with her eyes in the **gutter** looking for tin foil from cigarette packages or chewing gum wrappers. This was melted in the lid of a jar. The junkie wouldn't take an unmelted ball of **foil** because too many kids put iron washers in the middle to make it weigh heavier. Sometimes Neeley found a **seltzer** bottle. Francie helped him break the top off and melt it down for lead. The junkie wouldn't buy a complete top because he'd get into trouble with the soda water people. A seltzer bottle top was fine. Melted, it was worth a nickel.

译文

9 布鲁克林有棵树

贝蒂·史密斯

宁静这个词用于纽约的布鲁克林恰如其分。尤其是在1912年的夏天。沉静这个词大概更好些的，只是对布鲁克林的威廉斯堡不大合适。大草原的可爱，雪兰多的悦耳，用于布鲁克林都不合适。只能用宁静这个词，特别是夏日的一个周六下午。

下午的斜阳照在弗兰西·诺兰家爬满苔藓的院子里，把破旧的木篱笆晒得暖暖的。看着斜射下来的一缕缕阳光，弗兰西心头涌出一种美好的感觉来。这样的感觉，她回忆起一首诗歌时也有过。这首诗她在学校里背诵过，是这样的：

这是原始森林
松树和铁杉，低语阵阵
苔藓如须，翠绿满身
黄昏中伫立，依稀朦胧
如一个个德鲁伊老僧

弗兰西院子里的树既不是松树，也不是铁杉。树上的绿色枝条从树干向四周发散，枝条上长满了尖尖的叶子，整棵树看来如同无数撑开的绿伞。有人称之为天堂树。不管它的种子落到什么地方，都会长出一棵树来，向着天空，努力生长。这树长在四周围满木篱的空场子里，或是从无人留意的垃圾堆里钻出来；它也是唯一能在水泥地里长出来的树。它长得很茂密，而且只在居民区长。

星期天下午，你去散散步，走到一个不错的居民区，挺高档的居民区。你会从通往人家院子的铁门中看见这样一棵小树，这时候你就知道布鲁克林这一带会变成居民区了。树懂。树会打前站。到了后来，渐渐会有些贫穷的外国人跑过来，把破旧的褐砂石房子修成平方。他们把羽毛褥垫从窗户里推出来晒。天堂树长得郁郁葱葱。这种树就这习性。它喜欢穷人。

弗兰西院子里长的就是这树。在它的三楼太平梯附近，树上的小“伞”一个个蜷曲过来。一个坐在太平梯上的11岁女孩会觉得自己住在树上。夏天的每个星期六下午弗兰西都是这么想象的。

啊，布鲁克林的星期六多么美好啊！啊，到处都是那么美好啊！星期六是发薪日，也是个周末假日，却又不用守星期天那些清规戒律。人们有钱出去买东西，在这一天好好吃一顿饭、喝醉、约会、做爱、熬夜、唱歌、放音乐、打架、跳舞，而且因为次日就是自由自在的一天，还可以睡个懒觉——至少可以睡到晚场的弥撒。

星期天，大部分人会挤着去参加11点钟的弥撒。但是呢，也有一些人，很少的一些，会去参加六点钟的那场。人们夸他们赶得早，但其实他们不配这样的夸奖，因为他们根本是在外头待得太久，回到家的时候都已经是早晨了，所以才去这场弥撒。他们只想赶快应付过去，赶快清洗罪恶，然后回家安安心心睡一天大觉。

弗兰西的星期六是从去垃圾回收站开始的。和其他布鲁克林的小孩一样，她和弟弟尼力会在外头捡些碎布、纸张、金属、橡胶等破烂，藏在地下室上锁的箱子里，或是藏在床底下。星期一到星期五，每天放学回家的路上，弗兰西总是慢慢走，边走边看排水沟，希望能找到烟盒的锡纸或口香糖的包装纸。之后她会将这些东西放在小罐子的盖子上熔化；垃圾站不收没有熔化的锡球，因为很多孩子会将铁垫圈放在中间增加重量。有时候尼力会找到气泡矿泉水的罐子，弗兰西就帮他把壶嘴弄下来，熔化出其中的铅来，要不然垃圾站的人怕气泡水公司的人找麻烦，不敢回收完整的壶嘴。壶嘴是好货，化掉后能卖到五分钱。

（方柏林　译）

注释

1. serene[sə'rin] *adj.* 平静的
2. somber['sɔmbə] *adj.* 昏暗的
3. slant[slænt] *vi.* 倾斜
4. mossy['mɔsi] *adj.* 生苔的
5. primeval[prai'mi:vəl] *adj.* 原始的
6. hemlock['hemlɔk] *n.* 铁杉
7. radiate['reidieit] *vt.* 发散
8. bough[bau] *n.* 大树枝
9. tenement['tenimənt] *n.* 房屋
10. hack up：设计
11. morrow['mɔ:rəu] *n.* 次日
12. mass: 弥撒。基督教纪念耶稣牺牲的宗教仪式，拉丁文missa 的音译。认为是以不流血的方式，重复耶稣在十字架上对圣父的祭献。一般在教堂内的祭台上举行，由神父或主教将一种无酵的面饼和葡萄酒“祝圣”后，称它们已变成耶稣的“圣体”和“圣血”，并进行分食。
13. junkie['dʒʌŋki] *n.* 废旧品商人
14. hoard[hɔ:d] *vt.* 贮藏
15. gutter['ɡʌtə] *n.* 排水沟
16. foil[fɔil] *n.* 锡箔
17. seltzer['seltsə] *n.* 苏打水

赏析

贝蒂·史密斯(1896—1972)，美国女作家，德国移民的女儿。小时家境贫寒，成长于纽约布鲁克林的威廉斯堡。后来进入密歇根大学学习新闻、戏剧、写作和文学。其最主要作品是《布鲁克林有棵树》(1943)，曾被改编为电影(《天堂树》)、电视、音乐剧等多种形式，并获得过奥斯卡奖。她的经历与这部小说主人公弗兰西相似，早年也是靠自学完成了初步的知识积累，因此这部小说被视为贝蒂的自传体小说。贝蒂的其他作品有《明天会更好》(1947)、《快乐的早晨》(1963)，此外贝蒂的戏剧创作成就也很高，曾获洛克菲勒基金会和戏剧家协会基金会资助。

《布鲁克林有棵树》是一部关于生存与成长、梦想与尊严的小说。它描写了20世纪初经济大萧条背景下一个贫穷却光荣的美国家庭生存、奋斗的故事，主线是这一家人的感情故事，为读者描摹出了一组细致而不动声色的人物肖像。故事发生在纽约布鲁克林的威廉斯堡。小说一开始，11岁的主人公弗兰西·诺兰就和弟弟出现在垃圾收购站，他们姐弟靠周六捡废报纸、金属片、破布、橡胶轮胎和其他杂物，卖给收垃圾的人换得几枚硬币，然后把赚到的钱存入存钱罐，这个“银行”承载着他们全家人的富裕梦想。父亲因酗酒离世后，聪明好学的诺兰必须终止学业来帮助妈妈维持这个家，于是，她和弟弟第一次走出了布鲁克林，来到曼哈顿。在这里，她体验了第一次甜蜜而痛苦的恋爱，也不忘尽一切努力继续自己的学业。故事以弗兰西再次进入大学继续学习结尾，虽然她离开了从小生活的布鲁克林，但故乡在她的内心却永难忘怀。小说揭示的主题正如主人公弗兰西所说：“活着，奋斗着，爱着我们的生活，爱着生活馈赠的一切悲欢，那就是一种实现。生活的充实常在，人人皆可获得。”有评价说：“《布鲁克林有棵树》是一本让人洞悉个体如何能变得更坚强、坚定、睿智的书。最重要的，它谈及人要生存所需的人格力量，也就成了一篇关于爱、信任与磨难的文章。正是在读完这本书后，我平生第一次认识到，尽管磨难是一次艰难的考验，但它确实是个人所能体验的最积极的人生影响因素之一。”

本文选自小说第一章。主人公出场前，展现在读者面前的是宁静、祥和的布鲁克林，尤其是那种“懂人心”“喜欢穷人”“郁郁葱葱”的天堂树，它“不管种子落到什么地方，都会长出一棵树来，向着天空，努力生长”。天堂树的寓意由此可见一斑，主人公正是具备天堂树如此这般的品质，才能经受生活所赠与的一切，坚强地生存、有尊严地去实现梦想。接着，弗兰西出场，她的每周六都“是从去垃圾回收站开始的”……

原文

10 The Story of Mankind (Extract)

Hendrik Willem Van Loon

For Hansje and Willem,

When I was twelve or thirteen years old, an uncle of mine who gave me my love for books and pictures promised to take me upon a memorable expedition. I was to go with him to the top of the tower of Old Saint Lawrence in Rotterdam.

And so, one fine day, a **sexton** with a key as large as that of Saint Peter opened a mysterious door. "Ring the bell," he said, "when you come back and want to get out," and with a great grinding of rusty old hinges he separated us from the noise of the busy street and locked us into a world of new and strange experiences.

For the first time in my life I was confronted by the phenomenon of audible silence. When we had climbed the first flight of stairs, I added another discovery to my limited knowledge of natural phenomena — that of **tangible** darkness. A match showed us where the upward road continued. We went to the next floor and then to the next and the next until I had lost count and then there came still another floor, and suddenly we had plenty of light. This floor was on an even height with the roof of the church, and it was used as a storeroom. Covered with many inches of dust, there lay the abandoned symbols of a **venerable** faith which had been discarded by the good people of the city many years ago. That which had meant life and death to our ancestors was here reduced to junk and rubbish. The industrious rat had built his nest among the carved images and the ever watchful spider had opened up shop between the outspread arms of a kindly saint.

The next floor showed us from where we had derived our light. Enormous open windows with heavy iron bars made the high and **barren** room the roosting place of hundreds of pigeons. The wind blew through the iron bars and the air was filled with a **weird** and pleasing music. It was the noise of the town below us, but a noise which had been purified and cleansed by the distance. The **rumbling** of heavy carts and the clinking of horses' hoofs, the winding of cranes and **pulleys**, the hissing sound of the patient steam which had been set to do the work of man in a thousand different ways — they had all been blended into a softly rustling whisper which provided a beautiful background for the trembling cooing of the pigeons.

Here the stairs came to an end and the ladders began. And after the first ladder (a **slippery** old thing which made one feel his way with a cautious foot) there was a new and even greater wonder, the town-clock. I saw the heart of time. I could hear the heavy pulse beats of the rapid seconds-one-two-three — up to sixty. Then a sudden quivering noise when all the wheels seemed to stop and another minute had been chopped off **eternity**. Without pause it began again one-two-three — until at last after a warning rumble and the scraping of many wheels a thunderous voice, high above us, told the world that it was the hour of noon.

On the next floor were the bells. The nice little bells and their terrible sisters. In the centre, the big bell which made me turn stiff with fright when I heard it in the middle of the night telling a story of fire or flood. In **solitary** grandeur, it seemed to reflect upon those six hundred years during which it had shared the joys and the sorrows of the good people of Rotterdam. Around it, neatly arranged like the blue jars in an old-fashioned **apothecary** shop, hung the little fellows, who twice each week played a merry tune for the benefit of the country-folk who had come to market to buy and sell and hear what the big world had been doing. But in a corner — all alone and **shunned** by the others — a big black bell, silent and stern, the bell of death.

Then darkness once more and other ladders, steeper and even more dangerous than those we had climbed before, and suddenly the fresh air of the wide heavens. We had reached the highest gallery. Above us the sky. Below us the city — a little toy-town, where busy ants were hastily crawling hither and thither, each one intent upon his or her particular business, and beyond the **jumble** of stones, the wide greenness of the open country.

It was my first glimpse of the big world.

Since then, whenever I have had the opportunity, I have gone to the top of the tower and enjoyed myself. It was hard work, but it repaid in full the mere physical exertion of climbing a few stairs.

译文

10　人类的故事(节选)

亨德里克·威廉·房龙

汉斯及威廉:

我十二三岁时,那位曾让我爱上书画的舅舅答应带我去做一次探险。这次探险令我终生难忘,就是同他一起到鹿特丹圣劳伦斯教堂的塔顶去。

于是,天气晴好的一天,一个教堂司事拿一把钥匙给我们打开了那扇神秘的门——那钥匙就和圣彼得天国的钥匙一样大。“按门铃,”他说,“你们下来想出去的话。”他费了好大劲才转动了生锈的旧铰链,把我们与嘈杂、繁忙的街道隔开,锁进了一个新奇的世界里。

这是我生命中第一次面对有声的寂静。爬了一段楼梯,我又给自己有限的自然现象知识添加了另一个发现——有形的黑暗。借着火柴我们看清了继续向上的路。我们接着爬到第二层、第三层,就这样爬了一层又一层,也不知究竟爬了多少层后突然眼前一亮。这层是与教堂屋顶平齐的储藏室,里面堆满了善良的市民们多年前丢弃的圣像。这些以前可都是人们虔诚信仰的象征,祖先们视其为生死攸关的珍品,如今却躺在这里,上面落满了厚厚的灰尘,沦为一堆废物与垃圾了。勤快的老鼠在雕像间给自己搭了窝，时刻警醒的蜘蛛在仁慈圣徒张开的双臂间结网捕食。

又上了一层后，我们才发现亮光是从空房子巨大的窗户射进来的。窗户开着，上面装有沉重的粗铁条，正好为无数鸽子提供理想的栖息之处。清风透过铁条，送来了动听的音乐。这是我们脚下喧嚣的城市发出的噪声，但经过这段距离的净化与涤荡已经幻化为优美悦耳的音乐了。隆隆的马车声、嗒嗒的马蹄声、吱吖吱吖的起重机和滑轮声以及替人干着千百样工作的蒸汽机发出的嘶嘶声混合在一起，融汇成了一支轻柔的背景乐，刚好与鸽子震颤的咕咕声相配。

再往上就没有楼梯了，得爬梯子。爬完第一架梯子（又旧又滑，每一级都要摸索着爬）一幅新鲜而伟大的画面——城市大钟，展现在我们面前。我看到了时间的心脏，听到了飞逝的时间脉搏——一、二、三……直到六十。突然，一阵震颤声中，所有的齿轮同时停了下来，仿佛从永恒的时间中被切割掉了。紧接着它又开始搏动，一、二、三……低沉的隆隆声过后，齿轮就在我们头顶发出雷鸣般的响声，向世界宣告正午时刻的到来。

再上一层是许多大大小小的钟。有的灵巧优雅，有的体格庞大、令人生畏。正中央放着一口大钟，每每在它半夜响起，通告大火或洪水等事件时，我总是吓得浑身僵硬。而此刻的它则笼罩在一片庄严肃穆之中，仿佛在回顾六百多年来与鹿特丹人民共同经历的欢欣与苦楚。它身边整齐地挂着一排小钟，活像老式药店里陈列的大坛子。每周两次的集市时间，总有乡下人来赶集。他们买卖货物，打听大世界里形形色色的事情，每每此刻就会钟声齐鸣，为他们奏响生活的欢曲。角落里的黑大钟形只影单，冷峻无言，宛若一口死亡之钟。

再向上爬又是一片黑暗，梯子比之前更陡峭、更危险了。爬着爬着突然间呼吸到广阔天地的清新空气了。我们爬到了最高点，头顶着蓝天，脚踩着玩具般的城市。看着蚂蚁般的人们行色匆匆，专注于各自的事情。远处一堆乱石外是广阔的绿色田野。

这就是我对辽阔世界的最初一瞥。

从此一有机会，我就会爬到塔顶自娱自乐。爬上塔顶确实很费劲，却能得到充分的精神回报。

（王宁　译）

注释

1. sexton[ˈsekstən] *n.* 教堂司事
2. tangible[ˈtændʒəbl] *adj.* 有形的；可触摸的
3. venerable[ˈvenərəbl] *adj.* 庄严的；值得尊敬的
4. barren[ˈbærən] *adj.* 空洞的
5. weird[wiəd] *adj.* 超自然的
6. rumbling[ˈrʌmbliŋ] *n.* 隆隆声；辘辘声
7. pulley[ˈpuli] *n.* 滑轮
8. slippery[ˈslipəri] *adj.* 滑的

9. eternity[i 'tə:nəti] *n.* 来世，来生；不朽；永世

10. solitary['sɔlətri] *adj.* 孤独的

11. apothecary[ə'pɔθəkəri] *n.* 药剂师，药师；药材商

12. shun[ʃʌn] *vt.* 避开；回避

13. jumble['dʒʌmbl] *n.* 杂乱的一堆东西

赏析

亨德里克·威廉·房龙(1882—1944)，荷裔美国人，著名通俗历史学家，在历史、文化、文明、科学等方面都有著作，而且读者众多。他善于用轻巧俏皮的文字撰写历史、文化、文明和科学等方面的通俗著作，一生出版了三十多种著作。其代表作《宽容》《人类的故事》《圣经的故事》《房龙地理》《发明的故事》《太平洋的故事》《人类的艺术》《伦勃朗的人生苦旅》等，几乎本本畅销，影响了几代人。房龙的作品基本围绕人类生存发展的最本质问题，向人类的无知和偏见挑战，将知识和真理普及为人所共知的常识。文学家郁达夫先生盛赞房龙的写作手法，他说："房龙的笔，有一种魔力，但这也不是他的特创，这不过是将文学家的手法，拿来用以讲述科学而已。"

房龙的成名之作是《人类的故事》，写西方文明发展史，主要对象是少年。这本书在1921年11月推出，立即成为畅销书。在这部著作中，房龙用生动流畅的文字，将人类数千年的文明发展史呈现在读者的面前。

本文选自房龙《人类的故事》序言部分。作者以清新、流畅的笔调向读者描述了其舅舅为他开启历史这道大门的一次探险。这次探险让他终生难忘，在于他从这次探险中体会到了纵览辽阔世界的快感，于是他的故事从起源部分娓娓道来，一路走过辉煌的希腊、禁欲的中世纪、繁荣的文艺复兴、神秘的东方、理性的启蒙，最后见证了惨绝人寰的战争……

原文

11 The Happy Prince (Extract)

Oscar Wilde

All day long he flew, and at night-time he arrived at the city. "Where shall I put up?" he said, "I hope the town has made preparations."

Then he saw the statue on the tall column. "I will put up there," he cried, "it is a fine position with plenty of fresh air." So he **alighted** just between the feet of the Happy Prince.

"I have a golden bedroom," he said softly to himself as he looked round, and he prepared to go to sleep; but just as he was putting his head under his wing a large drop of water fell on him. "What a curious thing! " he cried, "there is not a single cloud in the sky, the stars are quite clear and bright, and yet it is raining. The climate in the north of Europe is really dreadful. The Reed used to like the rain, but that was merely her selfishness."

Then another drop fell.

"What is the use of a statue if it cannot keep the rain off?" he said, "I must look for a good chimney-pot," and he determined to fly away.

But before he had opened his wings, a third drop fell, and he looked up, and saw — Ah! What did he see?

The eyes of the Happy Prince were filled with tears, and tears were running down his golden cheeks. His face was so beautiful in the moonlight that the little Swallow was filled with pity.

"Who are you?" he said.

"I am the Happy Prince."

"Why are you weeping then?" asked the Swallow, "you have quite **drenched** me."

"When I was alive and had a human heart," answered the statue, "I did not know what tears were, for I lived in the palace of Sans-Souci, where sorrow is not allowed to enter. In the daytime I played with my companions in the garden, and in the evening I led the dance in the Great Hall. Round the garden ran a very lofty wall, but I never cared to ask what lay beyond it, everything about me was so beautiful. My courtiers called me the Happy Prince, and happy indeed I was, if pleasure be happiness. So I lived, and so I died. And now that I am dead they have set me up here so high that I can see all the ugliness and all the misery of my city, and though my heart is made of lead yet I cannot choose but weep."

"What, is he not solid gold?" said the Swallow to himself. He was too polite to make any personal remarks out loud.

"Far away," continued the statue in a low musical voice, "far away in a little street there is a poor house. One of the windows is open, and through it I can see a woman seated at a table. Her face is thin and worn, and she has **coarse**, red hands, all **pricked** by the needle, for she is a **seamstress**. She is embroidering passion-flowers on a satin gown for the loveliest of the Queen"s maids-of-honour to wear at the next Court-ball. In a bed in the corner of the room her little boy is lying ill. He has a fever, and is asking for oranges. His mother has nothing to give him but river water, so he is crying. Swallow, Swallow, little Swallow, will you not bring her the **ruby** out of my sword-hilt? My feet are fastened to this **pedestal** and I cannot move."

"I am waited for in Egypt," said the Swallow. "My friends are flying up and down the Nile, and talking to the large lotus-flowers. Soon they will go to sleep in the tomb of the great King. The

King is there himself in his painted coffin. He is wrapped in yellow **linen**, and embalmed with spices. Round his neck is a chain of pale green jade, and his hands are like withered leaves."

"Swallow, Swallow, little Swallow," said the Prince, "will you not stay with me for one night, and be my messenger? The boy is so thirsty, and the mother so sad."

"I don't think I like boys," answered the Swallow. "Last summer, when I was staying on the river, there were two rude boys, the miller's sons, who were always throwing stones at me. They never hit me, of course; we swallows fly far too well for that, and besides, I come of a family famous for its **agility**; but still, it was a mark of disrespect."

But the Happy Prince looked so sad that the little Swallow was sorry. "It is very cold here," he said, "but I will stay with you for one night, and be your messenger."

"Thank you, little Swallow," said the Prince.

So the Swallow picked out the great ruby from the Prince's sword, and flew away with it in his **beak** over the roofs of the town.

He passed by the cathedral tower, where the white marble angels were sculptured. He passed by the palace and heard the sound of dancing. A beautiful girl came out on the balcony with her lover. "How wonderful the stars are," he said to her, "and how wonderful is thc power of love! "

"I hope my dress will be ready in time for the State - ball," she answered, "I have ordered passion - flowers to be embroidered on it; but the seamstresses are so lazy."

He passed over the river, and saw the lanterns hanging to the masts of the ships. He passed over the Ghetto, and saw the old jews bargaining with each other, and weighing out money in copper scales. At last he came to the poor house and looked in. The boy was tossing feverishly on his bed, and the mother had fallen asleep, she was so tired. In he hopped, and laid the great ruby on the table beside the woman's thimble. Then he flew gently round the bed, fanning the boy's forehead with his wings. "How cool I feel," said the boy, "I must be getting better." And he sank into a delicious **slumber**.

Then the Swallow flew back to the Happy Prince, and told him what he had done. "It is curious," he remarked, "but I feel quite warm now, although it is so cold."

"That is because you have done a good action," said the Prince. And the little Swallow began to think, and then he fell asleep. Thinking always made him sleepy.

When day broke he flew down to the river and had a bath. "What a remarkable phenomenon," said the Professor of Ornithology as he was passing over the bridge. "A swallow in winter! " And he wrote a long letter about it to the local newspaper. Every one quoted it, it was full of so many words that they could not understand.

"Tonight I go to Egypt," said the Swallow, and he was in high spirits at the prospect. He visited all the public monuments, and sat a long time on top of the church steeple. Wherever he went the Sparrows **chirruped**, and said to each other, "What a distinguished stranger! " so he enjoyed himself very much.

When the moon rose he flew back to the Happy Prince. "Have you any commissions for Egypt?" he cried, "I am just starting."

"Swallow, Swallow, little Swallow," said the Prince, "will you not stay with me one night longer?"

"I am waited for in Egypt," answered the Swallow. "Tomorrow my friends will fly up to the Second Cataract. The river - horse couches there among the **bulrushes**, and on a great granite throne sits the God Memnon. All night long he watches the stars, and when the morning star shines he utters one cry of joy, and then he is silent. At noon the yellow lions come down to the water's edge to drink. They have eyes like green **beryls**, and their roar is louder than the roar of the cataract."

"Swallow, Swallow, little Swallow," said the Prince, "far away across the city I see a young man in a **garret**. He is leaning over a desk covered with papers, and in a tumbler by his side there is a bunch of withered violets. His hair is brown and crisp, and his lips are red as a **pomegranate**, and he has large and dreamy eyes. He is trying to finish a play for the Director of the Theatre, but he is too cold to write any more. There is no fire in the grate, and hunger has made him faint."

"I will wait with you one night longer," said the Swallow, who really had a good heart. "Shall I take him another ruby?"

"Alas! I have no ruby now," said the Prince, "my eyes are all that I have left. They are made of rare **sapphires**, which were brought out of India a thousand years ago. Pluck out one of them and take it to him. He will sell it to the jeweller, and buy food and firewood, and finish his play."

"Dear Prince," said the Swallow, "I cannot do that." And he began to weep.

"Swallow, Swallow, little Swallow," said the Prince, "do as I command you."

So the Swallow plucked out the Prince's eye, and flew away to the student's garret. It was easy enough to get in, as there was a hole in the roof. Through this he darted, and came into the room. The young man had his head buried in his hands, so he did not hear the flutter of the bird's wings, and when he looked up he found the beautiful sapphire lying on the withered violets.

"I am beginning to be appreciated," he cried, "this is from some great admirer. Now I can finish my play." And he looked quite happy.

The next day the Swallow flew down to the harbour. He sat on the mast of a large vessel and watched the sailors hauling big chests out of the hold with ropes. "Heave ahoy!" they shouted as each chest came up.

"I am going to Egypt!" cried the Swallow, but nobody minded, and when the moon rose he flew back to the Happy Prince.

译文

11 快乐王子(节选)

奥斯卡·王尔德

他飞了整整一天,夜晚时才来到这座城市。“我去哪儿过夜呢?”他说,“我希望城里已做好了准备。”

这时,他看见了高大圆柱上的雕像。“我就在那儿过夜,”他高声说,“这是个好地方,充满了新鲜空气。”于是,他就在快乐王子两脚之间落了窝。

“我有黄金做的卧室。”他朝四周看看后轻声地对自己说,随之准备入睡了。但就在他把头放在羽翅下面的时候,一颗大大的水珠落在他的身上。“真是不可思议!”他叫了起来,“天上没有一丝云彩,繁星清晰又明亮,却偏偏下起了雨。北欧的天气真是可怕。芦苇是喜欢雨水的,可那只是她自私罢了。”

紧接着又落下来一滴。

“一座雕像连雨都遮挡不住,还有什么用处?”他说,“我得去找一个好烟囱做窝。”他决定飞离此处。

可是还没等他张开羽翼,第三滴水又掉了下来,他抬头望去,看见了——啊!他看见了什么呢?

快乐王子的双眼充满了泪水,泪珠顺着他金黄的脸颊淌了下来。王子的脸在月光下美丽无比,小燕子顿生怜悯之心。

“你是谁?”他问对方。

“我是快乐王子。”

“那么你为什么哭呢?”燕子又问,“你把我的身上都打湿了。”

“以前在我有颗人心而活着的时候,”雕像开口说道,“我并不知道眼泪是什么东西,因为那时我住在逍遥自在的王宫里,那是个哀愁无法进去的地方。白天人们伴着我在花园里玩,晚上我在大厅里领头跳舞。沿着花园有一堵高高的围墙,可我从没想到去关心围墙那边有什么东西,我身边的一切太美好了。我的臣仆们都叫我快乐王子,的确,如果欢愉就是快乐的话,那我真是快乐无比。我就这么活着,也这么死去。而眼下我死了,他们把我这么高高地立在这儿,使我能看见自己城市中所有的丑恶和贫苦,尽管我的心是铅做的,可我还是忍不住要哭。”

“啊!难道他不是铁石心肠的金像?”燕子对自己说。他很讲礼貌,不愿大声议论别人的私事。

“远处,”雕像用低缓而悦耳的声音继续说,“远处的一条小街上住着一户穷人。一扇窗户开着,透过窗户我能看见一个女人坐在桌旁。她那瘦削的脸上布满了倦意,一双粗糙发红的手上到处是针眼,因为她是一个裁缝。她正在给缎子衣服绣上西番莲花,这是皇后最喜爱的,她将准备在下一次宫廷舞会上穿。在房间角落里的一张床上躺着她生病的孩子。孩子在发烧,嚷着要吃橘子。他的妈妈除给他喂几口河水外什么也没有,因此孩子老是哭个不停。燕子,燕子,小燕子,你愿意把我剑柄上的红宝石取下来送给她吗?我的双脚被固定在这基座上,不能动弹。"

"伙伴们在埃及等我,"燕子说,"他们正在尼罗河上飞来飞去,同朵朵大莲花说着话儿,不久就要到伟大法老的墓穴里去过夜。法老本人就睡在自己彩色的棺材中。他的身体被裹在黄色的亚麻布里,还填满了防腐的香料。他的脖子上系着一圈浅绿色翡翠项链,他的双手像是枯萎的树叶。"

"燕子,燕子,小燕子,"王子又说,"你不肯陪我过一夜,做我的信使吗?那个孩子太饥渴了,他的母亲伤心极了。"

"我觉得自己不喜欢小孩,"燕子回答说,"去年夏天,我到过一条河边,有两个顽皮的孩子,是磨坊主的儿子,他们老是扔石头打我。当然,他们永远也别想打中我,我们燕子飞得多快呀,再说,我出身于一个以快捷出了名的家庭;可不管怎么说,这是不礼貌的行为。"

可是快乐王子的满脸愁容叫小燕子的心里很不好受。"这儿太冷了,"他说,"不过我愿意陪你过上一夜,并做你的信使。"

"谢谢你,小燕子。"王子说。

于是燕子从王子的宝剑上取下那颗硕大的红宝石,用嘴衔着,越过城里一座连一座的屋顶,朝远方飞去。

他飞过大教堂的塔顶,看见了上面白色大理石雕刻的天使像。他飞过王宫,听见了跳舞的歌曲声。一位美丽的姑娘同她的心上人走上了天台。"多么奇妙的星星啊,"他对她说,"多么美妙的爱情啊。"

"我希望我的衣服能按时做好,赶得上盛大舞会,"她回答说,"我已要求绣上西番莲花,只是那些女裁缝们都太懒了。"

他飞过了河流,看见了高挂在船桅上的无数灯笼。他飞过了犹太区,看见犹太老人们在彼此讨价还价地做生意,还把钱币放在铜制的天平上称重量。最后他来到了那个穷人的屋舍,朝里面望去。发烧的孩子在床上辗转反侧,母亲已经睡熟了,因为她太疲倦了。他跳进屋里,将硕大的红宝石放在桌子上那女人的顶针旁。随后他又轻轻地绕着床飞了一圈,用羽翅扇着孩子的前额。"我觉得好凉爽,"孩子说,"我一定是好起来了。"说完就沉沉地进入了甜蜜的梦乡。

然后,燕子回到快乐王子的身边,告诉他自己做过的一切。"你说怪不怪,"他接着说,"虽然天气很冷,可我现在觉得好暖和。"

"那是因为你做了一件好事。"王子说。于是小燕子开始想王子的话,不过没多久便睡着了。对他来说,一思考问题就老是犯困。

黎明时分他飞下河去洗了个澡。"真是不可思议的现象,"一位鸟禽学教授从桥上走过时开口说道,"冬天竟会有燕子!"于是他给当地的报社关于此事写去了一封长信。每个人都引用他信中的话,尽管信中的很多词语是人们理解不了的。

"今晚我要到埃及去。"燕子说。一想到远方,他就精神百倍。他走访了城里所有的公共纪念物,还在教堂的顶端上坐了好一阵子。每到一处,麻雀们就叽叽喳喳地相互说:“多么难得的贵客啊!”所以他玩得很开心。

月亮升起的时候他飞回到快乐王子的身边。“你在埃及有什么事要办吗?”他高声问道,“我就要动身了。”

“燕子,燕子,小燕子,”王子说,“你愿意陪我再过一夜吗?”

“伙伴们在埃及等我呀,”燕子回答说,“明天我的朋友们要飞往第二瀑布,那儿的河马在灯芯草丛中过夜。古埃及的门农神安坐在巨大的花岗岩宝座上,他整夜守望着星星,每当星星闪烁的时候,他就发出欢快的叫声,随后便沉默不语。中午时,黄色的狮群下山来到河边饮水,他们的眼睛像绿色的宝石,咆哮起来比瀑布的怒吼还要响亮。”

“燕子,燕子,小燕子,”王子说,“远处在城市的那一头,我看见住在阁楼中的一个年轻男子。他在一张铺满纸张的书桌上埋头用功,旁边的玻璃杯中放着一束干枯的紫罗兰。他有一头棕色的卷发,嘴唇红得像石榴,他还有一双睡意蒙眬的大眼睛。他正力争为剧院经理写出一个剧本,但是他已经给冻得写不下去了。壁炉里没有柴火,饥饿又弄得他头昏眼花。”

“我愿意陪你再过一夜,”燕子说,他的确有颗善良的心,“我是不是再送他一块红宝石?”

“唉!我现在没有红宝石了,”王子说,“所剩的只有我的双眼。它们由稀有的蓝宝石做成,是一千多年前从印度出产的。取出一颗给他送去。他会将它卖给珠宝商,好买回食物和木柴,完成他写的剧本。”

“亲爱的王子,”燕子说,“我不能这样做。”说完就哭了起来。

“燕子,燕子,小燕子,”王子说,“就照我说的话去做吧。”

因此燕子取下了王子的一只眼睛,朝学生住的阁楼飞去了。由于屋顶上有一个洞,燕子很容易进去。就这样燕子穿过洞来到屋里。年轻人双手捂着脸,没有听见燕子翅膀的扇动声,等他抬起头时,正看见那颗美丽的蓝宝石放在干枯的紫罗兰上面。

“我开始受人欣赏了,”他叫道,“这准是某个极其钦佩我的人送来的。现在我可以完成我的剧本了。”他脸上露出了幸福的笑容。

第二天燕子飞到下面的海港,他坐在一艘大船的桅杆上,望着水手们用绳索把大箱子拖出船舱。随着他们“嘿哟!嘿哟!”的声声号子,一个个大箱子给拖了上来。

“我要去埃及了!”燕子喊道,但是没有人理会他。等月亮升起后,他又飞回到快乐王子的身边。

注释

1. alight[ə'lait] *vi.* 飞落
2. drench[drentʃ] *vt.* 使湿透
3. coarse[kɔːs] *adj.* 粗糙的
4. prick[prik] *vt.* 刺;戳
5. seamstress['simstrəs] *n.* 女裁缝师
6. ruby['rubi] *n.* 红宝石

7. pedestal['pedistl] *n.* 基座
8. linen['linin] *n.* 亚麻布
9. agility[ə'dʒiləti] *n.* 敏捷
10. beak[bik] *n.* 鸟嘴
11. slumber['slʌmbə] *n.* 睡眠
12. chirrup['tʃirəp] *vi.* 吱喳地叫
13. bulrush['bulrʌʃ] *n.* 芦苇；灯芯草
14. beryl['berəl] *n.* 绿宝石
15. garret['gærət] *n.* 阁楼；顶楼
16. pomegranate['pɔmigrænit] *n.* 石榴
17. sapphire['sæfaiə] *n.* 蓝宝石

赏析

奥斯卡·王尔德(1854—1900)，著名的爱尔兰剧作家、诗人、艺术家、童话家。他是19世纪与萧伯纳齐名的英国才子，也是英国唯美主义艺术运动的倡导者。王尔德出身于爱尔兰首都都柏林的贵族之家，父亲为医生，母亲是作家。王尔德自幼便显示出很高的天赋，精通法语、德语和古典文学，自都柏林圣三一学院毕业后，于1874年进入牛津大学学习。在牛津，王尔德接触了各种思想，为他之后成为唯美主义先锋作家确立了方向。1895年，王尔德因诽谤罪入狱两年。出狱后，他迁居法国，郁郁不得志，最后病死在巴黎的一家小客栈里。王尔德一生著有两本童话集《快乐王子和其他故事》《石榴屋》(又称《石榴之家》)，其中最著名的是《巨人的花园》《快乐王子》《夜莺与玫瑰》。在王尔德的墓碑上，他被誉为“才子和戏剧家”。但最能体现王尔德才华的，不是童话和短片小说，而是《道连·格雷的画像》《狱中记》等长篇小说，《斯芬克斯》等诗集以及《温德米尔夫人的扇子》《莎乐美》等戏剧作品，其戏剧作品堪称一时之绝唱。

唯美主义哲学尖锐批判了当时的物质社会和庸人主义，倡导人应该在生活中发现美、鉴别美、享受美，充分地展现个性。王尔德作为唯美主义的倡导者和实践者，从他的主张到个性和作品都充满着魅力。王尔德醉心于追寻艺术形式美，主张“为艺术而艺术”，并断言只有风格才能使艺术不朽。他的一生似乎就是一个巨大的悖论，是一个集天使与魔鬼于一身的矛盾人物。既世故又纯洁；既虚伪又真实；一面在取悦上流社会，一边又在讽刺上流社会。

王尔德一生中只写过九篇童话，但每一篇都是精华。他的童话作品可以与安徒生和格林童话相媲美。本文节选自《快乐王子》，是他最为世人称道的童话，却又远远超出了童话故事的界限。这篇童话讲述了一位有一颗"铅心"的王子浑身上下镶满黄金、珠宝,高高矗立在广场上。他看到宫墙外的世界与他生前在皇宫里感受到的世界大相径庭。这时的他更加富有人类的同情心,他拒绝人类的纵乐主义,也放弃了他的唯美主义。幸亏他在此时遇到了他的精神伴侣燕子,他对燕子哭泣道:"我看见我的城市里的一切丑恶、一切悲惨凄凉,尽管我的心脏是铅制的,可我不能选择,只好哭泣。"燕子在快乐王子心灵的召唤下,摒弃了世俗主义,开始了他们救助穷苦人民的自我牺牲之路。最后燕子因为寒冷死去了,快乐王子的心也在那个寒冷孤苦的寒夜破碎了。童话的结尾是上帝接他们进入天堂,因为他们是"这城市里最珍贵的两样东西"。

全文以清新、干净的文字传达了唯美的凄凉,读者感受到的不止是对穷人的怜悯、同情,还有对社会现状的鞭笞、对学者的讽刺,最重要的是对燕子与快乐王子超脱世俗的无私、对"爱"的顿悟的赞美,他们正是在彼此的相伴相惜中,找到了精神的伴侣、灵魂的归宿,把整篇文章提升到了对生命终极意义的追问层次上。

第四章 名人演讲

原文

1 Barack Obama's Victory Speech (2012) (Extract)

We want our kids to grow up in a country where they have access to the best schools and the best teachers — a country that lives up to its legacy as the global leader in technology and discovery and innovation — with all of the good jobs and new businesses that follow.

We want our children to live in an America that isn't burdened by debt, that isn't weakened by inequality, that isn't threatened by the **destructive** power of a warming planet.

We want to pass on a country that's safe and respected and admired around the world, a nation that is defended by the strongest military on earth and the best troops this — this world has ever known. But also a country that moves with confidence beyond this time of war, to shape a peace that is built on the promise of freedom and **dignity** for every human being.

We believe in a generous America, in a **compassionate** America, in a **tolerant** America, open to the dreams of an **immigrant**'s daughter who studies in our schools and **pledges to** our flag. To the young boy on the south side of Chicago who sees a life beyond the nearest street corner. To the furniture worker's child in North Carolina who wants to become a doctor or a scientist, an engineer or an **entrepreneur**, a diplomat or even a president.

That's the future we hope for.

That's the vision we share. That's where we need to go — forward.

That's where we need to go.

...

America, I believe we can build on the progress we've made and continue to fight for new jobs and new opportunities and new security for the middle class. I believe we can keep the promise of our founding, the idea that if you're willing to work hard, it doesn't matter who you are or where you come from or what you look like or where you love. It doesn't matter whether you're black or white or Hispanic or Asian or Native American or young or old or rich or poor, abled, disabled, gay or straight, you can make it here in America if you're willing to try.

译文

1 奥巴马胜选演讲(2012)(节选)

我们都希望自己的孩子生活在一个有最好学校和最好老师的国家,一个在科技、探索、创新方面引领世界的国家,一个能够创造优质工作和新兴实业的国家。

我们都希望自己的孩子生活在一个不会被债务所累的美国, 一个不会被不公侵蚀的美国,一个不会被全球变暖威胁的美国。

我们都希望留给自己的孩子一个安全无虞、广受尊敬的国家,一个被世界最强军事实力所捍卫的国家。同时,我们也希望留给他们一个这样的国家,能够以武力之外的自信去缔造植根于人类自由与尊严的和平。

我们相信这是一个慷慨的美国,一个富有同情心的美国,一个宽容的美国。在这里,新移民者的小女孩能够在我们的学校里接受教育,向我们的国旗宣誓,勇敢做梦。芝加哥南部的小男孩能够走出小小的街区,去追逐大大的梦想。北卡罗来纳产业工人家的孩子能够去实现自己的未来,当上医生、科学家、工程师、企业家、外交官,甚至总统。

这,是我们期待的未来。

这,是我们共同的理想;这,是我们要去的地方,勇往直前。

这,是我们的使命。

……

同胞们, 我相信我们能在业已开创的道路上有所建树, 继续努力为中产阶级提供新就业、新机会和新保障。我坚信我们能恪守这个国家的建国承诺,只要你愿意努力,不管你是谁、来自何处、外貌如何、心在何方,不论你是黑人、白人、西班牙裔、黄种人还是原住民,不论你年轻还是年老、富有抑或贫穷、健全还是残疾、异性恋还是同性恋,你都能在这里实现自己,只要你愿意努力。

(王一旸 译)

注释

1. destructive[di'strʌktiv] *adj.* 破坏的;毁灭性的;有害的;消极的
2. dignity['digniti] *n.* 尊严;高尚;自豪;自尊
3. compassionate[kəm'pæʃənət] *adj.* 有同情心的;表示怜悯的
4. tolerant['tɔlərənt] *adj.* 宽容的;容忍的;忍受的
5. immigrant['imigrənt] *n.* 移民;侨民
6. pledge to: 保证;许诺;发誓
7. entrepreneur[ˌɔntrəprə'nə] *n.* 企业家;主办人;承包人

赏析

奥巴马(Barack Hussein Obama Ⅱ,贝拉克·侯赛因·奥巴马二世),美国第44任总统,出生于美国夏威夷州火奴鲁鲁,他的父亲的祖籍是肯尼亚(The Republic of Kenya)。奥巴马是首位拥有黑人血统,并且童年在亚洲、印度尼西亚成长的美国总统,与不同地方和不同文化背景的人共同生活过。2008年11月5日,奥巴马当选美国第44届总统。2011年4月4日,奥巴马宣布竞选2012年美国总统。

演讲背景:2012年11月6日晚(当地时间),2012年美国总统大选尘埃落定。现任总统、民主党候选人奥巴马在美国大选中获得超过270张选举人票击败共和党挑战者罗姆尼,成功连任。长达一年的选战中,各种政治人物、商界精英、演艺明星、媒体名嘴带来各种精彩演讲。一起回顾2012年美国大选,近距离体验大洋彼岸的选战风云。

原文

2 Martin Luther King Jr.'s Speech: I Have a Dream (Extract)

Go back to **Mississippi**, go back to **Alabama**, go back to South **Carolina**, go back to **Georgia**, go back to **Louisiana,** go back to the **slums** and **ghettos** of our northern cities, knowing that somehow this situation can and will be changed. Let us not **wallow** in the valley of despair.

I say to you today, my friends. And so even though we face the difficulties of today and tomorrow, I still have a dream. It is a dream deeply rooted in the American dream.

I have a dream that one day this nation will rise up and live out the true meaning of its creed: "We hold these truths to be self-evident, that all men are created equal."

I have a dream that one day on the red hills of Georgia, the sons of former slaves and the sons of former slave owners will be able to sit down together at the table of brotherhood.

I have a dream that one day even the state of Mississippi, a state sweltering with the heat of injustice, sweltering with the heat of oppression, will be transformed into an oasis of freedom and justice.

I have a dream that my four little children will one day live in a nation where they will not be judged by the color of their skin but by the content of their character.

I have a dream today!

I have a dream that one day down in Alabama, with its vicious racists, with its governor having his lips dripping with the words of "**interposition**" and "**nullification**" — one day right there in Alabama little black boys and black girls will be able to join hands with little white boys and white girls as sisters and brothers.

I have a dream today!

I have a dream that one day every valley shall be **exalted**, and every hill and mountain shall be made low, the rough places will be made plain, and the crooked places will be made straight; and the glory of the Lord shall be revealed and all flesh shall see it together.

This is our hope. This is the faith that I go back to the South with. With this faith we will be able to hew out of the mountain of despair a stone of hope. With this faith we will be able to transform the jangling discords of our nation into a beautiful symphony of brotherhood. With this faith we will be able to work together, to pray together, to struggle together, to go to jail together, to stand up for freedom together, knowing that we will be free one day.

译文

2 马丁·路德·金"我有一个梦想"演讲稿(节选)

让我们回到密西西比去,回到阿拉巴马去,回到南卡罗莱纳去,回到佐治亚去,回到路易斯安那去,回到我们北方城市中的贫民区和少数民族居住区去,要心中有数,这种状况是能够也必将改变的。我们切不要在绝望的深渊里沉沦。

朋友们,今天我要对你们说,尽管眼下困难重重,但我依然怀有一个梦。这个梦深深植根于美国梦之中。

我梦想有一天,这个国家将会奋起,实现其立国信条的真谛:"我们认为这些真理不言而喻:人人生而平等。"

我梦想有一天,在佐治亚州的红色山冈上,昔日奴隶的儿子能够同昔日奴隶主的儿子同席而坐,亲如手足。

我梦想有一天,甚至连密西西比州——一个非正义和压迫的热浪逼人的荒漠之洲,也会改造成为自由和公正的青青绿洲。

我梦想有一天,我的四个小女儿将生活在一个不是以皮肤的颜色,而是以品格的优劣作为评判标准的国家里。

我今天怀有一个梦想。

我梦想有一天,亚拉巴马州会有所改变——尽管该州州长现在仍滔滔不绝地说什么要对联邦法令提出异议和拒绝执行——在那里,黑人儿童能够和白人儿童兄弟姐妹般地携手并行。

我今天有一个梦想。

我梦想有一天，幽谷上升，高山下降，坎坷曲折之路成坦途，圣光披露，满照人间。

这就是我们的希望。我怀着这种信念回到南方。有了这个信念，我们将能从绝望之岭劈出一块希望之石。有了这个信念，我们将能把这个国家刺耳的争吵声，改编成为一支洋溢着手足之情的优美交响曲。有了这个信念，我们将能一起工作，一起祈祷，一起斗争，一起坐牢，一起维护自由。因为我们知道，终有一天，我们会是自由的。

（徐立中　译）

注释

1. Mississippi[ˌmisiˈsipi] *n.* 密西西比河（发源于美国中北部湖沼区，南注墨西哥湾，是世界上最大的河流之一）；密西西比州（美国州名）
2. Alabama[ˌæləˈbæmə] *n.* 阿拉巴马州（美国州名）
3. Carolina[ˌkærəˈlainə] *n.* 卡罗莱纳州（美国州名）
4. Georgia[ˈdʒɔ:dʒə] *n.* 佐治亚州（美国州名）
5. Louisiana[lu:ˌi:ziˈænə] *n.* 路易斯安那州（美国州名）
6. slum[slʌm] *n.* 贫民窟；贫民区
7. ghettos[ˈgetəu] *n.* 贫民区；少数民族聚居区；犹太人区
8. wallow[ˈwɔləu] *vi.* 沉迷；打滚；颠簸
9. interposition[intəpəˈziʃən] *n.* 提出（异议）行为；插嘴（插入）行为；提出（异议）的事；插嘴（插入）的事
10. nullification[ˌnʌləfiˈkeʃən] *n.* 无效；废弃；取消；使无价值
11. exalted[iɡˈzɔ:ltid] *adj.* 高贵的；高尚的，崇高的；意气风发的；得意洋洋的

赏析

马丁·路德·金（Martin Luther King Jr.，1929年1月15日—1968年4月4日），著名的美国民权运动领袖，是一位出身于农民家庭的神学家，1964年度诺贝尔和平奖获得者，有“金牧师”之称。他最有影响力且最为人知的一场演讲是1963年8月28日的《我有一个梦想》，演讲词迫使美国国会在1964年通过《民权法案》，并宣布种族隔离和种族歧视政策为非法政策。

演讲背景：在20世纪60年代，美国人逐渐认识到，南北战争所致力的解放黑奴运动，并没有产生使美国黑人成为完全平等公民的预期效果。19世纪后期，美国黑人的公民权利受

到州和地方歧视黑人的法规和惯例层层约束和限制。在日常生活中，美国黑人常常被隔离开来，不能与白人同在一个学校上学、乘坐同一公共交通工具、同在一个地方居住。黑人不能充分参与美国社会生活，甚至在一百年后仍然和奴隶一样被剥夺各种权利，他们生活水准的提高与国家的发展并非完全相称。因此美国黑人的平等问题成为一个严重的社会问题。黑人志愿团体和各种教会以及其他各阶层关心此事的美国人团体，齐心协力掀起了一场争取民权的运动。

原文

3 Remarks by President Bush at Tsinghua University(Extract)

My country certainly has its share of problems, no question about that. And we have our faults. Like most nations, we're on a long journey toward achieving our own ideals of equality and justice. Yet there's a reason our nation shines as a beacon of hope and opportunity, a reason many throughout the world dream of coming to America.

It's because we're a free nation, where men and women have the **opportunity** to achieve their dreams. No matter your background or your **circumstance** of birth, in America you can get a good education, you can start your own business, you can raise a family, you can worship freely, and help elect the leaders of your community and your country. You can support the policies of our government, or you're free to openly disagree with them. Those who fear freedom sometimes argue it could lead to chaos, but it does not, because freedom means more than every man for himself.

Liberty gives our citizens many rights, yet expects them to exercise important **responsibilities**. Our liberty is given direction and purpose by moral character, shaped in strong families, strong communities, and strong religious institutions, and overseen by a strong and fair legal system.

My country's greatest symbol to the world is the Statue of Liberty, and it was designed by special care. I don't know if you've ever seen the Statue of Liberty, but if you look closely, she's holding not one object, but two. In one hand is the familiar torch we call the "light of liberty". And in the other hand is a book of law.

We're a nation of laws. Our courts are honest and they are independent. The President — me — I can't tell the courts how to rule, and neither can any other member of the **executive** or **legislative** branch of government. Under our law, everyone stands equal. No one is above the law, and no one is beneath it.

All political power in America is limited and it is **temporary**, and only given by the free vote of the people. We have a ***Constitution,*** now two centuries old, which limits and balances the power of the three branches of our government, the judicial branch, the legislative branch, and the executive branch, of which I'm a part.

Many of the values that guide our life in America are first shaped in our families, just as they are in your country. American moms and dads love their children and work hard and sacrifice for them, because we believe life can always be better for the next generation. In our families, we find love and learn responsibility and character.

And many Americans **voluntarily** devote part of their lives to serving other people. An amazing number — nearly half of all adults in America — volunteer time every week to make their communities better by mentoring children, or by visiting the sick, or caring for the elderly, or helping with thousands of other needs and causes. This is one of the great strengths of my country. People take responsibility for helping others, without being told, **motivated** by their good hearts and often by their faith.

America is a nation guided by faith. Someone once called us "a nation with the soul of a church." This may interest you — 95 percent of Americans say they believe in God, and I'm one of them.

译文

3 美国总统布什在清华大学的演讲(节选)

我们的国家也和其他国家一样有问题,这是毫无疑问的。也和大多数国家一样有我们的缺点。我们正在一条漫长的道路上,按照自己的理念努力营造一个平等公正的国家。但是美国被认为是世界上最具希望和发展机会的国家,全世界的许多人都梦想到美国来。

这是因为美国是一个自由的国家,人们享有实现梦想的同等机会。不论你的背景如何,不论你出生在什么地方,在美国你都可以受到很好的教育,开办企业,建立家庭,信仰自由,帮助选出社区和国家的领导人。你可以支持政府的政策,你也可以自由地反对这些政策。那些害怕自由的人有时争辩说,这样会引起混乱,但是这是不会的,因为自由意味着每个人不只为了自己的利益。

自由使我们的人民有很多权利,但是同时人们也必须负起他们的重要责任。自由的方向和目的受到道德的引导,这体现在坚实的家庭、社区和教会,并受到牢固和公正司法体系的监督上。

对于世界来说,美国最伟大的象征是自由女神。自由女神是经过精心设计的。不知道你们看到过没有,如果仔细看的话,你会发现,女神手持两样东西,而不是一个。她的一只手高举着自由明灯,另一只手拿的是法典。

美国是一个法治国家,我们的法庭是公正和诚实的。我作为总统不可能告诉法庭应该做出什么裁决,而且行政当局的任何官员和立法人员也都不可以这样做。根据我们的宪法,每个人都是平等的,没有人可以置于法律之上,也没有人不受到法律的保护。

美国所有的政治权力都不是无限的和永久的,权力只能通过公民自由选举产生。我们有一部《宪法》,已经有两百年的历史,它限制和平衡三个权力机构之间的权力,这三个权力机构是司法、立法和行政当局。我就是行政机构的一员。

指导我们的很多价值观是在家庭中形成的,就像中国一样。美国的妈妈和爸爸们疼爱自己的孩子,为他们辛勤地劳动,做出牺牲,因为我们相信,下一代的生活一定会更好。在我们的家庭中,我们可以找到关爱,可以学习如何负起责任,如何养成人格。

很多美国人都抽出时间为其他人服务,几乎一半的成年人每周都抽出时间,使得他们的社区办得更好。他们辅导儿童、探访病人、照顾老人,并且帮助做许许多多数不胜数的事情。这是我们国家的一大优势。人们主动承担起责任,主动帮助别人。他们这样做是出于善良的心和信仰。

美国是在信仰指导下的国家,一些人曾经称美国是"一个具有教会精神的国家"。你们对这种说法可能感兴趣。95%的美国人信仰上帝,我就是其中之一。

(岳永 译)

注释

1. opportunity[ˌɔpə'tunəti] *n.* 机会;适当的时机;良机
2. circumstance['səkəmstæns] *n.* 环境;境遇;事实,细节;典礼,仪式
3. liberty['libəti] *n.* 自由;许可权
4. responsibility[riˌspɔnsə'biliti] *n.* 责任,职责;责任感,责任心
5. executive [iɡ'zekjətiv] *n.* 行政部门 *adj.* 执行的;管理的;政府部门的
6. legislative['ledʒiˌsletiv] *adj.* (关于)立法的;立法机构的 *n.* 立法权;立法机关
7. temporary['tempərəri] *adj.* 临时的,暂时的;短暂的
8. Constitution['kɔnsti'tuʃən] *n.* 建立,组成;体格;构成方式;宪法
9. voluntarily[ˌvɔlən'terəli] *adv.* 志愿地;自动地,自发地
10. motivated ['motivetid] *adj.* 有动机的,有目的的;有积极性的

赏析

乔治·沃克·布什为美国第43任总统。布什在2001年1月20日就职,并且在2004年的选举中击败民主党参选人约翰·克里连任。在担任总统之前,布什于1995年至2000年间担任第46任的德州州长。布什家族很早就开始投入共和党以及美国政治,布什的父亲是之前曾担任第41任总统的乔治·赫伯特·沃克·布什,他的弟弟杰布·布什也曾是佛罗里达州的州长。由于与父亲同样都是美国总统,因此又常被称为小布什以区别,而他父亲就被称为老布什。在"美国在线"于2005年举办的票选活动"最伟大的美国人"中,布什被选为美国最伟

大的人物第6位。

2002年2月22日，美国总统布什在中国国家副主席胡锦涛的陪同下来到清华大学举行演讲。清华大学校长王大中先生主持演讲会，胡锦涛副主席首先致词，之后布什总统发表演讲并回答清华学子的提问。

原文

4 The Commencement Address by Steve Jobs(Extract)

My third story is about death.

When I was 17, I read a quote that went something like: "If you live each day as if it was your last, someday you'll most certainly be right." It made an impression on me, and since then, for the past 33 years, I have looked in the mirror every morning and asked myself, "If today were the last day of my life, would I want to do what I am about to do today?" And whenever the answer has been "No" for too many days in a row, I know I need to change something.

Remembering that I'll be dead soon is the most important tool I've ever encountered to help me make the big choices in life. Because almost everything — all external expectations, all pride, all fear of **embarrassment** or failure — these things just fall away in the face of death, leaving only what is truly important. Remembering that you are going to die is the best way I know to avoid the trap of thinking you have something to lose. You are already naked. There is no reason not to follow your heart.

About a year ago I was **diagnosed** with cancer. I had a scan at 7:30 in the morning, and it clearly showed a **tumor** on my **pancreas**. I didn't even know what a pancreas was. The doctors told me this was almost certainly a type of cancer that is **incurable**, and that I should expect to live no longer than three to six months. My doctor advised me to go home and get my affairs in order, which is doctor's code for prepare to die. It means to try to tell your kids everything you thought you'd have the next 10 years to tell them in just a few months. It means to make sure everything is buttoned up so that it will be as easy as possible for your family. It means to say your goodbyes.

I lived with that diagnosis all day. Later that evening I had a biopsy, where they stuck an endoscope down my throat, through my stomach and into my intestines, put a needle into my pancreas and got a few cells from the tumor. I was sedated, but my wife, who was there, told me that when they viewed the cells under a microscope the doctors started crying because it turned out to be a very rare form of pancreatic cancer that is curable with surgery. I had the surgery and I'm fine now.

This was the closest I've been to facing death, and I hope it's the closest I get for a few more decades. Having lived through it, I can now say this to you with a bit more certainty than when death was a useful but purely intellectual concept:

No one wants to die. Even people who want to go to heaven don't want to die to get there. And yet death is the destination we all share. No one has ever escaped it. And that is as it should be, because death is very likely the single best invention of life. It is life's change agent. It clears out the old to make way for the new. Right now the new is you, but someday not too long from now, you will gradually become the old and be cleared away. Sorry to be so dramatic, but it is quite true.

Your time is limited, so don't waste it living someone else's life. Don't be trapped by **dogma** — which is living with the results of other people's thinking. Don't let the noise of others' opinions drown out your own inner voice. And most important, have the courage to follow your heart and **intuition**. They somehow already know what you truly want to become. Everything else is secondary.

When I was young, there was an amazing publication called *The Whole Earth Catalog*, which was one of the bibles of my generation. It was created by a fellow named Stewart Brand not far from here in Menlo Park, and he brought it to life with his poetic touch. This was in the late 1960s, before personal computers and desktop publishing, so it was all made with typewriters, **scissors**, and **polaroid cameras**. It was sort of like Google in paperback form, 35 years before Google came along: it was idealistic, and overflowing with neat tools and great notions.

Stewart and his team put out several issues of *The Whole Earth Catalog*, and then when it had run its course, they put out a final issue. It was the mid-1970s, and I was your age. On the back cover of their final issue was a photograph of an early morning country road, the kind you might find yourself hitchhiking on if you were so adventurous. Beneath it were the words: "Stay Hungry. Stay Foolish." It was their farewell message as they signed off. Stay Hungry. Stay Foolish. And I have always wished that for myself. And now, as you graduate to begin anew, I wish that for you: Stay Hungry. Stay Foolish.

(*Stanford Report, June 14, 2005*)

译文

4　乔布斯对斯坦福毕业生的演讲(节选)

我的第三个故事是关于死亡的。

当我17岁的时候，我读到了一句话："如果你把每一天都当作生命中最后一天去生活的话，那么有一天你会发现你是正确的。"这句话给我留下了深刻的印象。从那时开始，过了33年，我在每天早晨都会对着镜子问自己："如果今天是我生命中的最后一天，我会不会完成我今天想做的事情呢？"当答案连续很多次被给予"不是"的时候，我知道自己需要改变某些事情了。

“记住你即将死去”是我一生中遇到的最重要的箴言。它帮我指明了生命中重要的选择。因为几乎所有的事情,包括所有的荣誉、所有的骄傲、所有对难堪和失败的恐惧,这些在死亡面前都会消失。我看到的是留下的真正重要的东西。你有时候会思考你将会失去某些东西,“记住你即将死去”是我知道的避免这些想法的最好办法。你已经赤身裸体了,你没有理由不去跟随自己的心一起跳动。

大概一年以前,我被诊断出癌症。我在早晨七点半做了一个检查,检查清楚地显示在我的胰腺有一个肿瘤。我当时都不知道胰腺是什么东西。医生告诉我那很可能是一种无法治愈的癌症,我还有三到六个月的时间活在这个世界上。我的医生叫我回家,然后整理好我的一切,那就是医生准备死亡的程序。那意味着你将要把未来十年对你小孩说的话在几个月里面说完;那意味着把每件事情都搞定,让你的家人会尽可能轻松地生活;那意味着你要说“再见”了。

我整天和那个诊断书一起生活。后来有一天早上我做了一个活切片检查,医生将一个内窥镜从我的喉咙伸进去,通过我的胃,然后进入我的肠子,用一根针在我胰腺上的肿瘤上取了几个细胞。我当时很镇静,因为我被注射了镇静剂。但是我的妻子在那里,后来告诉我,当医生在显微镜下观察这些细胞的时候他们开始尖叫,因为这些细胞最后竟然是一种非常罕见的可以用手术治愈的胰腺癌症。我做了这个手术,现在我痊愈了。

那是我最接近死亡的时候,我还希望这也是以后的几十年最接近的一次。从死亡线上又活了过来,相对于以前把死亡当成一个有用但是纯粹是知识上的概念的时候,我可以更肯定一点地对你们说:

没有人愿意死,即使人们想上天堂,人们也不会为了去那里而死。但是死亡是我们每个人共同的终点。从来没有人能够逃脱它。也应该如此。因为死亡就是生命中最好的一个发明。它将旧的清除以便给新的让路。你们现在是新的,但是从现在开始不久以后,你们将会逐渐地变成旧的然后被清除。我很抱歉这很戏剧性,但是这十分真实。

你们的时间很有限,所以不要将它们浪费在重复其他人的生活上。不要被教条束缚,那意味着你和其他人思考的结果一起生活。不要被其他人喧嚣的观点掩盖你真正的内心的声音。还有最重要的是,你要有勇气听从你直觉和心灵的指示——它们在某种程度上知道你想要成为什么样子,所以其他事情都是次要的。

当我年轻的时候,有一本叫作《整个地球的目录》的杂志,它是我们那一代人的圣经之一。它是一个叫Stewart Brand的家伙在离这里不远的Menlo Park书写的,他像诗一般神奇地将这本书带到了这个世界。那是20世纪60年代后期,在个人电脑出现之前,所以这本书全部是用打字机、剪刀还有偏光镜制造的。有点像用软皮包装的Google,在Google出现35年之前:这是理想主义的,其中有许多灵巧的工具和伟大的想法。

Stewart和他的伙伴出版了几期《整个地球的目录》,当它完成了自己使命的时候,他们做出了最后一期的目录。那是在70年代的中期,我正是你们的年纪。在最后一期的封底上是清晨乡村公路的照片(如果你有冒险精神的话,你可以自己找到这条路),在照片之下有这样一段话:“保持饥饿,保持愚蠢。”这是他们停止了发刊的告别语。“保持饥饿,保持愚蠢。”我总是希望自己能够那样，现在，在你们即将毕业、开始新的旅程的时候，我也希望你们能这样：保持饥饿，保持愚蠢。

（杨一兰　译）

注释

1. embarrassment[im'bærəsmənt] *n.* 窘迫；难堪；令人难堪或耻辱的事
2. diagnose[ˌdaiəg'nos] *vt.* 诊断；判断　*vi.* 做出诊断
3. tumor['tju:mə] *n.* 瘤
4. pancreas['pæŋkriəs] *n.* 胰；胰腺
5. incurable[in'kjurəbəl] *adj.* 无法治愈的；无法改变的
6. dogma['dɔgmə] *n.* 教义，教条，信条；武断的意见
7. intuition[ˌintu'iʃən] *n.* 直觉；凭直觉感知的知识；直觉力
8. scissors['sizəz] *n.* 剪刀
9. polaroid camera['poləˌrɔid 'kæmərə] 即显胶片照相机

赏析

史蒂夫·乔布斯（1955—2011），发明家，企业家，美国苹果公司联合创办人、前行政总裁。1976年乔布斯和朋友成立苹果电脑公司，他陪伴了苹果公司数十年的起落与复兴，先后领导和推出了麦金塔计算机、iMac、iPod、iPhone等风靡全球亿万人的电子产品，深刻地改变了现代通讯、娱乐乃至生活的方式。2011年10月5日他因病逝世，享年56岁。乔布斯是改变世界的天才，他凭敏锐的触觉和过人的智慧，勇于变革，不断创新，引领全球资讯科技和电子产品的潮流，把电脑和电子产品变得简约化、平民化，让曾经是昂贵稀罕的电子产品变为现代人生活的一部分。

这是一篇非常感人、励志的演讲。绝大多数人终生为生存而奋斗，且世世代代走不出来，并不去想为什么。也有太多人面对自己的内心，却生活得很惨，几人有乔布斯的能力？我们的时间有限，所以不要为别人而活，不要被教条所限，不要活在别人的观念里，不要让别人的意见左右自己内心的声音。最重要的是，勇敢地去追随自己的心灵和直觉，只有自己的心灵和直觉才知道你自己的真实想法，其他一切都是次要的。

原文

5 First Inaugural Address of Richard Milhous Nixon (Extract)

What kind of nation we will be, what kind of world we will live in, whether we shape the future in the image of our hopes, is ours to determine by our actions and our choices.

The greatest honor history can **bestow** is the title of peacemaker. This honor now **beckons** America — the chance to help lead the world at last out of the valley of turmoil, and onto that high ground of peace that man has dreamed of since the dawn of civilization.

If we succeed, generations to come will say of us now living that we mastered our moment, that we helped make the world safe for mankind.

This is our summons to greatness.

I believe the American people are ready to answer this call.

...

After a period of **confrontation**, we are entering an era of **negotiation**.

Let all nations know that during this **administration** our lines of communication will be open.

We seek an open world — open to ideas, open to the exchange of goods and people — a world in which no people, great or small, will live in angry isolation.

We cannot expect to make everyone our friend, but we can try to make no one our enemy.

Those who would be our adversaries, we invite to a peaceful competition — not in conquering territory or extending dominion, but in enriching the life of man.

As we explore the reaches of space, let us go to the new worlds together — not as new worlds to be conquered, but as a new adventure to be shared.

With those who are willing to join, let us cooperate to reduce the burden of arms, to strengthen the structure of peace, to lift up the poor and the hungry.

But to all those who would be tempted by weakness, let us leave no doubt that we will be as strong as we need to be for as long as we need to be.

Over the past twenty years, since I first came to this Capital as a freshman Congressman, I have visited most of the nations of the world.

I have come to know the leaders of the world, and the great forces, the hatreds, the fears that divide the world.

I know that peace does not come through wishing for it — that there is no substitute for days and even years of patient and **prolonged diplomacy**.

I also know the people of the world.

I have seen the hunger of a homeless child, the pain of a man wounded in battle, the grief of a mother who has lost her son. I know these have no ideology, no race.

I know America. I know the heart of America is good.

I speak from my own heart, and the heart of my country, the deep concern we have for those who suffer, and those who sorrow.

(*Monday, January 20, 1969*)

译文

5 理查德·尼克松第一次就职演讲(节选)

我们的国家将变成怎样的国家,我们将生活在怎样的世界上,我们要不要按照我们的希望铸造未来,这些都将由我们根据自己的行动和选择来决定。

历史所能赐予我们的最大荣誉,莫过于和平缔造者这一称号。这一荣誉现在正在召唤美国——这是领导世界最终脱离动乱的深谷,走向自文明开端以来人类一直梦寐以求的和平高坛的一个机会。

我们若获成功,下几代人在谈及现在在世的我们时会说,正是我们掌握了时机,正是我们协力相助,使普天之下国泰民安。

这是要我们创立宏伟大业的召唤。

我相信,美国人民准备响应这一召唤。

……

经过一段对抗时期,我们正进入一个谈判时代。

让所有国家都知道,在本届政府任期内,交流通道是敞开的。

我们谋求一个开放的世界——对各种思想开放,对物资和人员的交流开放,在这个世界中,任何民族,不论大小,都不会生活在怏怏不乐的孤立之中。

我们不能指望每个人都成为我们的朋友,可是我们能设法使任何人都不与我们为敌。

我们邀请那些很可能是我们对手的人进行一场和平竞赛——不是要征服领土或扩展版图,而是要丰富人类的生活。

在探索宇宙空间的时候,让我们一起走向新的世界——不是走向被征服的新世界,而是共同进行一次新的探险。

让我们同那些愿意加入这一行列的人共同合作,减少军备负担,加固和平大厦,提高贫穷挨饿的人们的生活水平。

但是,对所有那些见软就欺的人来说,让我们不容置疑地表明,我们需要多么强大就会多强大,需要强大多久,就会强大多久。

自从我作为新当选的国会议员首次来到国会大厦之后的20多年来,我已经出访过世界上大多数国家。

我结识了世界各国的领导人，了解到使世界陷于四分五裂的各种强大势力、各种深仇大恨、各种恐惧心理。

我知道，和平不会单凭愿望就能到来——这需要日复一日，甚至年复一年地进行耐心而持久的外交努力，除此别无他法。

我也了解世界各国人民。

我见到过无家可归的儿童在忍饥挨饿，战争中挂彩负伤的男人在痛苦呻吟，失去孩子的母亲在无限悲伤。我知道，这些并没有意识形态和种族之分。

我了解美国。我了解美国的心是善良的。

我从心底里，从我国人民的心底里，向那些蒙受不幸和痛苦的人们表达我们的深切关怀。

（杨一兰　译）

注释

1. bestow[bi'sto] *vt.* 赠给，授予；放置，安置；让……留宿
2. beckon['bekən] *vt. & vi.* (用头或手的动作)示意；召唤
3. confrontation[ˌkɔnfrʌn'teʃən] *n.* 对抗；面对；遭遇；对峙
4. negotiation[niˌgoʃi'eʃən] *n.* 协商，谈判；转让；通过
5. administration[ədˌmini'streʃən] *n.* 管理；实行；(政府)行政机关
6. ideology[ˌaidi'ɔlədʒi] *n.* 思想(体系)，思想意识；意识形态；观念学
7. prolonged[prə'lɔŋd] *adj.* 持续很久的；延长的；拖延的
8. diplomacy[di'ploməsi] *n.* 外交；外交手腕，交际手段；外交使团；处世之道

赏析

理查德·米尔豪斯·尼克松 (Richard Milhous Nixon，1913年1月9日—1994年4月22日)，美国第37位总统。1972年连任第47届总统。执政后，尼克松对内的目标是抑制通货膨胀，重振美国经济。对外，提出“尼克松主义”，与中华人民共和国直接接触。1972年2月访华，打开了两国关系的大门，成为访问新中国的第一位美国总统。1974年8月8日因“水门事件”被迫辞去总统职务，成为美国历史上第一个为了躲避国会对其滥用职权进行弹劾而辞职的总统。

在上述著名就职演讲中，演讲者反复使用“我们”和“我”代替“你们”或“你”使自己融入美国铜版纸中，这样既可以表达事实、号召听众行动，也更易于赢得听众。有些攻击政府机关的人们，虽然显得声势浩大，但实际上却并非是多数，而绝大多数美国人的声音却被这些激进的呼喊所掩盖；绝大多数美国人都是爱国的，不希望国家走入颓势，只是种种原因，他们并未站出来表达自己的意见，而是处于沉默状态。但他们也不得不承认，尼克松的这番话还真取得了不凡的效果，听过其演说的人，对他的支持率将近八成，而随后1972年的大选，尼克松以压倒性的胜利获得连任。

原文

6 The Queen Elizabeth II's Address to Parliament

My Lords and Members of the House of Commons,

Over such a period, one can observe that the experience of **venerable** old age can be a mighty guide but not a prerequisite for success in public office.

I am therefore very pleased to be addressing many younger **Parliamentarians** and also those bringing such a wide range of background and experience to your vital, national work.

During these years as your Queen, the support of my family has, across the generations, been beyond measure.

Prince Philip is, I believe, well-known for declining compliments of any kind. But throughout he has been a constant strength and guide.

He and I are very proud and grateful that the Prince of Wales and other members of our family are travelling on my behalf in this **Diamond Jubilee** year to visit all the Commonwealth **Realms** and a number of other Commonwealth countries.

These overseas tours are a reminder of our close affinity with the Commonwealth, encompassing about one-third of the world's population.

My own association with the Commonwealth has taught me that the most important contact between nations is usually contact between its peoples.

An organization dedicated to certain values, the Commonwealth has **flourished** and grown by successfully promoting and protecting that contact.

At home, Prince Philip and I will be visiting towns and cities up and down the land.

It is my sincere hope that the Diamond Jubilee will be an opportunity for people to come together in a spirit of neighbourliness and celebration of their own communities.

We also hope to celebrate the professional and voluntary service given by millions of people across the country who are working for the public good.

They are a source of vital support to the welfare and wellbeing of others, often unseen or overlooked.

And as we reflect upon public service, let us again be mindful of the remarkable sacrifice and courage of our Armed Forces.

Much may indeed have changed these past sixty years but the valour of those who risk their lives for the defence and freedom of us all remains undimmed.

The happy relationship I have enjoyed with Parliament has extended well beyond the more than three and a half thousand Bills I have signed into law.

I am therefore very touched by the magnificent gift before me, generously subscribed by many of you.

Should this beautiful window cause just a little extra colour to shine down upon this ancient place, I should gladly settle for that.

We are reminded here of our past, of the continuity of our national story and the virtues of **resilience**, **ingenuity** and **tolerance** which created it.

I have been **privileged to** witness some of that history and, with the support of my family, rededicate myself to the service of our great country and its people now and in the years to come.

译文

6 英国女王伊丽莎白二世登基60周年演讲稿

我的上议院和下议院的成员们：

在这样一个时代，年长者的经验很管用，但对于担任公职来说却不是成功的先决条件。

我也很高兴向很多年轻议员提建议，我也把广泛的背景知识和经验运用到日常国家事务中。

当女王的这些年，来自我家庭的几代人的支持难以衡量。

菲利普亲王因为拒绝各种赞扬而出名。但是，他是一个坚定的支持者和向导。

威尔士王子和其他家人将代表我在钻禧年出访所有的英联邦王国和部分英联邦国家，他和我都感到非常高兴和自豪。

这些海外行程将使占世界三分之一的人口的联邦成员国紧紧联系着。

我与英联邦国家交往的亲身经历告诉我，国家之间最重要的联系通常是人民之间的联系。

该机构提供固定的价值，鼓励和保持成员之间的联系，促进联邦国繁荣和发展。

在国内，菲利普亲王和我将会访问南北方的城市和郡县。

我真诚地希望，钻禧典礼将成为人们团结的一个良好契机，传递友善的邻里关系和他们的社区价值。

我也希望能够表彰那些在公共领域工作的，来自全国各地自愿提供服务的数百万人民和专家。

他们是为公众福祉提供重要支持的源泉，却往往被忽视。

我们对公共服务进行思考，让我们再一次注意到我们军队做出的卓越贡献和勇敢。

在过去的60年里，许多已经改变，但是为了守护国家和我们的自由而献身的勇气会永存。

我和议员之间的愉快关系很好地延续着，已经超过我签署3500份法案的时间。

结果我收到了非常壮观的礼物，你们中许多人慷慨地付出了。

如果这扇漂亮的窗户能为这个古老的地方增添色彩，我将为此感到高兴。

在这里，我们想起过去我们国家的故事，国民的坚韧性、创造力和宽容心。

我亲历了其中的一些历史，在我家人的支持下，现在和将来，我将致力于为我们伟大的国家和人民服务。

（倪宁　译）

注释

1. venerable['venərəbəl] *adj.* 令人尊重的；庄严的；珍贵的
2. parliamentarian['pɑrləmən'təriən] *n.* 国会议员
3. diamond jubilee['daiəmənd 'dʒubili] *n.* 第60周年纪念；钻禧年
4. realm[rəlm] *n.* 领域，范围；王国；(学术的)部门，界
5. flourish['flʌriʃ] *vi.* 挥舞；茂盛，繁荣；活跃，蓬勃 *vt.* 挥动，挥舞
6. resilience[ri'ziliəns] *n.* 弹性，弹力；快速恢复的能力；回弹
7. ingenuity[ˌindʒə'nuiti] *n.* 心灵手巧；独创性；独出心裁；巧妙
8. tolerance['tɔlərəns] *n.* 宽容，容忍；限度；公差；耐药量，耐药性
9. privilege to ['privəlidʒ] *vt.* 给予……特权；特免

赏析

伊丽莎白·亚历山德拉·玛丽·温莎(Elizabeth Alexandra Mary Windsor)，即伊丽莎白二世，英国女王，英联邦元首，国教(圣公会)的捍卫者。现任英国君主，英国、英联邦及15个成员国国家元首，国教会最高首领。2012年6月2日至5日，英国举办英女王钻禧庆典，纪念女王登基60周年。2012年12月18日，参加内阁会议，她成为百年来和平时期出席政府内阁会议的第一位英国君主。

演讲背景：英国女王伊丽莎白二世于2012年在威斯敏斯特大厅向议会发表登基60周年(钻禧年)演讲。女王在演讲中承诺，将牢记英国历史，继续全身心服务国家，称赞丈夫菲利普亲王不断给予力量和引导。她在位时间仅次于维多利亚女王的63年，女王已经完成了君主该做的事情：尽职地在公开场合露面，到各地旅行，在时局好或不好的时候访问她的臣民。

原文

7 EU Commission President Jose Manuel Barroso's Speech at China National School of Administration (Extract)

The trend towards a more **multi - lateral** world is getting clearer. It is positive that other nations are ready and willing to take on global responsibilities.

The case for increased cooperation between China and EU is stronger than ever. Together, the EU and China can contribute to solving the problems the world is facing.

Relations between China and the EU are good and **dynamic**. Together, we have developed a strategic partnership in which we cooperate on numerous issues. We are currently **elaborating** a partnership and cooperation agreement, to better reflect how our relations have developed and to boost those relations for the future.

People - to - people exchanges have increased. Our bilateral trade has grown. Today China is the most important source of imports for the EU, and the EU is China's largest trading partner. Our political, economic and people - to - people contacts have increased **exponentially** over the last decade.

The people of Europe were quick to respond to the devastating earthquake in Sichuan. Many citizens as well as European governments offered help and financial contributions. This Sunday we will hold a conference in Chengdu together with our Chinese partners on how to advance reconstruction and attract investment in that area.

Earlier this spring, I headed the biggest Commission delegation ever to travel to a third country, for a meeting with Premier Wen Jiabao to strengthen EU–China cooperation on **sustainable** development and trade. Indeed, new vistas of cooperation were opened up on that occasion. I am confident that tomorrow's ASEM Summit and our EU/China Summit on 1 December in Lyon will move our partnership further forward.

One issue, however, deserves sustained political attention from leaders on both sides: the trade deficit. We know that this in part reflects the growing **competitiveness** of Chinese products. But we must also recognize that other factors are involved, which can and must be corrected. We need to work together, in a spirit of reciprocity, to eliminate obstacles preventing the access, in many sectors, of European goods and services to the Chinese market.

Our cooperation in the fight against climate change is particularly important. We all now know that climate change is real, that it is caused by human activity, and that its consequences are universal and will be felt first and foremost by the poorest. Yes, it is true that the state of our planet today is a result of **industrialization** that began generations ago in developed countries. At that time none of us was aware of the consequences. But now we know, and we know that there is no solution without unity.

(*Beijing, 23 October, 2008*)

译文

7 欧盟委员会主席若泽·曼努埃尔·巴罗佐先生在中国国家行政学院的演讲(节选)

世界多极化的趋势日益清晰。许多其他国家准备并愿意承担全球责任,这将产生积极的影响。

中国和欧盟日益加深的合作规模是空前的。欧盟和中国能够共同为解决世界面临的问题做出贡献。

中国和欧盟之间的关系是良好而有活力的。我们建立了战略伙伴关系,在众多事务上开展了合作。目前,我们正在细化伙伴合作协议,以反映我们业已存在的关系并着眼未来推动这些关系的发展。

中欧间的人员交流也已加强。中欧双边贸易得到了扩大。中国今天已成为欧盟最重要的进口商品来源国,欧盟是中国最大的贸易伙伴。中欧间的政治、经济和人员交流在过去十年得到了显著加强。

欧洲人民对发生在四川的破坏性大地震做出了快速反应。许多欧洲人和政府提供了帮助和资金支援。本周日,我们将与我们的中国合作伙伴在成都共同举办一个旨在推动灾区重建和吸引投资的会议。

今年春天早些时候,我率领欧盟委员会历史上最大规模的出访第三国的代表团来到中国,与温家宝总理进行了会谈,讨论如何加强欧盟与中国在可持续发展和商贸方面的合作。事实上,那次会议已经为中欧间合作开启了新的前景。我相信,明天召开的亚欧首脑会议和12月1日在里昂召开的欧中峰会将会进一步推动我们的伙伴关系向前发展。

然而,有一个问题需要我们双方领导人从政治方面加以不断的关注,这就是贸易赤字问题。我们知道贸易赤字部分地反映出中国产品不断增加的竞争力。但是我们也必须认识到这其中还有一些可以而且必须纠正的其他因素。我们需要共同努力,本着互惠的精神,在许多领域为欧洲商品和服务进入中国市场清除障碍。

我们在应对气候变化方面的合作尤其重要。我们现在都认识到气候的变化是实实在在的,这一变化由人类活动引发,其影响是全球性的并且将首先波及最贫困的人口。是的,我们星球的现状是发达国家数代人以前开启的工业化进程造成的。当时,没有人意识到这些后果。但是,我们现在认识到了这一点,并且知道只有团结起来才能找到解决问题的办法。

(2008年10月23日于北京)

(纵向东 译)

注释

1. EU: *abbr.* 欧盟 European Union
2. multi-lateral:多边
3. dynamic[dai'næmik] *adj.* 动态的;动力的,动力学的;充满活力的
4. elaborating: elaborate的现在分词。变得复杂;详细制定;详尽阐述
5. exponentially[ˌikspo'nənʃəli] *adv.* 以指数方式
6. sustainable[sə'stenʃəbl] *adj.* 可持续的;可以忍受的;可支撑的
7. competitiveness[kəm'petətivnis] *n.* 竞争;竞争性
8. industrialization[inˌdʌstriələ'zeʃən] *n.* 工业化

赏析

若泽·曼努埃尔·杜朗·巴罗佐(Jose Manuel Durao Barroso,1956年3月22日—),出生于葡萄牙里斯本,是一位葡萄牙和欧洲联盟的政治家。从2004年11月22日开始担任欧盟委员会主席,此前他任葡萄牙总理。曾任内政部副国务秘书,外交和国际合作国务秘书,外交部长和葡萄牙总理。在他任期内他的一些政策遭到国内的反对,而他本人认为出于恶劣的经济状况和前任的社会党遗留下来的财政缺陷这些步骤是必需的,此外为了实现"稳定和增长协定"这些措施也是无法避免的。此外他在任期间试图改善欧洲联盟与美国之间的关系。巴罗佐很擅长外交,作为葡萄牙的外交部长甚至连反对党也不得不对他出色的工作表示赞赏。

演讲背景:2008年10月23日欧盟委员会主席若泽·曼努埃尔·巴罗佐来北京出席第七届亚欧首脑会议并到国家行政学院发表演讲。国务委员兼国务院秘书长、国家行政学院院长马凯会见了巴罗佐并主持演讲会。中国政府一贯高度重视发展同欧盟的关系,中欧加强全面战略伙伴关系符合双方的根本利益。国家行政学院多年来与欧盟有关方面进行了广泛而深入的交流与合作,希望双方进一步拓宽合作领域,创新合作形式,提高合作成效。

原文

8 Blood, Sweat and Tears

Winston Churchill

On Friday evening last I received from His **Majesty** the mission to form a new **administration**.

It was the evident will of **Parliament** and the nation that this should be conceived on the broadest possible basis and that it should include all parties.

I have already completed the most important part of this task. A war cabinet has been formed of five members, representing, with the Labor, Opposition and Liberals, the unity of the nation.

It was necessary that this should be done in one single day on account of the extreme urgency and rigor of events. Other key positions were filled yesterday. I am submitting a further list to the King tonight. I hope to complete the appointment of principal **Ministers** during tomorrow.

The appointment of other Ministers usually takes a little longer. I trust when Parliament meets again this part of my task will be completed and that the administration will be complete in all respects.

I considered it in the public interest to suggest to the Speaker that the House should be summoned today. At the end of today's proceedings, the **adjournment** of the House will be proposed until May 21 with provision for earlier meeting if need be. Business for that will be notified to M. P. 's at the earliest opportunity.

I now invite the House by a resolution to record its approval of the steps taken and declare its confidence in the new government. The resolution:

"That this House welcomes the formation of a government representing the united and inflexible resolve of the nation to prosecute the war with Germany to a victorious conclusion."

To form an administration of this scale and **complexity** is a serious undertaking in itself. But we are in the preliminary phase of one of the greatest battles in history. We are in action at any other points — in Norway and in Holland — and we have to be prepared in the Mediterranean. The air battle is continuing, and many preparations have to be made here at home.

In this crisis I think I may be pardoned if I do not address the House at any length today, and I hope that any of my friends and colleagues or former colleagues who are affected by the political reconstruction will make all allowances for any lack of ceremony with which it has been necessary to act.

I say to the House as I said to Ministers who have joined this government, I have nothing to offer but blood, toil, tears and sweat. We have before us an ordeal of the most grievous kind. We have before us many, many months of struggle and suffering.

You ask, what is our policy? I say it is to wage war by land, sea and air. War with all our might and with all the strength God has given us, and to wage war against a **monstrous tyranny** never surpassed in the dark and **lamentable** catalogue of human crime. That is our policy.

You ask, what is our aim? I can answer in one word, it is victory. Victory at all costs — victory in spite of all terrors — victory, however long and hard the road may be, for without victory there is no survival.

Let that be realized. No survival for the British Empire, no survival for all that the British Empire has stood for, no survival for the urge, the impulse of the ages, that mankind shall move forward toward his goal.

I take up my task in **buoyancy** and hope. I feel sure that our cause will not be suffered to fail among men.

I feel entitled at this juncture, at this time, to claim the aid of all and to say, "Come then, let us go forward together with our united strength."

译文

8 铁血泪

丘吉尔

上星期五晚上，我奉陛下之命，组织新的一届政府。

按国会和国民的意愿，新政府显然应该考虑建立在尽可能广泛的基础上，应该兼容所有的党派。

我已经完成了这项任务的最主要的部分。战时内阁已由五人组成，包括工党、反对党和自由党，这体现了举国团结一致。

由于事态的极端紧急和严峻，新阁政府须于一天之内组成，其他的关键岗位也于昨日安排就绪。今晚还要向国王呈报一份名单。我希望明天就能完成几位主要大臣的任命。

其余大臣们的任命照例得晚一些。我相信，在国会下一次召开时，任命将告完成，臻于完善。

为公众利益着想，我建议议长今天就召开国会。今天的议程结束时，建议休会到5月21日，并准备在必要时提前开会。有关事项会及早通知各位议员。

现在我请求国会做出决议，批准我所采取的各项步骤，记录在案，并且声明信任新政府。决议如下：

"本国会欢迎新政府的组成，它体现了举国一致的坚定不移的决心：对德作战，直到最后胜利。"

组织如此规模和如此复杂的政府原本是一项重大的任务。但是我们正处于历史上罕见的一场大战的初始阶段。我们在其他许多地点作战——在挪威，在荷兰，我们还必须在地中海做好准备。空战正在继续，而且在本土也必须做好许多准备工作。

值此危急关头，我想，即使我今天向国会的报告过于简略，也当能见谅。我还希望所有在这次改组中受到影响的朋友、同僚和旧日的同僚们对必要的礼仪方面的任何不周之处能毫不介意。

我向国会表明，一如我向入阁的大臣们所表明的，我所能奉献的唯有热血、辛劳、眼泪和汗水。我们所面临的将是一场极其严酷的考验，将是旷日持久的斗争和苦难。

若问我们的政策是什么？我的回答是：在陆上、海上、空中作战。尽我们的全力，尽上帝赋予我们的全部力量去作战，对人类黑暗、可悲的罪恶史上空前凶残的暴政作战。这就是我们的政策。

若问我们的目标是什么？我可以用一个词来回答，那就是胜利。不惜一切代价，去夺取胜利——不惧一切恐怖，去夺取胜利——不论前路如何漫长、如何艰苦，去夺取胜利。因为没有胜利就不能生存。

我们务必认识到，没有胜利就不复有大英帝国，没有胜利就不复有大英帝国所象征的一切，没有胜利就不复有多少世纪以来的强烈要求和冲动：人类应当向自己的目标迈进。

我精神振奋、满怀信心地承担起我的任务。我确信，大家联合起来，我们的事业就不会遭到挫败。

在此时此刻的危急关头，我觉得我有权要求各方面的支持。我要说："来吧，让我们群策群力，并肩前进！"

（牛晨怡　译）

注释

1. majesty[ˈmædʒisti] *n.* 陛下
2. parliament[ˈpɑrləmənt] *n.* 议会；国会
3. minister[ˈministə] *n.* 大臣；部长
4. adjournment[əˈdʒəːnmənt] *n.* 休会；延期；休会期；休庭期
5. complexity[kəmˈpleksiti] *n.* 复杂性；错综复杂的状态
6. monstrous[ˈmɑnstrəs] *adj.* 丑陋的；巨大的；畸形的
7. tyranny[ˈtirəni] *n.* 暴虐；专横；暴行
8. lamentable[ləˈmentəbəl] *adj.* 可悲的；令人惋惜的
9. buoyancy[ˈbɔiənsi] *n.* 浮力；恢复正常的能力；维持力

赏析

温斯顿·丘吉尔（Winston Leōnard Spencer Churchill，1874—1965），英国最伟大的政治家，记者，画家，演说家，作家，1953年诺贝尔文学奖得主(获奖作品《第二次世界大战回忆录》)。曾于1940—1945年及1951—1955年期间两度任英国首相，被认为是20世纪最重要的政治领袖之一，带领英国获得第二次世界大战的胜利。丘吉尔以超乎寻常的惊人敏感力和极大的勇气，冒着和平主义浪潮的巨大压力和"在政治上几乎有被消灭的危险"，一天也不放弃向国人发出预言式的战争警告，使英国人做好了战争来临的精神准备。

演讲背景：1940年5月8日，由于前首相张伯伦遭到不信任质疑动议，被迫辞职。5月10日下午6时，国王召见丘吉尔，令其组阁。一小时后丘吉尔会见工党领袖艾德礼，邀请工党加入内阁并获得支持。三天后丘吉尔首次以首相身份出席下议院会议，发表了著名的讲话："我所能奉献的唯有热血、辛劳、眼泪和汗水……若问我们的目标是什么？我可以用一个词来回答，那就是胜利。不惜一切代价，去夺取胜利——不惧一切恐怖，去夺取胜利——不论前路如何漫长、如何艰苦，去夺取胜利。因为没有胜利就不能生存。"下议院最终以381票对0票的绝对优势表明了对丘吉尔政府的支持。

第五章　名人书信

原文

1　Letter to a Young Friend

Benjamin Franklin

My dear friend,

I know of no medicine fit to **diminish** the violent natural **inclination** you mention; and if I did, I think I should not communicate it to you. Marriage is the proper **remedy**. It is the most natural state of man, and therefore the state in which you will find solid happiness. Your reason against entering into it at present appears to be not well founded. The **circumstantial** advantages you have in view by postponing it, are not only uncertain, but they are small in comparison with the thing itself, the being married and settled. It is the man and woman united that makes the complete human being, separate she wants his force of body and strength of reason; he wants her softness, sensibility and acute discernment. Together they are most likely to succeed in the world. A single man has not nearly the value he would have in that state of union. He is an incomplete animal. He **resembles** the odd half of a pair of scissors.

If you get a prudent, health wife, your industry in your profession, with her good economy, will be a fortune sufficient.

Your affectionate friend

译文

1　给年轻朋友的一封信

本杰明·富兰克林

我亲爱的朋友：

我知道没有药物能够消除你们所提到的那种疯狂的自然倾向；即使我知道，我想我也不该告诉你。婚姻是适当的药物。它是人类最本能的状态，因此是一种最幸福的生活状态。你拒绝现在进入婚姻殿堂的理由显得不够充分。你认为推迟婚姻可能存在好处,但这不仅不一定实现,而且,那些利益跟婚姻本身以及婚后的安定相比起来就微不足道了。男人和女人只有联合起来才能组成完整的人。女人缺乏男人的力量和周密的推理,而男人缺乏女人的温柔、感性和敏锐的洞察力。因此当男人和女人联合起来,就能够无往不胜。单身和离婚生活的男男女女不可能具有婚姻生活中的价值,是一种不完善的动物。这简直好比半把剪刀——孤掌难鸣。

如果你拥有一位健康而谨慎的妻子,你的辛勤工作,加上她的勤俭节约,必定会创造充足的财富。

您真挚的朋友

注释

1. diminish[di'miniʃ] *vt.* 使减少
2. inclination['inklə'neʃən] *n.* 倾向
3. remedy['remədi] *n.* 治疗
4. circumstantial[ˌsə:kəm'stænʃl] *adj.* 详细的
5. resemble[ri'zembl] *vt.* 类似

赏析

本杰明·富兰克林(1706—1790),18世纪美国伟大的科学家、政治家、文学家、哲学家、外交家、思想家、发明家等。富兰克林是美国"清教主义"的最杰出代表,"美国梦"的践行者,被誉为资本主义精神最完美的代表。他的一生是自我奋斗、自我教育、自我完善的过程,在众多不同的领域都取得了巨大的成就。有评价说他是18世纪仅次于华盛顿的名人。

出生在波士顿的富兰克林一生只在学校读了两年书,由于家庭经济拮据,他十几岁时就到小印刷所当学徒,做了近十年的印刷工人。这期间,他从未间断过自学。他的阅读范围很广,从自然科学、技术方面的通俗读物到著名科学家的论文以及名作家的作品都在他阅读的行列之内。后来他掌握了法文、意大利文、西班牙文及拉丁文,广泛地接受了世界科学文化的先进成果,为自己的科学研究奠定了坚实的基础。在美国独立过程中,富兰克林除了参加美洲殖民地第二届会议外,还加入一个五人委员会,负责起草《独立宣言》,并以大使身份前往法国寻求其对美国独立战争的支持,果然不辱使命。他的代表作《穷査理年鉴》成为当时13个殖民地区仅次于《圣经》的畅销书。富兰克林在他的自传中总结了自己毕生所践行的13种美德;他一生中还有无数发明，如避雷针、节能炉等，为此赢得了发明家的头衔。

本文是富兰克林给一位年轻朋友的信。寥寥数语中透露出的有富兰克林娴熟的语言驾驭能力，睿智、深刻的人生哲理及孜孜不倦的关爱。富兰克林曾说过“失去好妻子就是失去上帝的礼物”，所以他在这封信里对年轻人的劝慰就是“爱情、婚姻是一剂良药”。

原文

2 Helen Keller to Mrs. Laurence Hutton

12 Newbury Street, Boston, March 5, 1899

...I am now sure that I shall be ready for my examinations in June. There is but one cloud in my sky at present; but that is one which casts a dark shadow over my life, and makes me very anxious at times. My teacher's eyes are no better, indeed, I think they grow more troublesome, though she is very brave and patient, and will not give up. But it is most **distressing** to me to feel that she is **sacrificing** her sight for me. I feel as if I ought to give up the idea of going to college altogether: for not all the knowledge in the world could make me happy, if obtained at such a cost. I do wish, Mrs. Hutton, you would try to persuade Teacher to take a rest, and have her eyes treated. She will not listen to me.

I have just had some pictures taken, and if they are good, I would like to send one to Mr. Rogers, if you think he would like to have it. I would like so much to show in some way how deeply I appreciate all that he is doing for me, and I cannot think of anything better to do.

Every one here is talking about the Sargent pictures. It is a wonderful exhibition of portraits, they say. How I wish I had eyes to see them! How I should delight in their beauty and color! However, I am glad that I am not **debarred** from all pleasure in the pictures. I have at least the satisfaction of seeing them through the eyes of my friends, which is a real pleasure. I am so thankful that I can rejoice in the beauties, which my friends gather and put into my hands!

We are all so glad and thankful that Mr. Kipling did not die! I have his *Jungle - Book* in raised print, and what a **splendid**, refreshing book it is! I cannot help feeling as if I knew its **gifted** author. What a real, manly, lovable nature his must be! ...

译文

2 致劳伦斯·赫顿夫人

波士顿，纽伯里街12号

1899年3月5日

……现在我确信，我能够准备好6月份的考试。目前在我的天空中只有一块云，可是正是它在我的生活中投下了阴影，使我有时很焦急。老师的眼睛没有见好，实际上我认为是麻烦更大了，尽管她很勇敢坚韧，不肯放弃。但是感到她是为我牺牲了自己的视力，我难过极了。我觉得似乎应该完全放弃上大学的想法，因为如果是以这样的代价换来的，就是得到世界上全部的知识也不会让我高兴。我真的希望，赫顿夫人，你能尽力说服老师休息一段时间，治疗一下眼睛。她不肯听我的话。

我刚刚照了一些相，如果照得好，假如你觉得罗杰斯先生愿意要的话，我想寄一张给他。我非常希望用某种方式向他表示，我是多么深深地感谢他为我做的一切，我想不出更好的方法了。

我们这里人人都在谈论萨金特的画。他们说这是一个非常出色的肖像画展。我多么希望我的眼睛能够看到这些画！它们的美和色彩会使我多么陶醉！不过我很高兴我没有被完全排除在画带来的愉快之外。至少我得到了通过朋友的眼睛来观赏它们的满足，这确实是真正的快乐。我非常感谢自己能够享受美，是我的朋友收集起来放到我的手里的！

吉卜林先生没有死，我们大家都很高兴，也很欣慰！我有他的《丛林故事》的盲文版，这是一本多么美好清新的书啊！我禁不住感到仿佛自己认识它天才的作者。他的性格肯定是真诚的、高尚的、可爱的！……

（王家湘 译）

注释

1. distressing[di'stresiŋ] *adj.* 使烦恼的
2. sacrifice['sækrifais] *vt.* 牺牲
3. debar[di'bɑː] *vt.* 阻止；排除；防止
4. splendid['splendid] *adj.* 极好的
5. gifted['giftid] *adj.* 有才华的

赏析

海伦·凯勒(1880—1968)，美国盲聋女作家、教育家、慈善家、社会活动家。海伦在19个月的时候因为一场猩红热，永远失去了视力和听力。但她以自强不息的顽强毅力，在安妮·莎

莉文老师的帮助下，掌握了英、法、德等五国语言。海伦·凯勒一生一共写了14部巨作，《我的生活》是她的处女作，作品一经发表，立即在美国引起了轰动，被称为“世界文学史上无与伦比的杰作”，出版的版本超过百余种，在世界上产生了巨大的影响。最著名的是《我的生活》《走出黑暗》《老师》三本书以及发表在美国《大西洋月刊》上的著名散文《假如给我三天光明》。除此以外，她一生还致力于为残疾人造福，建立慈善机构，被美国《时代周刊》评为美国十大英雄偶像，荣获“总统自由勋章”等奖项。

海伦的世界暗淡无光、寂静无声，似乎上帝把太多的不幸降临在这位柔弱的女子身上了。可上帝就是要她来完成常人眼中的奇迹，安妮·莎莉文小姐就是上帝派来协助她的人。师生俩的关系保持了50多年，看似母女，胜似母女，所以海伦在《假如给我三天光明》里写到她第一个想看见的人就是莎莉文老师。当然，一个人自己不努力，即使是上帝亲自来也无法助他成功，海伦的奇迹更多来自她坚强的毅力、坚持不懈的努力。正如马克·吐温所言：19世纪出现了两个了不起的人物，一个是拿破仑，一个就是海伦·凯勒。

海伦无法接受正常的学校教育，但从她7岁时就走进她生命，并在此后半个多世纪都陪伴她的良师益友莎莉文给了她不亚于正常孩子的教育。1898年，海伦·凯勒进入马萨诸塞州的剑桥女子学校学习，并于1900年秋季再申请就读哈佛大学拉德克利夫学院。1904年，海伦以优异的成绩获得了文学学士学位，成为首位毕业于高等院校的聋盲人。

这封信写于海伦准备大学入学考试期间。信中首先表达了她内心的不安，让她深感不安的不是即将到来的考试，而是莎莉文老师的健康状况。海伦渴望学到更多的知识，但如果要以老师的健康为代价，那么她宁愿不要这些知识。正是海伦这种感恩和体谅老师的心情促使她写信给赫顿夫人，希望能劝服老师修养一段时间。信的后半部分记叙了海伦广泛的兴趣爱好和对知识极大的渴慕。整段文字语言规范、情感真挚，足见海伦在语言学习方面所付出的超乎常人想象的代价。

原文

3 Helen Keller to Mr. John Hitz

14 Coolidge Ave., Cambridge, Nov. 26, 1900

× × has already communicated with you in regard to her and my plan of establishing an **institute** for deaf and blind children. At first I was most **enthusiastic** in its support, and I never dreamed that any grave objections could be raised except indeed by those who are **hostile** to Teacher; but now, after thinking most seriously and consulting my friends, I have decided that × ×'s plan is by no means **feasible**. In my eagerness to make it possible for deaf and blind children to have the same advantages that I have had, I quite forgot that there might be many **obstacles** in the way of my accomplishing anything like what ×× proposed.

My friends thought we might have one or two pupils in our own home, thereby **securing** to me the advantage of being helpful to others without any of the disadvantages of a large school. They were very kind; but I could not help feeling that they spoke more from a business than a **humanitarian** point of view. I am sure they did not quite understand how passionately I desire that all who are **afflicted** like myself shall receive their rightful **inheritance** of thought, knowledge and love. Still I could not shut my eyes to the force and weight of their arguments, and I saw plainly that I must abandon ××'s scheme as impracticable. They also said that I ought to appoint an **advisory** committee to control my affairs while I am at Radcliffe. I considered this suggestion carefully, then I told Mr. Rhoades that I should be proud and glad to have wise friends to whom I could always turn for advice in all important matters. For this committee, I choose six, my mother, Teacher, because she is like a mother to me, Mrs. Hutton, Mr. Rhoades, Dr. Greer, and Mr. Rogers, because it is they who have supported me all these years and made it possible for me to enter college. Mrs. Hutton had already written to mother, asking her to telegraph if she was willing for me to have other advisers besides herself and Teacher. This morning we received word that mother had given her consent to this agreement. Now it remains for me to write to Dr. Greer and Mr. Rogers...

We had a long talk with Dr. Bell. Finally he proposed a plan which delighted us all beyond words. He said that it was a gigantic **blunder** to attempt to found a school for deaf and blind children, because they would lose the most precious opportunities of entering into the fuller, richer, freer life of seeing and hearing children. I had had misgivings on this point; but I could not see how we were to help it. However Mr. Bell suggested that ×× and all her friends who are interested in the scheme should organize an association for the promotion of the education of the deaf and blind, Teacher and myself being included of course. Under his plan they were to appoint Teacher to train others to instruct deaf and blind children in their own homes, just as she had taught me. Funds were to be raised for the teachers' **lodgings** and also for their salaries. At the same time Dr. Bell added that I could rest content and fight my way through Radcliffe in competition with seeing and hearing girls, while the great desire of my heart was being fulfilled. We clapped our hands and shouted; ×× went away beaming with pleasure, and Teacher and I felt more light of heart than we had for sometime. Of course we can do nothing just now; but the painful anxiety about my college work and the future welfare of the deaf and blind has been lifted from our minds. Do tell me what you think about Dr. Bell's suggestion. It seems most practical and wise to me; but I must know all that there is to be known about it before I speak or act in the matter ...

译文

3 致希茨先生

库利奇大道14号，剑桥

1900年11月26日

有关她和我建立一个盲聋儿童的公共机构的事情，某某已经给你写过信了。一开始我非常热情地支持这件事，连做梦也没有想到，除了那些对老师敌视的人之外，会有人提出什么严重的反对；但是现在，经过了极其认真的考虑并和朋友们商量了以后，我认为某某的计划根本不可行。在我急切地想要让盲聋儿童有可能获得我所享有的有利条件的情况下，我忘记了在我实现某某的任何建议的道路上可能会存在许多障碍。

我的朋友们认为我们可以在我们自己的家里收一两个学生，这样我既能得到帮助别人的好处，又没有一个大规模的学校具有的任何缺点。他们是好心；但是我总禁不住感到他们更多是从任务而不是从博爱的角度谈问题。我相信他们并不十分了解，我是多么强烈地渴望一切和我受到同样不幸的人，能够获得他们应有的思想、知识和爱的传承。然而我不能闭眼不看他们论据的分量，我清楚地看到我必须因其不切实际而放弃某某的计划。他们还说，在我就读于拉德克里夫学院期间，我应该指定一个顾问委员会来掌控自己的事务。我仔细地考虑了这个建议，然后对罗兹先生说，能有在一切重要事情上可以向他们征求意见的明智的朋友，我将感到骄傲和高兴。我选择了6个人组成这个委员会，我的母亲，老师，因为她就像我的母亲一样，赫顿夫人，罗兹先生，格里尔博士和罗杰斯先生，因为是他们在这些年里一直支持着我，使我有可能进入大学。赫顿夫人已经给母亲写过信，说如果她愿意除了她本人和老师之外我再有几个其他的顾问，就给她打电报。今天早上我们收到了消息，说母亲已经同意这个安排。现在剩下的就是我给格里尔博士和罗杰斯先生写信了。……

我们和贝尔博士进行了一次长谈。最后他提出了一个让我们大家都非常高兴的计划。他说企图为盲聋儿童建立一个学校是一个巨大的错误，因为那样的话，他们会失去进入有视力和听力的儿童的更全面、更丰富、更自由的生活的最宝贵的机会。在这一点上我也一直有顾虑，但是我看不出能有什么办法来解决这个问题。不过贝尔先生建议，某某夫人和对她的计划感兴趣的朋友们应该组织一个促进盲聋人教育的协会。老师和我当然都被包括在内。在他这个计划之下，他们要委派老师培训别的人在盲聋儿童的家庭里对他们进行教育，就像她教我那样。需要筹措资金为老师们提供住处和工资。贝尔博士还补充说，我可以放心满意地在和视力及听力正常的女孩子的竞争中奋力完成拉德克里夫的学业，与此同时，我心中伟大的愿望正在得到实现。我们鼓掌呼喊；某某快乐地满脸带着笑离去，老师和我的心情在相当一段时间里没有这么轻松过。当然，目前我们什么也没有做，但是对于我大学的学习和盲聋人未来的福利上的痛苦的焦虑已经从我们心头消失了。请一定告诉我你对贝尔先生建议的想法。我觉得它非常明智可行，但是在我在这件事上谈论或行动之前，我必须了解需要得知的一切情况。……

（王家湘 译）

注释

1. institute['institju:t] *n.* 学会
2. enthusiastic[inˌθju:zi'æstik] *adj.* 热心的
3. hostile['hɔstl] *adj.* 怀敌意的
4. feasible['fi:zəbl] *adj.* 可行的
5. obstacle['ɔbstəkl] *n.* 障碍
6. secure[si'kjur] *adj.* 固定住的
7. humanitarian[hju:ˌmæni'teəriən] *adj.* 人道主义的
8. afflict[ə'flikt] *vt.* 折磨；使痛苦
9. inheritance[in'heritəns] *n.* 遗产
10. advisory[əd'vaizəri] *adj.* 顾问的
11. blunder['blʌndə] *n.* 大错
12. lodging['lɔdʒiŋ] *n.* 住所

赏析

海伦·凯勒有正常人眼中的不幸，然而祸福相倚，谁又能否认不幸所带来的幸运呢？海伦深知她的幸运，因此她心存感恩，希望把这种幸运播撒在更多如她这般的不幸人身上，这是人道、大爱。

这封信就如何把爱的福音播撒给更多的盲聋人征求希茨先生的意见。这封信中，海伦在语言组织和措辞方面严谨审慎，足见她对这件涉及多人利益事情的重视以及集思广益、综合权衡利弊的做事态度。

原文

4 Helen Keller to Dr. Edward Everett Hale

Cambridge, Nov. 10, 1901

My teacher and I expect to be present at the meeting tomorrow in **commemoration** of the one hundredth anniversary of Dr. Howe's birth; but I very much doubt if we shall have an opportunity to speak with you; so I am writing now to tell you how delighted I am that you are to speak at the meeting, because I feel that you, better than any one I know will express the heartfelt **gratitude** of those who owe their education, their opportunities, their happiness to him who opened the eyes of the blind and gave the dumb lip language.

Sitting here in my study, surrounded by my books, enjoying the sweet and intimate companionship of the great and the wise, I am trying to realize what my life might have been, if Dr. Howe had failed in the great task God gave him to perform. If he had not taken upon himself the responsibility of Laura Bridgman's education and led her out of the pit of **Acheron** back to her human inheritance, should I be a sophomore at Radcliffe College today — who can say? But it is idle to **speculate** about what might have been in connection with Dr. Howe's great achievement.

I think only those who have escaped that death-in-life existence, from which Laura Bridgman was rescued, can realize how isolated, how **shrouded** in darkness, how **cramped** by its own **impotence** is a soul without thought or faith or hope. Words are powerless to describe the desolation of that prison-house, or the joy of the soul that is delivered out of its capacity. When we compare the needs and helplessness of the blind before Dr. Howe began his work, with their present usefulness and independence, we realize that great things have been done in our midst. What if physical conditions have built up high walls about us? Thanks to our friend and helper, our world lies upward; the length and breadth and sweep of the heavens are ours!

译文

4 致爱德华·埃弗里特·黑尔博士

剑桥，1901年11月10日

老师和我期待着出席明天举行的庆祝豪博士100周年诞辰的大会；但是我想我们恐怕不会有机会和你说话，因此我现在写信告诉你，我多么高兴你将要在会上发言，因为我感到你会比我认识的其他任何人更好地表达出这样一些人对他的衷心感谢，是他给了这些人教育、机会和幸福，使盲人睁开了眼睛，给了聋哑人唇语。

坐在自己的书房里，四周是我的书籍，享受着伟人和智者亲密美好的陪伴，我尽力在想象着如果豪博士没有完成上帝给予他的伟大任务，我的生活会是什么样子。如果他没有亲自担负起教育劳拉·布里奇曼的责任，将她带出了地狱的深渊，重回人类的传承，我今天会是拉德克里夫学院二年级的学生吗？——谁能知道呢？不过从豪博士的伟大成就来猜测原本会是怎样是毫无意义的。

我想，只有那些逃脱了虽生如死的生存的人，劳拉·布里奇曼就是从这种状态中被拯救出来的，才能够体会没有思想或信念或希望的灵魂是多么孤独，黑暗是多么紧地包裹着它，本身的无能为力是多么巨大的束缚。语言没有能力形容那个监狱的凄凉，也无法形容从囚禁中被解救出来的灵魂的喜悦。当我们把豪博士开始他的工作之前盲人的匮乏和无助状态与他们今天的作用和独立加以比较，我们意识到我们取得了伟大的成就。即使身体条件在我们周围筑起了高墙又怎么样？由于我们的朋友和帮助者，我们的世界在上方，整个辽阔的天空是属于我们的！

注释

1. commemoration[kəˌmeməˈreiʃn] *n.* 庆典；纪念会
2. gratitude[ˈgrætitu:d] *n.* 感谢的心情
3. Acheron[ˈækərɔn] *n.* 阿克隆，古代希腊、罗马神话里所称在地狱间的河流，称作冥河，也以此来称呼阴间、地狱、冥府。也就是悲伤之河或无喜悦之河。
4. speculate[ˈspekjuleit] *vi.* 推测
5. shroud[ʃraud] *vt.* 覆盖
6. cramped[kræmpt] *adj.* 狭窄的
7. impotence[ˈimpətəns] *n.* 虚弱

赏析

黑尔博士这位美国19世纪著名的特殊教育家就像盗取天火的普罗米修斯一样为那些处于黑暗深渊的聋哑人带来了光明。幸运的劳拉·布里奇曼在即使上帝向她关闭了看、听、说三扇窗后依然学会了用手语与人交流，她的幸运就来自于这位黑尔博士。对海伦来说，更大的幸运就是遇到劳拉·布里奇曼的学生安妮·莎莉文·梅西。

正是这样的薪火相传造就了海伦的成功，所以她在黑尔博士诞辰100周年纪念之际的心情是常人无法完全体会的。全文语言清新、文法规范、感情诚挚，主题就是感恩。海伦以一颗谦逊、悲悯、诚挚的心感谢造就了她目前生活的人。海伦的感恩是摈弃一切杂质的。

原文

5 Ernest Hemingway to His Father(C. E. Hemingway)

Dear Dad,

Thanks very much for your letter and for forwarding the letter to Uncle Tyley. I had a good letter from him yesterday. You cannot know how badly I feel about having caused you and Mother so much shame and suffering — but I could not write you about all of my and Hadley's troubles even if it were the thing to do. It takes two weeks for a letter to cross the Atlantic and I have tried not to transfer all the hell I have been through to anyone by letter. I love Hadley and I love Bumby — Hadley and I **split up** — I did not desert her nor was I committing **adultery** with anyone. I was living in the apartment with Bumby — looking after him while Hadley was away on a trip and it was when she came back from this trip that she decided she wanted the definite divorce. We arranged everything and there was no **scandal** and no **disgrace**. Our trouble had been going on for along time. It was entirely my fault and it is no one's business. I have nothing but love admiration and respect for Hadley and while we are busted up I have not in any way lost Bumby. He lived with me in Switzerland after the divorce and he is coming back in November and will spend this winter with me in the mountains.

You are fortunate enough to have only been in love with one woman in your life. For over a year I had been in love with two people and had been absolutely **faithful** to Hadley. When Hadley decided that we had better get a divorce the girl with whom I was in love was in America. I had not heard from her for almost two months. In her last letter she had said that we must not think of each other but of Hadley. You refer to "Love Pirates", "persons who break up your home etc." and you know that I am hot tempered but I know that it is easy to wish people in Hell when you know nothing of them. I have seen, suffered, and been through enough so that I do not wish anyone in Hell. It is because I do not want you to suffer with ideas of shame and disgrace that I now write all this. We have not seen much of each other for a long time and in the meantime our lives have been going on and there has been a year of tragedy in mine and I know you can appreciate how difficult and almost impossible it is for me to write about it.

After we were divorced if Hadley would have wanted me I would have gone back to her. She said that things were better as they were and that we were both better off. I will never stop loving Hadley nor Bumby nor will I cease to look after them. I will never stop loving Pauline Pfeiffer to whom I am married. I have now **responsibility** toward three people instead of one. Please understand this and know that it doesn't make it easier to write about it. I do understand how hard it is for you to have to make explanations and answer questions and not hear from me. I am a rotten correspondent and it is almost impossible for me to write about my private affairs. Without seeking it — through the success of my books — all the profits of which I have turned over to Hadley — both in America, England, Germany and the Scandinavian countries — because of all this there is a great deal of talk. I pay no attention to any of it and neither must you. I have had come back to me stories people have told about me of every fantastic and scandalous sort — all without foundation. These sorts of stories spring up about all writers — ball players — popular **evangelists** or any public performers. But it is through the desire to keep my own private life to myself — to give no explanations to anybody — and not to be a public performer personally that I have unwittingly caused you great anxiety. The only way I could keep my private life to myself was to keep it to myself — and I did owe you and Mother a statement on it. But I can't write about it all the time.

I know you don't like the sort of thing I write but that is the difference in our taste and all the **critics** are not Fanny Butcher. I know that I am not disgracing you in my writing but rather doing something that some day you will be proud of. I can't do it all at once. I feel that eventually my life will not be a disgrace to you either. It also takes along time to unfold.

You would be so much happier and I would too if you could have confidence in me. When people ask about me, say that Ernie never tells us anything about his private life or even where he is but only writes that he is working hard. Don't feel responsible for what I write or what I do. I take the responsibility, I make the mistakes and I take the punishment.

译文

5 欧内斯特·海明威致父亲(C. E. 海明威)

亲爱的爸爸：

非常感谢您的来信以及您转来的泰莱叔叔的来信。我昨天也收到了一封他好心写来的信。您也许不知道,我对我自己给您和母亲带来如此多的羞辱和痛苦而深感不安——但我不可能把我和哈德利之间的问题全部写信告诉您,即使这是我应该做的事。跨越大西洋的信得走两个星期,而且我努力不要把我所经历过的极大痛苦通过书信转移给任何人。我爱哈德利和本比——哈德利和我离婚了——我没有遗弃她,也没有与任何人通奸。我和本比住在一所公寓里——哈德利外出旅行时我照看她。正是当她旅行归来时,她决定与我离婚。我们安排好了一切,没有流言蜚语,也没有耻辱。我们之间的问题已持续了很长时间。这全是我的过错,不关别人的事。我对哈德利只有敬仰和尊重,当我们的婚姻破裂时,我无论如何不能失去本比。离婚后,我和本比居住在瑞士,他11月份将回来与我在山里度过冬季。

您很幸运,您在一生中只爱过一个女人。在一年多的时间里,我同时爱上两个人,但我始终完全地忠实于哈德利。当哈德利决定我们最好离婚时,我爱的那个女子正在美国。我已近两个月没有收到她的来信了。在她的最后一封信中,她说,我们不能只考虑彼此,而应该替哈德利考虑。您提到"爱情掠夺者""破坏你的家庭的人"等,您知道我脾气急躁,但我知道,当您不了解别人时很容易诅咒别人进地狱,而我已经目睹了、遭受了并经历了极大的痛苦,因此我不会诅咒别人进地狱。正是因为我不希望您蒙受耻辱和不体面之苦,现在我才给您写这一切。我们已有很长时间没有见面了,而同时我们的生活都在继续,悲剧发生在我的身上已有一年了,我知道您能懂得,对我来说写出这一切有多么困难,几乎无法表达。

我们离婚后,如果哈德利还需要我,我是会回到她身边去的。但她说一切都好转了,我们俩人的境况都很好。我将永远不会停止对哈德利和本比的爱,也不会停止照料他们。我也永远不会停止对与我结合的波琳·法伊弗的爱。我现在是对三个人而不是只对一个人负有责任,请您理解这一切,并理解我写出这一切也很不容易。我确实明白,对您来说,不得不向别人解释和回答提问,却又收不到我的信,这是多么困难。我是个不会写信的人,对我来说,把我的私事写出来几乎是不可能的。没有刻意追求——由于我的作品的成功——我转给哈德利的所有收益——包括美国、英国、德国、斯堪的纳维亚半岛上的国家——因为这一切,又引起了许多流言蜚语。我不在意这些闲话,您也不必在意。我已经回到了原来的自己,人们所谈论的关于我的每一个虚假的、流言蜚语类的故事,都是没有根据的。这类故事出现在每一个作家、运动员、受欢迎的福音传道士及任何演员的身上。但由于我渴望使自己的私人生活属于我自己,因此,我没有对任何人解释,我个人不愿成为演员以至于无意中给您带来了巨大的焦虑。唯一使我的个人生活只属于自己的办法就是把它保留给自己——我的确应该向您和母亲说明这件事,但我不能总是写信谈论它。

我知道您不喜欢我写的这类作品,但这是我们的品味的不同,而且并非所有的评论家都是范妮·布彻这种人。我知道我没有在我的作品中使您蒙受耻辱,而是做了一件将来会使您引以为自豪的事。我不可能立刻使您感到自豪。我觉得最终我的生活将不会给您带来耻辱。这需要很长的时间才能显示出来。

如果您相信我,您会感到快乐得多,我也会感到快乐得多。当人们问起我,您就说欧尼从来不告诉我们他的个人生活,甚至不告诉我们他在哪里,而只写信说他在努力工作。您不必为我所写的和我所做的负责。我自己负一切责任,如果我犯了错误,我会接受惩罚。

注释

1. split up:(使)断绝关系
2. adultery[ə'dʌltəri] *n.* 通奸;私通
3. scandal['skændl] *n.* 丑闻
4. disgrace[dis'ɡreis] *n.* 丢脸;不光彩
5. faithful ['feiθfl] *adj.* 忠实的;忠诚的
6. responsibility[ri'spɔnsə'biliti] *n.* 责任;职责
7. evangelist[i'vændʒəlist] *n.* 福音传道者
8. critic['kritik] *n.* 批评家;评论家

赏析

欧内斯特·米勒尔·海明威 (Ernest Miller Hemingway,1899—1961),美国小说家,诺贝尔文学奖获得者,出生于美国伊利诺伊州芝加哥市郊区的奥克帕克。代表作有《老人与海》等。海明威被誉为美利坚民族的精神丰碑,他的写作风格以简洁著称,对美国文学及20世纪文学的发展有极深远的影响。

海明威习惯写信,对他来讲,通信是生活必需品。他一生写了六七千封信。海明威的"致父亲信"是历史的精神财富,能使我们欣赏伟大心灵中那深邃的思想、闪光的智慧和隐秘的悲欢;它也是人类的艺术瑰宝,透过感人至深的语句、随意而又抒情的笔调,享受文字之美、艺术之美。

原文

6 Thomas Jefferson to His Nephew

Paris, August 10, 1787

Dear Peter,

I have received your two letters of December the 30th and April the 18th, and am very happy to find by them, as well as by letters from Mr. Wythe, that you have been so fortunate as to attract his notice and good will; I am sure you will find this to have been one of the most fortunate events of your life, as I have ever been sensible it was of mine. I enclosed you a **sketch** of the sciences to which I would wish you to apply, in such order as Mr. Wythe shall advise; I mention, also, the books in them worth your reading, which submit to his correction. Many of these are among your father's books, which you should have brought to you. As I do not recollect those of them not in his library, you must write to me for them, making out a catalogue of such as you think you shall have occasion for, in eighteen months from the date of your letter, and consulting Mr. Wythe on the subject. To this sketch, I will add a few particular observations:

1. Italian. I fear the learning of this language will **confound** your French and Spanish. Being all of them degenerated dialects of the Latin, they are apt to mix in conversation. I have never seen a person speaking the three languages, who did not mix them. It is a delightful language, but late events having **rendered** the Spanish more useful, lay it aside to prosecute that.

2. Spanish. Bestow great attention on this, and endeavor to acquire an accurate knowledge of it. Our future connections with Spain and Spanish America, will render that language a valuable acquisition. The ancient history of that part of America, too, is written in that language. I send you a dictionary.

3. Moral Philosophy. I think it lost time to attend lectures on this branch. He who made us would have been a pitiful **bungler**, if he had made the rules of our moral conduct a matter of science. For one man of science, there are thousands who are not. What would have become of them? Man was destined for society. His morality, therefore, was to be formed to this object. He was endowed with a sense of right and wrong, merely relative to this. This sense is as much a part of his nature, as the sense of hearing, seeing, feeling; it is the true foundation of morality, and not the "to kalon" (Greek: The beautiful), truth, &c., as fanciful writers have imagined. The moral sense, or **conscience**, is as much a part of man as his leg or arm. It is given to all human beings in a stronger or weaker degree, as force of members is given them in a greater or less degree. It may be

strengthened by exercise, as may any particular limb of the body. This sense is **submitted**, indeed, in some degree, to the guidance of reason; but it is a small stock which is required for this: even a less one than what we call common sense. State a moral case to a ploughman and a professor. The former will decide it as well, and often better than the latter, because he has not been led **astray** by artificial rules. In this branch, therefore, read good books, because they will encourage, as well as direct your feelings. The writings of Sterne, particularly, form the best course of morality that ever was written. Besides these, read the books mentioned in the enclosed paper; and, above all things, lose no occasion of exercising your **dispositions** to be grateful, to be generous, to be charitable , to be humane, to be true, just, firm, orderly, courageous, &c. Consider every act of this kind, as an exercise which will strengthen your moral faculties and increase your worth.

4. Religion. Your reason is now mature enough to examine this object. In the first place, **divest** yourself of all bias in favor of novelty and **singularity** of opinion. Indulge them in any other subject rather than that of religion. It is too important, and the consequences of error may be too serious. On the other hand, shake off all the fears and **servile** prejudices, under which weak minds are servilely crouched. Fix reason firmly in her seat, and call to her **tribunal** every fact, every opinion. Question with boldness even the existence of a God; because, if there be one, he must more approve of the homage of reason, than that of blindfolded fear. You will naturally examine first, the religion of your own country. Read the *Bible*, then as you would read Livy or Tacitus. The facts which are within the ordinary course of nature, you will believe on the authority of the writer, as you do those of the same kind in Livy and Tacitus. The testimony of the writer weighs in their favor, in one scale, and their not being against the laws of nature, does not weigh against them. But those facts in the *Bible* which contradict the laws of nature, must be examined with more care, and under a variety of faces.

5. Travelling. This makes men wiser, but less happy. When men of sober age travel, they gather knowledge, which they may apply usefully for their country; but they are subject ever after to recollections mixed with regret; their affections are weakened by being extended over more objects; and they learn new habits which cannot be **gratified** when they return home. Young men, who travel, are exposed to all these inconveniences in a higher degree, to others still more serious, and do not acquire that wisdom for which a previous foundation is requisite, by repeated and just observations at home. The glare of pomp and pleasure is analogous to the motion of the blood; it absorbs all their affection and attention, they are torn from it as from the only good in this world, and return to their home as to a place of exile and **condemnation**. Their eyes are forever turned back to the object they have lost, and its recollection poisons the **residue** of their lives. Their first and most delicate passions are **hackneyed** on unworthy objects here, and they carry home the dregs, insufficient to make themselves or anybody else happy. Add to this, that a habit of idleness, an inability to apply themselves to business is acquired, and renders them useless to themselves and their country. These observations are founded in experience. There is no place where your

pursuit of knowledge will be so little **obstructed** by foreign objects, as in your own country, nor any, wherein the virtues of the heart will be less exposed to be weakened. Be good, be learned, and be industrious, and you will not want the aid of travelling, to render you precious to your country, dear to your friends, happy within yourself. I repeat my advice, to take a great deal of exercise, and on foot. Health is the first requisite after morality. Write to me often, and be assured of the interest I take in your success, as well as the warmth of those sentiments of attachment with which I am, dear Peter.

Your affectionate friend

译文

6 杰斐逊致侄子的信

巴黎，1787年8月10日

亲爱的彼得：

我已收到你12月30日和4月18日的两封来信。从你和威思先生的来信中，我很高兴地发现，你已经幸运地引起了他的注意，并赢得了他的好感。我相信你会发现这是你一生之中最幸运的事情，正如我的直觉告诉我的，那也是我最幸运的事情。我随信附上一份学科概要，我希望你在威思先生的建议下去申请这些学科。我也提到了这些学科中值得一读的书，当然你还是应该在威思先生的指导下去选择阅读。有些书在你父亲的藏书之中，你应该已经随身带去。由于我记不清哪些书是你父亲的书房中所没有的，你一定要写信告诉我，并把你认为从写信那天起之后的十八个月中你有机会接触到的书列一个清单，并就此请教威思先生。关于这个概要，我还要特别补充几点我的看法：

1.意大利语。我怕学习这种语言会使你把法语和西班牙语与之混淆。由于这几种语言都是由拉丁语退化衍生出来的，所以在会话中很容易混淆。我还从来没有见过一个人能同时说这三种语言而不弄混的。意大利语是一门令人愉快的语言，但近来发生的事倒使西班牙语更有用处。这个问题先放到一边吧。

2.西班牙语。你要把更多的精力投入到这门学科上来，并尽力去扎实地掌握。我们国家的未来同西班牙及西班牙语及美洲国家之间的关系，将使掌握这种语言变得至关重要。美洲历史中关于那片地区的部分也是以西班牙语来记载的。我给你寄去了一本词典。

3.道德哲学。我认为听这门课纯属浪费时间。如果那个要我们去听课的人使我们的道德行为准则变成一门学科，那他一定是个工作拙劣的可怜的家伙。对于懂得这种学问的人来说，会有无数不懂的人，他们应该怎么办呢？人是社会的一分子，因此，他的道德也是以此为目标来形成的。他被赋予仅与此有关的是非感，这种是非感就像听、看、感觉等一样，是人的本能的一部分，它才是道德准则的真正基础，而不是如那些富于幻想的作家所想象的那样是美、真等的基础。是非感或良知，就像腿或手臂一样，是一个人的身体的一部分，它以一种或强或弱的形式被赋予全人类，就像每个人的力量也是有大有小一样。道德可以通过实践得到加强，就像身体的任何一个部分都可以通过锻炼变得强壮一样。在某种程度上，道德确实服从于理智的引导，但服从理智引导的道德只是很小的一部分，甚至比我们所说的常识还要少。如果对一个农民和一个教授陈述一宗道德案件，前者往往会做出很好的判定，而且通常比后者的判定要好得多，因为他没有被人为制定的清规戒律引入歧途。因此，在学这门课程的时候，你要多读好书，因为它们不但能给你鼓励，还能引导你的感觉，尤其是斯特恩的书，它们是已有的道德教科书中最好的。除此之外，你还要读我在信里提到的那些书；最重要的，要随时陶冶你的性情，要有感激之心，要慷慨大方，要仁慈，要讲人道，要真诚、公正、坚定、有序、勇敢等。你要把这其中每一个方面的实践活动都看作是一种可以增强你的道德修养、提高你的自身价值的锻炼。

4.宗教。你的理智现在已经足够成熟，可以研究一下这门学科了。首先，你要摒除一切对新颖独特见解的偏好，要把它们投入到其他学科中去，而不是在宗教上。这一点非常重要，因为在宗教方面，错误的言论也许会造成很严重的后果。另一方面，你要摆脱所有的畏惧和奴性心理，它会使人心理脆弱、行为畏缩；要坚决保持理智，无论遇到任何事、任何意见，都要以理智去面对。你要学会做任何事都要三思而后行，否则，即使真的有上帝存在，也帮不了你，因为上帝也一定会赞同理智的行为，而不是盲目的敬畏。你一定要首先研究自己国家的宗教，那就先看《圣经》吧，然后再看李维和塔西陀的书。看了李维和塔西陀的书之后，你也会像他们一样，开始思考普通自然学科中所包含的真理。从某种程度上说，他们的观点中掺杂了个人的喜好，但是由于他们的喜好并不违背自然规律，所以也无可厚非。需要注意的是，《圣经》中有一些明显同自然规律相抵触的观点，一定要小心对待，并从多种角度去理解。

5. 旅行。旅行能使人变得聪明，但乐趣却不是很多。中年人在旅行时积累知识，并可能会用到这些知识来为他们的国家服务，但在以后的岁月里，他们容易产生伴随着遗憾的回忆；他们的情感因投入到过多的事物上而被减弱；他们养成了新习惯，但回到家后却感觉不适应。年轻人旅行时，更容易遇到这些麻烦，因为他们的见识不够，这种见识需要以往的知识和经历作为基础，而这个基础只有通过日积月累的观察和学习才能建立起来。外面世界的精彩使他们心花怒放、热血沸腾，吸引了他们的全部情感和注意力，使他们难以割舍，此时对他们来说，回家就像被流放或服刑一样；他们的目光永远在回顾已经逝去的事物，这种回忆会毒害他们的余生。这些毫无价值的事情消耗了他们最原始、最美好的感情，他们将这些糟粕带回家中，使自己及身边的人都闷闷不乐。此外，他们还养成了懒散的习惯，丧失了对事业的上进心，这使他们变成了既无助于自己，也无助于国家的废人。这些都是我在观察中所得来的经验，没有什么地方能像自己国家一样，使你在追求知识时免于受到外物的阻碍，也使你心灵的美德不会受到影响。还有，你要有教养、要有学问、要勤奋，这样你就不会借助旅行来使自己热爱祖国、珍视朋友，并善待自己。我再重复我的建议，要多运动，多走路，健康是紧随道德之后人类最重要的需求。亲爱的彼得，要常给我写信，并保证让我对你的成功总是充满兴趣和热情。

你的挚友

（安娜 译）

注释

1. sketch[sketʃ] *n.* 梗概
2. confound[kən'faund] *vt.* 使混乱
3. render['rendə] *vt.* 致使
4. bungler['bʌŋglə] *n.* 笨拙者
5. conscience['kɔnʃəns] *n.* 道德心;良心
6. submit[səb'mit] *vi.* 服从
7. astray[ə'strei] *adv.* 误入歧途地
8. disposition[ˌdispə'ziʃn] *n.* 性情
9. divest[dai'vest] *vt.* 迫使放弃
10. singularity[ˌsiŋgjə'lærəti] *n.* 奇异;稀有
11. servile['sə:vail] *adj.* 奴性的
12. tribunal[trai'bju:nl] *n.* 裁决
13. gratify['grætifai] *vt.* 使高兴
14. condemnation[ˌkɔndem'neiʃn] *n.* 定罪
15. residue['rezidu:] *n.* 剩余
16. hackney['hækni] *vt.* 役使;出租
17. obstruct[əb'strʌkt] *vt.* 妨碍;阻塞

赏析

托马斯·杰斐逊(1743—1826),第三任美国总统,政治家、思想家、哲学家、科学家、教育家、发明家。他与约翰·亚当斯和本杰明·富兰克林等人一起起草了美国《独立宣言》,是美国独立战争期间的主要领导人之一,可以被称为美国的缔造者之一。美利坚合众国成立后,杰斐逊先后担任过第一任国务卿、第二任副总统和第三任总统。他在任期间保护农业,发展民族资本主义工业。从法国手中购买路易斯安那州,使美国领土近乎增加了一倍,被普遍视为美国历史上最杰出的总统之一,同华盛顿、林肯和罗斯福齐名。

杰斐逊出身于弗吉尼亚的富裕家庭,从小受到良好的教育。在取得律师资格后就积极投身国家独立运动,发挥了不可磨灭的作用。杰斐逊是美国历史上屈指可数的伟大的思想家,他所创造出来的博大精深的民主思想体系带有浓厚的人文主义色彩,他所倡导的自由、平等思想成为数百年来美国精神的重要内涵,即:人民言论自由、出版自由、宗教自由。杰斐逊也是一位杰出的政治家,他从政60余年,表现出了许多高贵的品质。在任总统期间,他提倡平民作风,以平等的态度对待一切人。杰斐逊还是杰出的教育家,他重视教育,制定出一套大、中、小三级教育制度,并亲自筹建了弗吉尼亚大学。杰斐逊还是位文学家,他一生著述颇多,涉及问题相当广,写下大量书信文稿,后人为纪念他而出版了他的20卷文集。晚年的杰斐逊还致力于建筑学研究,亲自设计建造了蒙蒂塞洛庄园和弗吉尼亚大学的校园建筑风格。

本文是杰斐逊写给侄子的信。全文以庄重、质朴的语言既表达了长者对晚辈所取得成就的欣喜安慰,又不失语重心长的谆谆教诲。读来让人既能感受到浓浓的亲情,又能体会到长者对后辈精神的引领。

原文

7 Napoleon to Josephine

I have your letter, my **adorable** love. It has filled my heart with joy... since I left you I have been sad all the time. My only happiness is near you. I go over endlessly in my thought of your kisses, your tears, your **delicious** jealousy. The charm of my wonderful Josephine **kindles** a living, blazing fire in — my heart and senses. When shall I be able to pass every minute near you, with nothing to do but to love you and nothing to think of but the pleasure of telling you of it and giving you proof of it? I loved you some time ago; since then I feel that I love you a thousand times better. Ever since I have known you I **adore** you more every day. That proves how wrong is that saying of La Bruyere "Love comes all of a sudden."

Ah, let me see some of your faults; be less beautiful, less graceful, less tender, less good. But never be jealous and never shed tears. Your tears send me out of my mind ... they set my very blood on fire. Believe me that it is utterly impossible for me to have a single thought that is not yours, a single fancy that is not **submissive** to your will. Rest well. Restore your health. Come back to me and then at any rate before we die we ought to be able to say: "We were happy for so very many days!" Millions of kisses even to your dog.

译文

7 拿破仑致约瑟芬

我收到了你的信,我崇拜的心上人。你的信使我充满了欢乐……自从与你分手以后,我一直闷闷不乐,愁眉不展。我唯一的幸福就是伴随着你。你的吻给了我无限的思索和回味,还有你的泪水和甜蜜的嫉妒。我迷人的约瑟芬的魅力像一团炽热的火在心里燃烧。什么时候我才能在你身旁度过每分每秒，除了爱你什么也不需做；除了向你倾诉我对你的爱并向你证明爱的那种愉快，什么也不用想了？我不敢相信不久前爱上你，自那以后我感到对你的爱更增一千倍。自我与你相识，我一天比一天更崇拜你。这正好证明了拉布吕耶尔说的"爱，突如其来"多么不切合实际。

唉，让我看你的一些美中不足吧。再少几分甜美，再少几分优雅，再少几分温柔妩媚，再少几分姣好吧。但决不要嫉妒，决不要流泪。你的眼泪使我神魂颠倒，你的眼泪使我热血沸腾。相信我，我每时每刻无不想你，不想你是绝无可能的，没有一丝意念能不顺着你的意愿。好好休息，早日康复。回到我的身边，不管怎么说，在我们谢世之前，我们应当能说："我们曾有多少个幸福的日子啊！"千百万次吻，甚至吻你的爱犬。

注释

1. adorable[ə'dɔ:rəbl] *adj.* 值得崇拜的
2. delicious[di'liʃəs] *adj.* 有趣的
3. kindle ['kindl] *vt* 点燃；激起
4. adore [ə'dɔ:] *vt.* 爱慕；喜爱；极喜欢
5. submissive[səb'misiv] *adj.* 顺从的

赏析

拿破仑·波拿巴（Napoleon Bonaparte，1769—1821），法国军事家与政治家，法兰西第一共和国执政、法兰西第一帝国皇帝，出生在法国科西嘉岛。西欧和中欧的广大领土曾被拿破仑占领过，使整个欧洲的地图为之改动，威震半个欧洲，使法国资产阶级革命的思想得到了更为广阔的传播。在位前期是法国人民的骄傲，直至今日一直受到法国人民的尊敬与热爱。拿破仑是一位卓越的军事天才，而且在情场上的感情与爱情谋略则更具一番情味。1796年经巴黎司令部保罗巴拉斯介绍娶了约瑟芬。

《拿破仑致约瑟芬》是一封言语轻松、感情真挚的情书，也是一封热情洋溢、充满柔情蜜意的情书。约瑟芬比拿破仑大6岁，当时是有两个孩子的寡妇，但是约瑟芬的娇柔、纯洁、善良，深得拿破仑喜爱，她的美貌和坦诚深深地打动了拿破仑。拿破仑相信爱情，选择和她结为半路夫妻。这是一篇赞美诗，凝结了真挚的感情。信中运用了比喻、排比、夸张等修辞方法，使得文章极富感染力，令我们感受到了这位叱咤风云的人物的温柔一面，堪称情书中的经典之作。

原文

8 Winston Churchill to His Wife

My dearest one,

Alex and his aide-de-camp, who is the son of Lord Templemore, have left us after staying two nights. I hope Alex will come back again next weekend. He certainly enjoyed himself painting, and produced a very good picture considering it is the first time that he has handled a brush for six years. I have now four pictures, three of them large, in an advanced state, and I honestly think they are better than any I have painted so far. I gave Alex your message and he was very pleased.

The painting has been a great pleasure to me, and I have really forgotten all my **vexations**. It is a wonderful cure, because you really cannot think of anything else. This is Saturday, and it is a week since we started. We have had newspapers up till Wednesday. I have skimmed through them, and it certainly seems we are going to have a pretty hard time. I cannot feel the Government are doing enough about **demobilization**, still less about getting our trade on the move again. I do not know how we are ever to pay our debts, and it is even difficult to see how we shall pay our way. Even if we were all united in a Coalition, gathering all the strength of the nation, our task might well be beyond our powers. However, all this seems already quite remote from me on this lovely lake, where nearly all the days are full of sunshine and the weather bright and cool.

Much better than the newspapers was your letter, with its amusing but rather **macabre** account of the Journey to Woodford. I am longing to hear how our affairs are progressing. I do hope you are not **overtaxing** yourself with all the business that there is to do. We shall certainly not forget about Mary's birthday; but let me know what you have done about a present.

Considering how pleasant and delightful the days have been, I cannot say they have passed quickly. It seems quite a long time since I arrived, although every day has been full of interest and occupation. I have **converted** my enormous bathroom into a studio with **makeshift easels**, and there all this morning Alex and I tried to put the finishing touches on our pictures of yesterday. He has set his heart on buying a villa here on a **promontory**. I have not seen it inside, but from the outside it looks the most beautiful **abode** one can possibly imagine, and I understand that inside it is even more romantic, going back to the fifteenth century. He was a little startled when I pointed out to him that no one will be allowed to buy a foreign property across the exchange perhaps for many years.

He begged me to stay on here as long as I like, but I think I shall come back the 18th or 19th. I am doubtful whether I shall stop in Paris. I expect in another ten or eleven days I shall be very keen to get home again. Sarah has been a great joy, and gets on with everybody. She and I both drive the speed-boats. They are a wonderful way of getting about this lake, and far safer than the awful winding roads around which the Italians career with motorcars and lorries at all sorts of speeds and angles.

Charles plays golf most days. There is a very pretty link here, and he has fierce contests with himself or against Ogier. His devoted care of me is deeply touching.

You maybe amused to see the **elaborate** form in which your telegram, which I rejoiced to receive today, was sent.

My darling I think a great deal of you and last night when I was driving the speed-boat back there came into my mind your singing to me *In the Gloaming* years ago. What a sweet song and tune and how beautifully you sang it in all its **pathos**. My heart thrills and I love to feel you near me in thought. I feel so tenderly towards you my darling and the more pleasant and agreeable the scenes and days, the more I wish you were here to share them and give me a kiss.

You see I have nearly forgotten how to write with a pen. Isn't awful my **scribbles**?

Miss Layton has heard from her "boy-friend" in S. Africa that she is to go out there (not Canada) immediately if possible to marry him. So she is very happy. Yesterday the South African officers came from their hotel and took her out to "water-plane" behind their speed boat. She looked very handsome whirling along in the water and made three large circles in front of the villa before she tumbled in. Sarah is writing you now. The DB is starting.

Always your loving husband

译文

8 温斯顿·丘吉尔致妻子的信

我最亲爱的：

亚历克斯和他的副官——坦普莫尔勋爵的儿子，在我们这里住了两晚之后，已经走了。我希望亚历克斯下周末能再来。他十分喜欢绘画，而且还画了一幅很不错的画，这也是他从学习绘画至今六年来画的最出色的画。我现在已经有了四幅作品，其中三幅还是大幅的；说实话，我真的认为这是迄今为止我画得最好的画。我把你的情况告诉了亚历克斯，他听后很高兴。

对我来说，绘画真是其乐无穷，使我忘记了一切烦恼。绘画是一种神奇的疗法，因为它可以使人消除一切杂念。今天是星期六，从我们出发至今已经一个星期了，可直到星期三我们才收到一些报纸。我浏览了一下这些报纸，感觉似乎我们必将经历一段艰难的日子。我感到我们的政府并没有在裁军问题上尽最大的努力，也没有重新大力开展我们的贸易。我不知道我们究竟应该如何去偿还债务，更不知道怎样才能不增加负债。即使我们全部组成一个联盟，集中起全国的所有力量，也无法完成我们所面临的任务。不过，这一切似乎离我很遥远，身处在这片美丽的湖上，每天所感受到的几乎都是明媚的阳光和清爽的天气。

你的那封有趣且惊险的乌德福之旅的信，比报纸可好看得多。我想知道我们的事情进展得怎么样了，真希望你不要为这些事给自己太多的压力。我们当然不会忘记玛丽的生日，不过你要告诉我你准备了什么礼物。

这样的日子虽然很轻松愉快，但仍感觉过得很慢；虽然每天过得都很有趣、充实，但依然觉得我们来这里似乎已经很长时间了。我把那间大浴室改成了带有临时画架的画室，今天一上午亚历克斯和我都在那里努力完成昨天的画。他决定在这里的一个海角处买一幢别墅。从外表上看，这幢别墅确实是人所能想象到的最漂亮的住宅，我没有见过别墅的内部装饰风格，但听说非常浪漫，充满了15世纪情调。不过，当我告诉他已经多年不允许私自购买外国地产时，他有点惊讶。

亚历克斯说如果我愿意的话，他希望我继续住在这儿，但我想十八日或十九日就回来。我在考虑途中是否应在巴黎逗留，但我多么希望再过十天或十一天之后就能回到我渴望已久的家中。萨拉给我们带来了极大的快乐，她和每个人都相处得很好。我们俩一起驾驶快艇在湖上飞驰，非常惊险、刺激，但比起意大利职业赛车手在条件恶劣的崎岖小路上全方位、全速驾驶小汽车或卡车，可要安全多了。

查尔斯大多数时间都在打高尔夫球。这里有一个很漂亮的高尔夫球场，他有时自己打，有时和奥吉尔打。他对我的悉心照顾使我深为感动。

很高兴今天收到了你的电报，想必你也对自己精心策划的电文格式感到好笑吧。

亲爱的，我非常想念你。昨晚当我驾着快艇返航时，脑海中回荡的便是你多年前唱给我的一首歌《黄昏》。多么动听的歌！多么优美的曲调！你唱得又是那么哀婉动人！我的心在颤抖，真挚的爱使我感觉你就在我的身边，你是那样温柔！亲爱的，这里的景色越是赏心悦目，我就越希望你能在这里与我共同分享这一切。来吻我吧！

你看，我几乎不知道如何拿笔了，我一定写得很乱吧？

雷顿小姐已经收到了她“男朋友”从南非来的信。如果有可能，她会立即去南非(不是加拿大)与他结婚，因此她非常高兴。昨天几个南非官员从旅馆来把她带到一架停在他们的快艇后面的“水上飞机”上。她在水面上盘旋着，在别墅的前方绕了三个大圈才落下来，真是太美了！萨拉现在正在给你写信。晚餐铃响了。

永远爱你的丈夫

(安娜 译)

注释

1. vexation[vek'seiʃn] *n.* 令人烦恼的事
2. demobilization[di:ˌməubiai'zeˌʃn] *n.* 复员
3. macabre[mə'kɑ: br(ə)] *adj.* 可怕的
4. overtax[ˌəuvə'tæks] *vt.* 负担过度
5. convert[kən'və:t] *vt.* 转换

6. makeshift[ˈmeikʃift] *adj.* 临时的
7. easel[ˈi:zl] *n.* 画架
8. promontory[ˈprɔməntri] *n.* 海角
9. abode[əˈbəud] *n.* 住处
10. elaborate[iˈlæbəret] *adj.* 精心制作的
11. pathos[ˈpeiθɔs] *n.* 悲怅
12. scribble[ˈskribl] *n.* 潦草写成的东西

赏析

温斯顿·丘吉尔(1874—1965),英国政治家、演说家、作家、画家以及记者。丘吉尔曾于1940—1945年及1951—1955年期间两度任英国首相，被认为是20世纪最重要的政治领袖之一,带领英国获得第二次世界大战的胜利。他最著名的作品是《第一次世界大战回忆录》,六卷本的《第二次世界大战回忆录》，还创作了《伦道夫·丘吉尔勋爵传》《英语民族史》等多部小说和回忆录。1953年因《不需要战争》而获得诺贝尔文学奖,瑞典文学院在授予他诺贝尔文学奖的颁奖词中说:“丘吉尔成熟的演说，目的敏捷准确,内容壮观动人。犹如一股铸造历史环节的力。……丘吉尔在自由和人性尊重的关键时刻的滔滔不绝的演说,却另有一番动人心魄的魔力。也许他自己正是以这伟大的演说,建立了永垂不朽的丰碑。”2002年,BBC举行了一个名为“最伟大的100名英国人”的调查,结果丘吉尔获选为有史以来最伟大的英国人。

丘吉尔与出身贵族却家境贫寒的克莱门蒂娜·霍齐尔结婚,一生共育有5个孩子。本文是丘吉尔在度假之余写给妻子的信，讲述的是丘吉尔这位政治人物在一处湖光山色的别墅以作画来放松身心,但同时又心系国家;虽然身处风景宜人之处,却无法与爱妻共享美景,因此思家心切。透过这段平实、温暖的文字,读者可以看到一个在政坛上叱咤风云的伟人非常温情的一面。

原文

9 Shelley to Keats

Pisa, July 27th, 1820

My dear Keats,

I hear with great pain the dangerous accident that you have undergone, Mr. Gisborne who gives me the account of it, adds, that you continue to wear a **consumptive** appearance. This consumption is a disease particularly fond of people who write such good verses as you have done, and with the assistance of an English writer it can often indulge its selection; — I do not think that young and **amiable** poets are at all bound to gratify its taste; they have entered into no bond with the **Muses** to that effect.

But seriously (for I am joking on what I am very anxious about) I think you would do well to pass the winter after so **tremendous** an accident in Italy, and (if you think it as necessary as I do) so long as you could find Pisa or its neighborhood agreeable to you, Mrs. Shelley unites with myself in urging the request, that you would take up your residence with us. — You might come by sea to Leghorn, (France is not worth seeing, and the sea air is particularly good for weak lungs) which is within a few miles of us. You ought at all events to see Italy, and your health which I suggest as a motive, might be an excuse to you.

I spare declamation about the statues and the paintings and the ruins — and what is a greater piece of **forbearance** — about the mountains the streams and the fields, the colors of the sky, and the sky itself.

I have lately read you *Endymion* again and ever with a new sense of the treasures of poetry it contains, though treasures poured forth with indistinct **profusion**. This, people in general will not endure, and that is the cause of the comparatively few copies which have been sold. — I feel persuaded that you are capable of the greatest things, so you but will.

I always tell Ollier to send you copies of my books. — *Prometheus Unbound* I imagine you will receive nearly at the same time with this letter. The *Cenci* I hope you have already received — it was **studiously** composed in a different style "below the good how far! But far above the great". In poetry I have sought to avoid system and mannerism; I wish those who excel me in genius, would pursue the same plan .

Whether you remain in England, or journey to Italy, — believe that you carry with you my anxious wishes for your health happiness and success, wherever you are or whatever you undertake — and that I am.

Yours sincerely

P. B. Shelley

译文

9 雪莱致济慈

比萨,1820年7月27日,

亲爱的济慈:

听说你遭到极为危险的意外,我深为担忧。这一不幸的消息是吉斯伯恩先生告诉我的,他还说你至今仍带有患肺病的样子。这种结核病特别喜欢光顾像你那样能写出美妙诗篇的人,再加上英国的严冬,病情往往会越发严重。鄙人并不认为年轻宽厚的诗人们一定要慷慨地任它肆意折磨,我们诗人在那一方面并不受缪斯的约束。

然而说正经的我心里非常着急,可还在跟你要笑,我觉得你在经受如此巨大的不幸之后来意大利过冬,对你的身体一定会有所裨益。若你也像我一样感到有此必要,只要你还喜欢比萨及其周围地区,我和我的夫人都切望你能和我们住在一起。你可以乘船到里窝那,法国不值得游览,而大海对病弱的肺部特别有益,里窝那与我们这儿相隔仅有几英里之遥。你无论如何应该到意大利来看看。我认为你的健康问题满可以作为你到这里来的理由。

这里的雕塑、绘画和古迹之美妙无须我赘述,此处山间的小溪和田野、绚丽多姿的云彩和天空就更令人神往了。

最近,我重读了你的《恩底弥翁》,使我对诗的内涵甚至产生一种珍贵新奇的感觉,而我的心灵则又一次感受到罕见的奔放诗意。诚然,华章销售不畅,这也只是因为凡夫俗子难以领受佳作而已。事实使我确信你一定能写出最伟大的诗篇,也只有你才能吟出这样的传世佳句。

我一直关照奥利尔将我的书寄几本给你,我想你或许在接到此信的同时收到《解放了的普罗米修斯》。我希望你已经收到《钦契一家》,这是我着意打破传统风格而创作的。"'善'之下是多么遥远,却高高凌驾于'伟大'之上。"

在诗歌创作上,我一直力求避免落入俗套。我希望才识过我者也能采取同样的方针。请相信,无论你留在英国还是来意大利,无论你居留何处或写些什么,我们都热切地祝愿你身体健康、生活幸福、创作成功。

你真诚的

P. B. 雪莱

注释

1. consumptive[kən'sʌmptiv] *adj.* 肺病的
2. amiable['eimiəbl] *adj.* 和蔼可亲的
3. the Muses(缪斯):是主管音乐、诗歌、舞蹈、天文等九位女神的总称。他们居于希腊南帕那萨斯山脚下以及赫利孔山上的名泉之中。因此，至今仍有fountain of knowledge(知识的源泉)，springs of inspiration(灵感的源泉)的说法。出于对缪斯女神们的敬仰，古希腊人把艺术作品以及自然科学方面的物品放置在缪斯神庙，即mouseion里面。

4. tremendous[tri'mendəs] *adj.* 巨大的
5. forbearance[fɔ:'beərəns] *n.* 忍耐
6. profusion[prə'fju:ʒn] *n.* 丰富；充沛
7. studiously ['stju:diəsli] *adv.* 专心地

赏析

珀西·比西·雪莱 (1792—1822)，19世纪英国著名的积极浪漫主义诗人，与拜伦、济慈齐名。雪莱一生见识广泛，是一位典型的空想社会主义者和理想主义者。他以笔为武器，宣扬无神论，抨击封建制度的专横无道、英国资本主义制度的剥削，反映劳动人民的悲惨境遇并支持爱尔兰的民族独立运动，从而引起了英国资本主义阶级对他的仇视。诗人被迫迁居意大利，利用文学阵地来表达自己的思想。长诗《麦布女王》《伊斯兰的起义》，诗剧《解放了的普罗米修斯》，诗体悲剧《钦契一家》，政治抒情诗《致英国人民》《1819年的英国》《暴政的假面游行》，抒情诗《云》《致云雀》《西风颂》等作品中既有诗人情感炽热、慷慨激昂的强烈政治诉求，又有想象丰富、音韵和谐、节奏明快的直抒胸臆。但不幸天妒英才，诗人于1822年7月驾小艇旅行途中，偶遇风暴，溺水于斯佩齐亚海湾，时年30岁。

本文是雪莱向济慈发出的邀请信。雪莱被迫离开英国前往意大利之前，对济慈了解得并不多，定居比萨期间，他听说济慈的新诗集在伦敦问世并首次获得好评的同时健康状况恶化，于是发出这封信，邀请济慈前往比萨休养。全文措辞委婉谨慎、感情真挚，从中能读出雪莱对济慈成就的由衷欣慰，对其才华的惺惺相惜，对其健康的深深忧虑及对异地相逢的急切企盼。

原文

10 Keats to Shelley

Hampstead, August 16th, 1820

My dear Shelley,

I am very much gratified that you, in a foreign country, and with a mind almost over-occupied, should write to me in the **strain** of the letter beside me. If I do not take advantage of your invitation, it will be prevented by a circumstance I have very much at heart to **prophesy**. There is no doubt that an English winter would put an end to me, and do so in a **lingering** hateful manner. Therefore, I must either voyage or journey to Italy, as a soldier marches up to a battery.

My nerves at present are the worst part of me, yet they feel **soothed** when I think that come what extreme may, I shall not be destined to remain in one spot long enough to take a hatred of any four particular bedposts. I am glad you take any pleasure in my poor poem, which I would willingly take the trouble to unwrite, if possible, did I care so much as I have done about reputation. I received a copy of the *Cenci*, as from yourself from Hunt. There is only one part of it I am judge of — the poetry and dramatic effect — which by many spirits nowadays is considered the **Mammon**.

A modern work, it is said must have a purpose, which may be the God. An artist must serve Mammon; he must have "self- concentration", selfishness perhaps. You, I am sure, will forgive me for sincerely remarking that you might **curb** your **magnanimity,** and be more of an artist, and "load every **rift**" of your subject with ore. The thought of such discipline must fall like cold chains upon you, who perhaps never sat with your wings furled for six months together.

And is not this extraordinary talk for the writer of *Endymion*, whose mind was like a pack of scattered cards? I am picked up and sorted to a pip.

My imagination is a monastry and I am its monk. You must explain my **metaphysics** to yourself. I am in expectation of *Prometheus* every day. Could I have my own wish for its interest effected you would have it still in manuscript, or be but now putting an end to the second act. I remember you advising me not to publish my first- blights, on Hampstead **Heath**. I am returning advice upon your hands. Most of the poems in the volume I send you have been written above two years, and would never have been published but from a hope of gain; so you see I am inclined enough to take your advice now. I must express once more my deep sense of your kindness, adding my sincere thanks and respects for Mrs. Shelley.

In the hope of soon seeing you, I remain.

most sincerely yours

John Keats

译文

10 济慈致雪莱

汉普斯台得,1820年8月16日

亲爱的雪莱:

您客居异邦,思念万千,仍不辞劳苦给我写信(您的信此刻就在我身边),表达了您对我的关心,这真让我感激不尽!万一不能应邀前往,那肯定是由于我的病情又在作怪,这也应是预料之中的。至于这儿的天气,就不用说了,这儿的严冬会毫不留情地日益侵袭我这本来就很虚弱的身体,或许会让我命归九泉。因此,我或取水路,或走陆路,就像奔赴疆场的战士一样,一定前往意大利。

时下,我最糟的病情就是神经紧张。然而,无论有什么不测,我将不为命运所摆布,而久卧病榻厌恶人生,每当我一想起这些,我就感到宽慰许多了。拙作承蒙错爱,让我兴奋不已。如果我仍能如昔日那样看重自己的名誉,很可能就会把它付之一炬。我从亨特那儿收到了一册《钦契一家》,同您亲自寄来的一样。只有其中的一点我可做评——就是诗歌与戏剧效果,这为现代许多人所崇尚。

一部现代作品据说一定要主题明确,它可能就是上帝。艺术家必须有所追求,他必须"孤芳自赏"——或者说是私心而已。我敢肯定您会宽恕我的直言不讳,您不妨少一点体现您那高尚的品质,多一点艺术家的风格,让字里行间都洋溢着您的主题。想一想这样的框架,您一定像是上了冰冷的镣铐,或许您从未收起翅膀,安然坐上半载吧。

我作为《安狄米恩》的作者,以往总是思绪紊乱,就像散在地上的纸牌。如今说起这些,岂非多谈?幸好我能把这些牌收起来,并能重新理顺。

我的想象力是座庙宇,而我就是庙宇中的和尚。每天我都在期盼《普罗米修斯》。假如您在写作的时候,采纳了我的意见,那部作品肯定还未完成,或许正在写第二幕的结尾。记得您曾劝我不要发表那些无病呻吟、以汉普斯台德荒原为背景的组诗。现在该轮到我奉劝您的时候了。我寄给您的诗歌集都是两年前写的。假如不是为了生活所迫的话,我决不会让它们贻笑大方的,由此您也能看出,我是多么愿意听取您的忠告的。再次感激您的关心和盛情邀请。谨此,请转达我对您夫人的诚挚谢意和敬意!

盼望着和您见面的那一刻!

你最真诚的朋友
约翰·济慈

注释

1. strain[stren] *n.* 负担
2. prophesy['prɔfəsai] *vt.* 预言
3. lingering['liŋgəriŋ] *adj.* 拖延的
4. soothe[suð] *vt.* 使平静
5. Mammon (玛蒙):喜爱金银财宝的恶魔。Mammon也被称为Amaimon,在叙利亚语中有着"富有"和"金钱"的含义。这位恶魔出现在《旧约圣经》与《新约圣经》之间的年代,在《玛太福音书》中曾有关于他的描绘:"一个人不能侍奉两个主人,热爱一方则必须憎恶另一方。如果你敬爱神,那么就不能执着于财富!"
6. curb[kə:b] *vt.* 控制
7. magnanimity[mægnə'nimiti] *n.* 宽宏大量
8. rift[rift] *n.* 裂缝;不和

9. metaphysics[metə'fiziks] *n.* 形而上学

10. heath[hiθ] *n.* 荒野

赏析

约翰·济慈（1795—1821），19世纪英国杰出的浪漫主义诗人。济慈出身于伦敦一个小业主家庭，当过药剂师的学徒，后来放弃医学，专事写作。济慈早期的作品大多是仿作；1817年出版的第一本诗集受到了褒贬不一的评价；随后的几年里，济慈一直受到疾病与经济问题的困扰，但这也是他诗歌创作的巅峰期。期间，济慈写出了大量优秀作品，其中包括《伊莎贝拉》《圣亚尼节前夜》《海伯利安》等著名长诗，最脍炙人口的《夜莺颂》《希腊古翁颂》《秋颂》《拉弥亚》等名篇，表现出诗人对大自然的强烈感受和热爱，赢得巨大声誉。由于家族病史，济慈感染上了肺结核，并于1821年2月23日前往意大利疗养的途中逝世，年仅25岁。

济慈虽与拜伦、雪莱同被列为英国浪漫主义诗歌的杰出代表，但他的诗作主要以刻画鲜明具体而取胜，他所描摹的景物具有实体感，这与他追求美感以逃避现实的思想有密不可分的关系。虽然他也同雪莱、拜伦一样表达对社会现实的不满，但他的诗作表现了突出的唯美主义色彩。

本文是济慈就雪莱邀请其去比萨疗养的回信。济慈以同样谨慎婉转的语气向其精神之友表达了感激、欣赏、敬仰之情，同时还透露他预感自己将不久于人世，但他无所畏惧。这就是伟大人物在面对死神时所表现出的坦然不惧的精神，并能在生命的最后时刻奏出最强音。

第六章 经典影片

影片一:《傲慢与偏见》(*Pride and Prejudice*, 2005)

赏析

该电影根据简·奥斯汀同名小说改编。由乔·怀特(Joe Wright)执导,凯拉·奈特利(Keria Knightley)、马修·麦克费登(Matthew Macfadyen)等主演。电影于2005年9月16日上映。奥斯汀这部写于1797年但直到1813年才出版的小说是英语文学中最具有杀伤力的言情小说之一。

这部作品以日常生活为素材,一反当时社会上流行的感伤小说的内容和矫揉造作的写作方法,生动地反映了18世纪末到19世纪初处于保守和闭塞状态下的英国乡镇生活和世态人情。这部社会风情画式的小说不仅在当时吸引着广大的读者,时至今日,仍给读者和观影者以独特的艺术享受。

奥斯汀在这部小说中通过班纳特五个女儿对待终身大事的不同处理,表现出乡镇中产阶级家庭出身的少女对婚姻爱情问题的不同态度,从而反映了作者本人的婚姻观:为了财产、金钱和地位而结婚是错误的;而结婚不考虑上述因素也是愚蠢的。因此,她既反对为金钱而结婚,也反对把婚姻当儿戏。她强调理想婚姻的重要性,并把男女双方感情作为缔结理想婚姻的基石。书中的女主人公伊丽莎白出身于小地主家庭,为富豪子弟达西所热爱。达西不顾门第和财富的差距,向她求婚,却遭到拒绝。伊丽莎白对他的误会和偏见是一个原因,但主要的是她讨厌他的傲慢。因为达西的这种傲慢实际上是地位差异的反映,只要存在这种傲慢,他与伊丽莎白之间就不可能有共同的思想感情,也不可能有理想的婚姻。以后伊丽莎白亲眼观察了达西的为人处世和一系列所作所为,特别是看到他改变了过去那种骄傲自负的神态,发现他其实是一个优越而有教养的年轻人,在他势利而傲慢的外表下藏着一颗敏感细腻的心灵。伊丽莎白消除了对他的误会和偏见,从而与他缔结了美满姻缘。伊丽莎白对达西先后两次求婚的不同态度,实际上反映了女性对人格独立和平等权利的追求。

原文

1 The Quarrel

Darcy: Miss Elizabeth. I have struggled **in vain** and can bear it no longer. These past months have been a **torment**. I came to Rosings only to see you. I have fought against judgement, my family's expectation, **the inferiority of your birth**, my rank. I will put them aside and ask you to end my **agony**.

Elizabeth: I don't understand.

Darcy: I love you. Most **ardently**. Please do me the honour of accepting my hand.

Elizabeth: Sir, I appreciate the struggle you have been through, and I am very sorry to have caused you pain. It was unconsciously done.

Darcy: Is this your reply?

Elizabeth: Yes, sir.

Darcy: Are you laughing at me?

Elizabeth: No.

Darcy: Are you rejecting me?

Elizabeth: I'm sure the feelings which **hindered** your regard will help you overcome it.

Darcy: Might I ask why with so little **civility** I am thus **repulsed**?

Elizabeth: I might enquire why you told me you liked me against your better judgement? If I was uncivil, then that is some excuse. But you know I have other reasons.

Darcy: What reasons?

Elizabeth: Do you think anything might tempt me to accept the man who has ruined the happiness of a most beloved sister? Do you deny that you separated a young couple who loved each other, exposing your friend to **censure for caprice** and my sister to **derision** for disappointed hopes, involving them both in acute misery?

Darcy: I do not deny it.

Elizabeth: How could you do it?

Darcy: I believed your sister indifferent to him. I realized his attachment was deeper than hers.

Elizabeth: She's shy!

Darcy: Bingley was persuaded she didn't feel strongly.

Elizabeth: You suggested it.

Darcy: For his own good.

Elizabeth: My sister hardly shows her true feelings to me. I suppose his fortune had some bearing?

Darcy: I wouldn't do your sister the dishonour. It was suggested...

Elizabeth: What was?

Darcy: It was clear an advantageous marriage...

Elizabeth: Did my sister give that impression?

Darcy: No! No! There was, however, your family...

Elizabeth: Our want of **connection**?

Darcy: No, it was more than that.

Elizabeth: How, sir?

Darcy: The lack of propriety shown by your mother, younger sisters and your father. Forgive me. You and your sister I must **exclude from** this.

Elizabeth: And what about Mr. Wickham.

Darcy: Mr. Wickham?

Elizabeth: What excuse can you give for your behaviour?

Darcy: You take an eager interest.

Elizabeth: He told me of his misfortunes.

Darcy: Oh, they have been great.

Elizabeth: You ruin his chances yet treat him with sarcasm.

Darcy: So this is your opinion of me? Thank you. Perhaps these offences might have been overlooked had not your pride been hurt by my scruples about our relationship. I am to rejoice in the inferiority of your circumstances?

Elizabeth: And those are the woof a gentleman. Your **arrogance and conceit**, your selfish disdain for the feelings of others made me realize you were the last man in the world I could ever marry.

Darcy: Forgive me, madam, for taking up so much of your time.

译文

1 争 吵

达西:伊丽莎白小姐,我实在没有办法撑下去了,这几个月对于我来说是一种折磨。我来罗新斯只是为了见你,理智的想法和家族的期望阻挠着我,你卑微的出身和我爵位的悬殊也令我迟疑不决,但我要把这一切统统抛开,请你终结我的痛苦。

伊丽莎白:我不明白你在说什么。

达西:我爱你,最真挚的爱。请赐予我荣幸,接受我的手吧。

伊丽莎白:先生,我感激你的挣扎,很抱歉引起你的痛苦,我完全是无心的。

达西:这就是你的回复?

伊丽莎白:是的,先生。

达西:你是在嘲笑我吗?

伊丽莎白:不。

达西:你是在拒绝我?

伊丽莎白:我确信,你心中阶级的门槛会帮助你克服痛苦。

达西:我能否问问,为什么我竟会遭受如此无礼的拒绝?

伊丽莎白:那么我能否问问,为什么你说喜欢我是违背了你自己的理智?若说我是无礼的,那这就是我无礼的理由之一吧,但我还有别的理由。

达西:什么理由?

伊丽莎白:一个毁了我最亲爱的姐姐幸福的人,怎么会打动我的心去爱他呢?你能否认你拆散了一对相爱的恋人,让你的朋友被大家指责为朝三暮四,让我的姐姐被大家嘲笑为奢望空想,让他们双方都受尽了痛苦?

达西:我并不否认。

伊丽莎白:你怎么能做出这样的事情?

达西:我认为你姐姐觉得他无关紧要。我觉得他的爱要比她更多。

伊丽莎白:那是因为她害羞!

达西:我说服彬格莱认为,她的感觉并不强烈。

伊丽莎白:那都是你说的。

达西:我这样做是为了他好。

伊丽莎白:我想你是担心她是看上了他的钱吧?

达西:我无意使你姐姐难堪。有迹象表明……

伊丽莎白:什么?

达西:这门婚事明显是为了谋取利益的……

伊丽莎白:我姐姐给你那种印象?

达西:不!你姐姐没,然而你的家人……

伊丽莎白:你以为我们是为了攀高枝?

达西:不,比那更甚。

伊丽莎白:怎样更甚,先生?

达西:你母亲、你妹妹们还有你父亲有失身份的表现。请原谅我,你和你姐姐当然没有。

伊丽莎白:那韦翰先生又是怎么回事?

达西:韦翰先生?

伊丽莎白:你对他的所作所为,又能给出什么借口?

达西:你对他倒是十分关心。

伊丽莎白:他告诉了我他的不幸遭遇。

达西:哦,他的确太不幸啦。

伊丽莎白：你毁了他，现在还讥讽他。

达西：这就是你对我的看法？谢谢，只怪我老老实实地，把我以前一误再误、迟疑不决的原因说了出来，所以伤害了你的自尊心。否则你也许就不会计较我得罪你的这些地方了，难道你指望我会为你那些微贱的亲戚而欢欣鼓舞吗？

伊丽莎白：这像是个绅士说的话吗？你十足狂妄自大、自私自利、看不起别人，我早就想好了，哪怕天下男人都死光了，我也不愿意嫁给你。

达西：请原谅，小姐，耽搁了你这么多时间。

注释

1. in vain: 徒然；无效
2. torment['tɔ:ment] *n.* 痛苦；折磨
3. the inferiority of sb.'s birth: 某人卑微的出身
4. agony['æɡəni] *n.* 苦恼；极大的痛苦
5. ardently['ɑ:dntli] *adv.* 热烈地；热心地
6. hinder['hində] *vt.* 阻碍；打扰
7. civility[si'viləti] *n.* 礼貌；礼仪
8. repulse[ri'pʌls] *vt.* 拒绝；击退
9. censure for caprice: 因反复无常而受谴责
10. derision[di'riʒən] *n.* 嘲笑的对象
11. connection[kə'nekʃən] *n.* 连接；关系，此处指高攀
12. exclude from: 排斥；把……排除在外
13. arrogance and conceit: 狂妄自负

对白二

原文

2 Early-Morning Encounter

Elizabeth: I couldn't sleep.

Darcy: Nor I. My aunt...

Elizabeth: Yes, she was here.

Darcy: How can I ever **make amends for** such behaviour?

Elizabeth: After what you've done for Lydia and, I suspect, for Jane, it is I who should be making amends.

Darcy: You must know. Surely you must know it was all for you. You are too generous to **trifle with** me. You spoke with my aunt last night and it has taught me to hope as I'd scarcely allowed myself before. If your feelings are still what they were last April, tell me so at once. My **affections** and wishes have not changed. But one word from you will silence me forever. If, however, your feelings have changed... I would have to tell you, you have **bewitched** me, body and soul, and I love... I love... I love you. I never wish to be parted from you from this day on.

Elizabeth: Well, then.

Darcy: Your hands are cold.

译文

2　清晨遇见

伊丽莎白：我睡不着。

达西：我也是，我姑妈……

伊丽莎白：是的，她昨晚来过。

达西：我可以为昨晚的事情做出补偿吗？

伊丽莎白：经过丽迪雅的事情后，还有吉英的事情，我想做补偿的人应该是我。

达西：你得知道，你一定得知道，我做这一切都是为了你。你是个爽快的人，绝不会开我的玩笑。昨晚你与我姑妈的谈话，倒让我觉得事情有了希望，以前我几乎不敢奢望。请你老实告诉我，你的心情是否还和4月里一样，我的心愿和情感依然如旧，只要你说一句话，我便再也不提这桩事。如果，你的感觉有所改变的话……我想告诉你，你把我的躯体和灵魂都占据了，我爱……我爱……我爱你。从今天起我不想与你分开。

伊丽莎白：唔。

达西：你的手好冷。

（根据大家论坛影视英语网资料整理）

注释

1. make amends for：补偿；赔偿损失
2. trifle with：玩弄；视同儿戏
3. affection[ə'fekʃn] *n.* 喜爱；感情
4. bewitch[bi'witʃ] *v.* 蛊惑；使着迷

影片二:《肖申克的救赎》

(*The Shawshank Redemption*, 1994)

赏析

《肖申克的救赎》(*The Shawshank Redemption*) 改编自斯蒂芬·金《不同的季节》(*Different Seasons*)中收录的《丽塔海华丝及萧山克监狱的救赎》。影片《肖申克的救赎》在牢狱题材电影中突破了类型片的限制, 拍出了同类作品罕见的人情味和温馨感觉,因而在公映时成为卖座的黑马。

毫无疑问,这是一部上乘佳作,没有动作,没有特技,甚至没有美人,却依然能深深打动观众,并且历经十几年而魅力不减。究其原因,它并不是一部简单的、纯粹的商业片,而是一部揭露美国司法黑幕(judicial lowdown)的巨片,也是一幅用友谊和希望描绘的生命画卷, 一部蕴含人生哲理的喻世之作(realistic works)。这是一部在学习电影的过程中必看的作品,它在技巧的层面接近完美。故事悬念的设计、人物的设置、主要情节的展开、道具的设计、音响的处理、成功的剪辑、流畅的镜头语言,包括演员的表演都令观者满意。

1946年,保守稳重的银行家安迪(蒂姆·罗宾斯 Tim Robbins 饰)被冤枉杀了他的妻子和其情人,两个无期徒刑将他后半生推入无底深渊。他没有就此沦落,却通过自己的智慧,很快成为狱长的私人助理,这是由于银行家出身的安迪懂得如何帮助狱卒逃税,帮监狱长将他收到的非法收入“洗白”。他在贪婪、残暴的狱卒手下为犯人们赢得了冰啤酒、图书馆以及与尊严和自由更为靠近的牢笼生活。在知道翻案出狱无望的真相后,他用一把小石槌在美女海报后面凿了20年,凿开了瑞德认为600年都无法凿穿的隧洞,爬过500码的下水道,在电闪雷鸣的大雨中轻笑着拥抱久违的自由。我们仿佛看到信念刺穿重重黑幕,在暗夜中打了一道夺目霹雳。

这是一部崇尚自由的电影。重要的是,它向人展现了取得自由的过程,它告诉你,自由不可能那么轻而易举,它也许要曲折,也许要在黑暗里瑟瑟发抖,甚至可能会依靠向强权妥协来换取自身的生存,它告诉你自由是那样一个艰难甚至是必须穿越猥琐与肮脏的过程。换句话说,它给了自由甚至说是理想一个完整的定义。

电影告诉我们,自由可以依靠妥协来苟延残喘,却不能依靠妥协来取得自由。片中有这样一段,一个在狱中度过大半生的老管理员出狱后,由于多年的牢狱生活已经使他体制化,面对自由的人生突然失去了生存下去的信心,自杀在房间里。正如在重重挤压之下的牢狱里待了三十年的瑞德所说,希望是危险的东西,是精神苦闷的根源。“刚入狱的时候,你痛恨周围的高墙;慢慢地,你习惯生活在其中;最终你会发现自己不得不依靠它而生存。那就是体制化”。(These walls are kind of funny like that. First you hate them, then you get used to them.

Enough time passed, get so you depend on them. That's institutionalizing.）影片给了我们一个悖论：当自由突然而至的时候，它也许已经失去了光辉，因为没有了生活的支持，没有了生存意义的赋予，自由对于你来说，不过是另一座监狱。安迪的自由虽然艰难，虽然屈辱，但有了信念的支撑，才有了它本应有的光泽。

《肖申克的救赎》从情节来看，讲述的是主人公安迪成功越狱、重获自由的经历，但实质上描述的是安迪从灵魂到肉体获得拯救的过程。这部影片触及了人类灵魂最深处的东西，它反映的是一个关于体制化与反体制化、希望与绝望、灵魂救赎的深刻的主题。体制化(institutionalized)、希望(hope)、救赎(redemption)是该片三个最为关键的反映影片主题的词语。

对白一

原文

3 Black Label Beer

RED: And that's how it **came to pass**, that **on the second-to-last day** of the job, the convict crew that tarred the plate factory roof in the spring of 49 wound up sitting in a row at ten o'clock in the morning, drinking icy cold **Black Label beer**, **courtesy of** the hardest screw that ever walked a turn at Shawshank State Prison.

HADLEY: Drink up, boys. While it's cold, ladies.

RED: The colossal prick even managed to sound **magnanimous**. We sat and drank with the sun on our shoulders, and felt like free men. We could have been tarring the roof of one of our own houses. We were the **lords of all creation**. As for Andy, he spent that break hunkered in the shade, a strange little smile on his face, watching us drink his beer.

HEYWOOD: Want a cold one, Andy?

ANDY: No thanks. I gave up drinking.

RED: You could argue he'd done it to **curry favor with** the guards. Or maybe make a few friends among us cons. Me, I think he did it just to feel normal again...if only for a short while.

译文

3 黑标啤酒

瑞德：这就是事情的经过，在这件工作完成的倒数第二天，这群在房顶涂沥青的囚犯在

49年的春天,在早晨10点钟坐成一排,喝着冰凉的肖申克州立监狱有史以来最狠的狱卒请客的黑标啤酒。

哈雷:都喝了吧,孩子们,趁着凉。

瑞德:那个凶狠的家伙竟试着显示出他的宽宏来。我们坐着喝酒,身披阳光,感觉就像个自由的人,就像在为自己的房子涂房顶,仿佛我们是一切的主宰。至于安迪,他蹲坐在阴影下小息,奇怪的笑容挂在脸上,看着我们喝着他的啤酒。

海沃德:这儿有瓶凉的,安迪。

安迪:不,谢谢。我戒酒了。

瑞德:你可以认为他这样做是为了讨好守卫,或者想与我们这些人交朋友。我却认为,他之所以这样做是想再次回到正常的生活,即使是一小会儿……

注释

1. came to pass:发生;经过
2. on the second-to-last day:倒数第二天
3. Black Label beer:黑标啤酒
4. courtesy of:经由提供
5. magnanimous[mæg'næniməs] *adj*. 宽宏大量的;有雅量的;宽大的
6. lords of all creation:一切生物的主宰
7. curry favor with:巴结;拍马屁

对白二

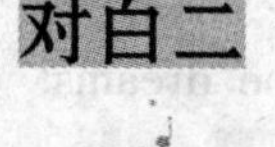

原文

4 The Agreement

ANDY: My wife used to say I'm a hard man to know. Like a closed book. Complained about it all the time. (pause) She was beautiful. I loved her. But I just didn't know how to show it, that's all. I killed her, Red. I didn't **pull the trigger**. But I drove her away. That's why she died. Because of me, the way I am.

RED: That don't make you a murderer. Bad husband, may be. Feel bad about it if you want to. But you didn't pull the trigger.

ANDY: No. I didn't. Someone else did, and I **wound up** here. Bad luck, I guess.

RED: Bad luck? Jesus.

ANDY: It floats around. Has to land on somebody. Say a storm comes through. Some folks sit in their living rooms and enjoy the rain. The house next door **gets torn out of** the ground and smashed flat. It was my turn, that's all. I was in the path of the **tornado**. (softly) I just had no idea the storm would go on as long as it has. (glances to him) You think you'll ever get out of here?

RED: Sure. When I got a long white beard and about three marbles left rolling around upstairs.

ANDY: Tell you where I'd go. **Zihuatanejo**.

RED: Zihuatanejo?

ANDY: Mexico. Little place right on the Pacific. You know what the Mexicans say about the Pacific? They say it has no memory. That's where I'd like to **finish out my life**, Red. A warm place with no memory. Open a little hotel right on the beach. Buy some worthless old boat and fix it up like new. Take my guests out charter fishing. (beat) You know, a place like that, I'd need a man who can get things.

RED: Jesus, Andy. I couldn't hack it on the outside. Been in here too long. I'm an **institutional man** now. Like old Brooks Hatlen was.

ANDY: You underestimate yourself.

RED: Bullshit. In here I'm the guy who can get it for you. Out there, all you need are Yellow Pages. I wouldn't know where to begin. (derisive snort) Pacific Ocean? Hell. Like to scare me to death, something that big.

ANDY: Not me. I didn't shoot my wife and I didn't shoot her lover, and whatever mistakes I made I've paid for them and then some. That hotel and that boat...I don't think it's too much to want. To look at the stars just after sunset. Touch the sand. Wade in the water. Feel free.

RED: Goddamn it, Andy, stop! Don't do that to yourself! Talking shitty pipe dreams! Mexico's down there, and you're in here, and that's the way it is!

ANDY: You're right. It's down there, and I'm in here. I guess it comes down to a simple choice, really. **Get busy living or get busy dying**.

RED: What the hell does that mean?

译文

4 约定

安迪:我妻子曾说我是个难于理解的人,像一本合着的书,她总在抱怨。(停了一下)她很美,我爱她,但是也许我表示得不够。是我杀了她,瑞德。不是我开的枪,但是我把她赶走的,那是她死去的原因。因为我,因为我那样对她。

瑞德:那你并不是凶手,顶多是个不好的丈夫。你可以为此难过,但不是你开的枪。

安迪:是的,不是我开的。别人杀了她,我却在这里受罪。我想是运气不好吧。

瑞德:运气不好?天!

安迪:它一旦来临,就一定会降临到某个人的身上。比如一场暴雨来临,有些人在他们的卧室里坐着享受,隔壁却被折磨、摧毁。这次轮上了我,就这样。我碰到了这场龙卷风,(轻轻地)只是没想到时间会这么长。(看看瑞德)你想过离开这儿吗?

瑞德:当然。等到我长着长长的白胡子的时候,等到我老糊涂的时候。

安迪:告诉你我会去哪儿,泽华塔尼。

瑞德:泽华塔尼?

安迪:墨西哥,地处太平洋的一个小地方。你知道墨西哥人是怎样谈论太平洋的吗?他们说那里没有回忆。在海滩上开一个小旅馆,买些不值钱的旧船翻新,让客人们包船钓鱼。(拍拍瑞德)要知道,像这样的地方,我需要一个能找到东西的人。

瑞德:天!安迪,我外面是混不下去的,在这儿待得时间太长啦,我现在是一个被制度化了的人,就像老布鲁克斯·哈特兰。

安迪:你小看自己了。

瑞德:废话。我在这里是能提供东西的人,在外面,你只需要电话黄页就够了,我可不知道该怎么开始。(鼻子里哼了一声)太平洋?见鬼。那么大的地方,还不把我吓得要死!

安迪:不应该这样。我没杀死我的妻子,也没杀死她的情夫,而且无论什么样的错误我已经受到惩罚。旅馆和船……我不认为这有什么难以得到。日落看星辰,走到沙滩,踩着海浪,感受自由。

瑞德:天杀的!安迪,停止!别那样想!也别说那些狗屁的白日梦!墨西哥远在天边,而你却在这儿,情况就是这样。

安迪:你说得对,它在那儿,我在这儿。我想是该做选择的时候了,该做了。要么忙着活,要么忙着死。

瑞德:那到底是什么意思?

注释

1. pull the trigger: 扣动扳机
2. wound up: 上足发条;紧张。此处指受罪
3. get torn out of: 撕开;扯下。此处指被折磨、摧毁
4. tornado[tɔr'nedo] *n.* 龙卷风;旋风;暴风;大雷雨
5. Zihuatanejo: 泽华塔尼,墨西哥西南部的一座城市,格雷罗州第四大城市
6. finish out my life: 度过余生
7. institutional man: 制度化的人
8. get busy living or get busy dying: 要么忙着活,要么忙着死

原文

5 Money Laundry

RED: And behind every **shady deal**, behind every dollar earned... there was Andy, keeping the books.

ANDY: Two deposits, Casco Bank and New England First. **Night drop**, like always, sir.

NORTON: Get my stuff down to laundry. Two suits for dry - clean and a bag of **whatnot**. Tell them if they over - starch my shirts again, they're gonna hear about it from me. (adjusts his tie) How do I look?

ANDY: Very nice.

NORTON: Big charity to - do up Portland way. Governor's gonna be there. (indicates pie) Want the rest of that? Woman can't bake worth shit.

ANDY: Thank you, sir.

RED: He's got his fingers in a lot of pies, from what I hear.

ANDY: What you hear isn't half of it. He's got scams you haven't dreamed of. **Kickbacks on his kickbacks**. There's a river of dirty money flowing through this place.

RED: Money like that can be a problem. Sooner or later you gotta explain where it came from.

ANDY: That's where I come in. I channel it, funnel it, filter it...stocks, **securities**, tax free municipals... I send that money out into the big world. And when it comes back...

RED: It's clean as a virgin's whistle?

ANDY: Cleaner. By the time Norton retires, I will have made him a millionaire.

RED: Jesus. They ever catch on, he's gonna **wind up** wearing a number himself.

ANDY: I thought you had more **faith in** me than that.

RED: I'm sure you're good, but all that paper leaves a trail. Anybody gets too curious — FBI, IRS, whatever — that trail's gonna lead to somebody.

ANDY: Sure it will. But not to me, and certainly not to the warden.

RED: All right, who?

ANDY: Peter Stevens.

RED: Who?

ANDY: The silent, silent partner. He's the guilty one, your honor. The man with the bank accounts. That's where the filtering process starts. They trace it back, all they're gonna find is him.

RED: But who the hell is he?

ANDY: A **phantom**. An apparition. Second cousin to Harvey the Rabbit. (off Red's look) I conjured him out of thin air. He doesn't exist...except on paper.

RED: You can't just make a person up.

ANDY: Sure you can, if you know how the system works, and where the cracks are. It's amazing what you can accomplish by mail. Mr. Stevens has a birth certificate, social security card, driver's license. They ever track those accounts, they'll wind up chasing a figment of my imagination.

RED: Jesus. Did I say you were good? You're Rembrandt.

ANDY: It's funny. On the outside, I was an honest man. Straight as an arrow. I had to come to prison to be a crook.

RED: Does it ever bother you?

ANDY: I don't run the scams, Red, I just process the profits. That's a fine line, maybe. But I've also built that library, and used it to help a dozen guys get their high school diplomas. Why do you think the warden lets me do all that? To keep you happy and doing the laundry. Money instead of sheets.

RED: I work cheap. That's the trade-off.

译文

5 洗 钱

瑞德：在每笔幕后的交易下，赚来的每一美元……都由安迪登记入账。

安迪：两笔存款，凯斯科和新格兰第一银行，夜存，如同往常，先生。

诺顿：把我的东西拿到洗衣房，两套西装要干洗，还有架子上的包。告诉他们，如果再浆洗过了的话，我就要找他们麻烦了。(整理领带)看上去如何？

安迪：非常好！

诺顿：有个大型慈善会，州长会去。(示意馅饼)要剩下的这些吗？女人只能烤出恶心的东西。

安迪：谢谢！

瑞德：他把手伸到了许多的馅饼里，我听说的。

安迪：你听说的还不到一半，他做的勾当你做梦都想不到。一层又一层回扣，那些黑钱如河一般在此流淌。

瑞德：像那样得来的钱会有麻烦的，迟早要解释它从哪儿来。

安迪：那就是用我的原因。我把钱流通、汇集、过滤……什么股票、证券、免税公债……我把钱投入这大千世界中，当它再返回的时候……

瑞德：干净得就像处女吗？

安迪:还要干净。诺顿退休时,我将把他变成百万富翁。

瑞德:天! 要是被逮住,他也会完蛋穿上号衣的。

安迪:我以为你相信我的能力。

瑞德:我当然知道你很棒,但文件会留下痕迹的。任何有着强烈好奇心的人——联邦调查局、国税局,不管是谁——他们顺着痕迹会找到的。

安迪:的确会找到。但不是我,当然更不会是典狱长。

瑞德:那是谁?

安迪:皮特·斯蒂文斯。

瑞德:谁?

安迪:沉默的、无声的合伙人。他是有罪的,大人。银行账户是他的,洗钱就是从那儿开始的。他们如果追查,最终只会找到他。

瑞德:但他到底是谁?

安迪:一个影子,一个幻影,哈维兔子(电影)的远房亲戚。(看看瑞德的表情)我凭空变出了他,他并不真实存在,只存在于文件上。

瑞德:你怎么能编造出一个人呢!

安迪:当然可以,如果你知道制度是如何运作的,漏洞又在哪里的话。只通过邮件就可以做成这件事,令人惊奇。斯蒂文斯先生有出生证、社保卡、驾驶执照。他们去查些账户,只能追踪到我想象出来的虚构物。

瑞德:天哪! 我说过你很棒吗? 你简直就是伦布兰特(著名画家)。

安迪:这很好笑,在外面时,我是一个正直人,直如利箭。可我不得不来到监狱做一个骗子。

瑞德: 这使你苦恼过吗?

安迪: 阴谋不是我出的,瑞德,我只是处理利润,那也许是个分界线吧。可我还建造了图书馆,并用它帮助十几个狱友获得中学文凭。你凭什么认为监狱长允许我做这些?

瑞德: 我工作廉价。这就是交易。

注释

1. shady deal: 幕后交易
2. night drop: 夜存
3. whatnot['hwɔtˌnɔt] *n.* 古董架;陈设架
4. kickbacks on his kickbacks: 一层又一层回扣
5. securities[si'kjuritis] *n.* (金融)有价证券;担保
6. wind up: 完蛋
7. faith in: 对……有信心
8. phantom['fæntəm] *n.* 幽灵;幻影

对白四

原文

6 The Recollection

RED: Andy Dufresne, who **crawled through** a river of shit and came out clean on the other side. Andy Dufresne, **headed for** the Pacific. Those of us who knew him best talk about him often. I swear, the stuff he pulled. It always makes us laugh. Sometimes it makes me sad, though, Andy being gone. I have to remind myself that some birds aren't **meant to be** caged, that's all. Their feathers are just too bright...and when they fly away, the part of you that knows it was a sin to lock them up does rejoice...but still, the place you live is that much more **drab and empty** that they're gone. I guess I just miss my friend.

译文

6 回 忆

瑞德：安迪·杜弗兰，爬过污垢的河流，在彼岸洗净重生，奔向海洋。我们这些熟悉他的人，经常地谈论他。无疑，有关他的话题，总会引起我们的笑声。安迪的离去，有时会让我难过。我必须承认有些鸟是关不住的，关不住。它们的羽毛是如此鲜亮……当它们飞走时，因摆脱了罪恶，你会替它们高兴。但是，你仍然还得生活在这个枯燥、乏味的地方。我想我失去了朋友。

（根据原版英语网资料整理）

注释

1. crawl through: 爬过；穿过
2. head for: 前往；出发
3. meant to be: 命中注定
4. drab and empty: 枯燥；乏味

影片三：《阿甘正传》(*Forrest Gump*, 1994)

赏析

《阿甘正传》(*Forrest Gump*)，是一部根据同名小说改编的美国电影，小说作者温斯顿·格卢姆(*Winston Groom*)。电影荣获1995年奥斯卡最佳影片奖、奥斯卡最佳男主角奖、奥斯卡最佳导演奖等6项大奖。美国百部经典名片之一，美国“反智电影”的代表作，充满着好莱坞电影回归的保守主义精神，是一部展现历史与个人的约定，以小人物的经历透视美国政治社会史的影片。

20世纪90年代，美国社会的反智情绪高涨，好莱坞于是推出了一批贬低现代文明、崇尚低智商和回归原始的影片，美国媒体称之为“反智电影”。《阿甘正传》就是这一时期反智电影的代表作，通过对一个智商为75的智障者生活的描述，反映了美国生活的方方面面，并以独特的角度对美国几十年来社会政治生活中的重要事件做了展现。它使美国人重新审视国家和个人的过去，重新反省美国人的本质。

阿甘(汤姆·汉克斯 Tom Hanks 饰)在影片中被塑造成了美德的化身，诚实、守信、认真、勇敢而重视感情，对人只懂付出不求回报，也从不介意别人拒绝，他只是豁达、坦荡地面对生活。他把自己仅有的智慧、信念、勇气集中在一点，他什么都不顾，只知道凭着直觉在路上不停地跑，他跑过了儿时同学的歧视、跑过了大学的足球场、跑过了炮火纷飞的越战泥潭、跑过了乒乓外交的战场、跑遍了全美国，并且最终跑到了他的终点。

“Mama always said life was like a box of chocolates. You never know what you're gonna get.”妈妈说生活就像一盒巧克力，你永远都不知道你会得到什么。每个看过《阿甘正传》的人都会从中得到些许感悟：生命就像那空中白色的羽毛，或迎风搏击，或随风飘荡，或翱翔蓝天，或堕入深渊……

对白一

原文

7 Like Peas and Carrots

Mrs. Gump: You do your very best now, Forrest.

Young Forrest: I sure will, Mama.

Forrest: I remember the bus ride on the first day of school very well.

Bus Driver: Are you coming along?

Young Forest: Mama said not to be taking rides from strangers.

Bus Driver: This is the bus to school.

Young Forrest: I'm Forrest — Forrest Gump.

Bus Driver: I'm Dorothy Harris.

Young Forrest: Well, now we aren't strangers anymore.

Boy 1: This seat's taken.

Boy 2: It's taken.

Boy 3: You can't sit here.

Forrest: You know, it's funny what a young man **recollects**, 'cause I don't remember being born. I don't recall what I got for my first Christmas, and I don't know when I went on my first outdoor picnic, but I do remember the first time I heard the sweetest voice in the wide world.

Girl: You can sit here if you want.

Forrest: I had never seen anything so beautiful in my life. She was like an angel.

Girl: Well, are you going to sit down or aren't you? What's wrong with your legs?

Young Forrest: Um, nothing at all, thank you. My legs are just **fine and dandy**.

Forest: I just sat next to her on that bus and had a conversation all the way to school.

Young Forrest: My back's crooked like a question mark. Next to Mama, no one ever talked to me or asked me questions. Are you stupid or something? Mama says, "**Stupid is as stupid does.**"

Girl: I'm Jenny.

Young Forrest: I'm Forrest — Forrest Gump.

Forest: From that day on, we was always together. Jenny and me was **like peas and carrots**. She taught me how to climb. Come on, Forrest, you can do it. I showed her how to **dangle**. "A good little..." She helped me learn how to read, and I showed her how to **swing**. Sometimes, we'd just sit out and wait for the stars. Mama's going to worry about me.

Girl: Just stay a little longer.

Forest: For some reason, Jenny didn't never want to go home.

Young Forrest: OK, Jenny, I'll stay.

Forest: She was my most special friend. My only friend. Now, my mama always told me that miracles happen every day. Some people don't think so, but they do.

译文

7 形影不离

甘夫人:你要开始努力学习了,福雷斯。

福雷斯·甘:我一定会的,妈妈。

福雷斯·甘:我非常清楚记得第一次乘校车去上学。

校车司机:你上不上车?

福雷斯·甘:妈妈说不要上陌生人的车子。

校车司机:这是校车。

福雷斯·甘:我是福雷斯——福雷斯·甘。

校车司机:我是多萝西·哈里斯。

福雷斯·甘:嗯,现在我们不是陌生人了。

男孩一:这位子有人了。

男孩二:有人了。

男孩三:你不准坐这儿。

福雷斯·甘:你知道,孩子记事实在奇怪,我不记得我的出生,我不记得我的第一份圣诞礼物,我也不记得我第一次去野餐,但我却记得,我第一次听到最甜的声音,在整个世界上。

女孩:你愿意的话可以坐这儿。

福雷斯·甘:我一生再没见过如此美丽的人,她就像一位天使。

女孩:你想坐还是不想坐?你的腿怎么啦?

福雷斯·甘:没什么,谢谢你,我的腿好得很。

福雷斯·甘:我和她并排坐在校车里,去学校途中我们一直在说话,当时我的背像个问号那么弯,除了妈妈,没有人和我说话,或问我问题,你是不是有点傻?妈妈说,"做傻事的才是傻瓜"。

女孩:我叫珍妮。

福雷斯·甘:我叫福雷斯——福雷斯·甘。

福雷斯·甘:由那天开始,我们经常在一起,珍妮和我形影不离,她教我怎么爬树。"快,福雷斯,你能做到。"我教她怎么摇摆,"一个好小……"她帮我学怎么认字,我教她怎么倒挂。有时,我们就那么坐着,等星星出来。"妈妈会担心我的。"

女孩:再待一会儿。

福雷斯·甘:不知为什么,珍妮从来不爱回家。

福雷斯·甘：好吧，珍妮，我再待一会儿。

福雷斯·甘：她是我最好的朋友，我唯一的朋友，妈妈总是对我说，每天都会有奇迹，有些人并不同意，但这是真的。

注释

1. recollect[ˌrekəˈlekt] *v.* 回忆；想起

2. fine and dandy: 令人满意的；十全十美的

3. stupid is as stupid does: 做傻事的才是傻瓜

4. like peas and carrots: 形影不离

5. dangle[ˈdæŋg(ə)l] *vi.* 摇晃地悬挂着

6. swing[swiŋ] *vi.* 摇摆；悬挂

对白二

原文

8 Recruited in the Army

Forest: Hello. I'm Forrest. Forrest Gump.

Army Bus Driver: Nobody gives a horse's shit who you are, pus ball! You're not even a lowlife, scum-sucking maggot! Get your maggoty ass on the bus! You're in the army now!

Recruit 1: Seat's taken.

Recruit 2: Taken.

Forrest: At first it seemed like I made a mistake. It was only my induction day, and I was getting **yelled at.**

Bubba: Sit down if you want to.

Forrest: I didn't know who I might meet or what they might ask.

Bubba: You ever been on a real **shrimp boat**?

Forrest: No.

Bubba: But I been on a real big boat. I'm talking about a shrimp catching boat. I been working on shrimp boats all my life. I started out on my uncle's boat when I was about maybe 9. I was just looking into buying my own boat and got drafted. My given name is Benjamin Buford Blue. People call me Bubba, just like one of them old red neck boys. Can you believe that?

Forrest: My name's Forrest Gump. People call me Forrest Gump. So Bubba was from Bayou La Batre, Alabama, and his mama cooked shrimp. And her mama before her cooked shrimp and her mama before her mama cooked shrimp, too. Bubba's family knew everything, there was to know about the shrimping business.

Bubba: I know everything there is to know about the shrimping business. I'm going into the shrimping business for myself, after I get out of the army.

Forrest: OK.

Drill Sergeant: Gump! What's your **sole purpose** in this army?

Forrest: To do whatever you tell me, Drill Sergeant!

Drill Sergeant: God damn it, Gump, you're a goddamn genius. That's the most outstanding answer I've ever heard. You must have a goddamn IQ of 160. You are goddamn gifted, **Private** Gump. Listen up, people!

Forest: Now for some reason, I fit in the army, **like one of them round pegs**. It's not really hard. You just make your bed neat, remember to stand up straight, and always answer every question with "Yes, Drill Sergeant".

Drill Sergeant: Is that clear?

Forest: Yes, Drill Sergeant!

译文

8 应征入伍

福雷斯·甘:你好。我是福雷斯,福雷斯·甘。

部队司机:根本没人会关心你叫什么名字,脓包!你还不如低等生物,吃屎的虮!你赶快坐到座位上!你现在到部队了!

新兵一:有人坐了。

新兵二:有人。

福雷斯·甘:开始我觉得我犯了个错误,入伍第一天,我就给骂得狗血喷头。

布巴:你愿意的话可以坐下。

福雷斯·甘:我不知我会遇到谁,或他们会问我什么。

布巴:你有没有乘过真正的捕虾船?

福雷斯·甘:没有。

布巴:可我乘过一条真正的大捕虾船,我指的是一种专门捕虾的船,我一直都在捕虾船上干活,开始是我叔叔的船,那时我大概9岁,我刚在考虑自己去买一条船,然后就应征入伍了。我的名字叫本杰明·巴弗·布鲁。人们都管我叫布巴,好像个乡下佬的名字,很难以置信吧?

福雷斯·甘:我叫福雷斯·甘,人们都管我叫福雷斯·甘。布巴来自亚拉巴州拉巴特湾,他的妈妈是煮虾的,他的妈妈的妈妈也是煮虾的,还有他的妈妈的妈妈的妈妈也是煮虾的。布巴家的人了解所有跟捕虾有关的事情。

布巴：我知道所有跟捕虾有关的事情，我自己也准备去捕虾，等我退伍之后。

福雷斯·甘：好的。

教官：阿甘！你到部队来干什么？

福雷斯·甘：干你叫我干的事，教官！

教官：他妈的，阿甘，你他妈的真是个天才。这是我听过的最了不起的回答，你他妈的智商一定有160，你他妈的真有天赋，列兵阿甘。大家都听着！

福雷斯·甘：不知什么原因，我很适合当兵，就像一对插销那么适合。其实一点都不苦，你只需把你的床铺好，记着要站得笔直，不管回答什么问题都说“是，教官”。

教官：听清楚没有？

福雷斯·甘：是，教官！

注释

1. yell at: 对……吼叫
2. shrimp boat: 捕虾船
3. sole purpose: 唯一目的
4. private[ˈpraivət] *n.* 列兵；二等兵
5. like one of them round pegs: 像一对插销那么适合

对白三

原文

9 President Nixon and the Watergate Scandal

Anchorman: The U.S. Ping-Pong team met with President Nixon today...

Forrest: Wouldn't you know it? A few months later, they invited me and the Ping-Pong team to visit the White House. So I went again. And I met the President of the United States again. Only this time, they didn't get us rooms in a real fancy hotel.

President Nixon: Are you enjoying yourself in our nation's capital, young man?

Forrest: Yes, sir.

President Nixon: Well, where are you staying?

Forrest: It's called the Hotel Ebbott.

President Nixon: Oh, no, no, no. I know a much nicer hotel. It's brand-new. Very modern. I'll have my people take care of it.

Security Guard: Security. Frank Wills.

Forrest: Yeah. Sir, you might want to send a **maintenance man** over to that office **across the way**. The lights are off and they must be looking for a **fuse box**, 'cause them flashlights, they're keeping me awake.

Security Guard: OK, sir. I'll check it out.

Forrest: Thank you. Good night.

President Nixon: Therefore, I shall **resign the presidency effective at noon tomorrow**. Vice President Ford will **be sworn in** as President at that hour in this office.

Officer: Forrest Gump.

Forrest: Yes, sir!

Officer: As you were. I have your **discharge papers**. Service is up, son.

Forrest: Does this mean I can't play Ping-Pong no more?

Officer: For the army, it does.

Forrest: And just like that, my service in the United States Army was over. So I went home.

译文

9 尼克松总统和水门丑闻

主持人:美国乒乓球队今天与尼克松总统见面……

福雷斯·甘:你知道吧?几个月后他们邀请我和乒乓球队去白宫,所以我去了。并且第二次见到了合众国的总统。不过这次他们没有给我们安排房间。

尼克松总统:你在我们的首都玩得愉快吗,年轻人?

福雷斯·甘:是的,先生。

尼克松总统:很好,你住在哪儿?

福雷斯·甘:埃伯特酒店。

尼克松总统:啊,不,不。我知道有家更好的酒店,是新开张的水门酒店,设备很先进。我会叫人安排你入住的。

保安:安全。

福雷斯·甘:是,先生,你能不能叫人派维修人员去对面办公室看看,里面灯不亮,他们大概正在找保险丝盒,因为他们打着手电,把我都照醒了。

保安:好的,先生。我去查一下。

福雷斯·甘:谢谢,晚安。

尼克松总统:因此,我将辞去总统职位,从明天中午起生效。明天此时在这间办公室,福特副总统,将宣誓就任总统。

官员:福雷斯·甘。

福雷斯·甘：是，长官！

官员：我收到你的退役批文，根据条例服役期结束了，孩子。

福雷斯·甘：是不是说我不能再打乒乓球了？

官员：对军队来说，是的。

福雷斯·甘：就这样，我在合众国军队的生活结束了。所以我回家了。

（根据大家论坛影视英语网资料整理）

注释

1. maintenance man: 维修人员
2. across the way: 街对面；路对面
3. fuse box: 保险丝盒
4. resign the presidency: 辞去总统职位
5. effective at noon tomorrow: 明天中午起生效
6. be sworn in: 发誓
7. discharge papers: 退役批文

影片四：《加勒比海盗1》(*Pirates of the Caribbean I*, 2003)

赏析

加勒比海盗(Pirates of the Caribbean)，早在20世纪60年代，最先出现在美国加州的迪士尼乐园。作为其中一个景点，游客可以乘坐在水上漂流的机动船，进入室内看不同的布景。电影则是根据这个景点而制作的。之后，以此为名拍摄了一系列电影作品。

放浪不羁亦正亦邪的杰克·史派罗(约翰尼·德普 Johnny Depp饰)，是活跃在加勒比海上的年轻海盗，拥有令人闻风丧胆的“黑珍珠号”海盗船。对他来说，最惬意的生活就是驾驶着“黑珍珠”在加勒比海上游荡，自由自在地打劫过往船只。杰克是彻彻底底的自由派，与威尔的爱情至上形成了鲜明的对比。影片的最大矛盾冲突就在于爱情和自由的冲突，两者的冲突贯穿于整部影片，体现在每一个角落。影片的一开始，威尔跟伊丽莎白的爱情就一直纠结着我们，本来没有任何悬念的恋爱史却偏偏被弄得如此曲折。杰克最后——或者说自始至终都有选择的自由，他的小船、他的藏宝图以及他放荡不羁的个性都是他自由的表现。影片之所以波折，不是因为杰克也不是因为威尔，而是因为伊丽莎白的内心矛盾，也就是她心中对爱情和自由的选择的矛盾。但影片的结局却不适合让伊丽莎白跟杰克在一起，因为这需要以牺牲杰克的自由为代价，海盗没了自由那还叫什么海盗？

现实生活中爱情和自由理应是可以兼得的，但影片却将两者完完全全地对立起来。伊丽莎白的罗盘指向杰克，其实是她心中对自由的追求高于对爱情的渴望，这也是她与威尔的感情出现危机的时候。而影片的结局，威尔与伊丽莎白得到了盼望已久的爱情，却失去了自由，以十年一见的代价换来了永恒的爱情，这正是影片主题所在。威尔为给他老爸自由，需要以自己的爱情为代价。同样另一方面，那个喜欢伊丽莎白的将军，当他真正选择爱情的时候也是他生命终结的时候。这样的矛盾影片中无处不在。

"因为地平线一直在那儿"。你想到达那儿，但你永远到达不了。就是那样，遥不可及难以放弃。"约翰尼·德普说看过的一部法国水手写的书中，问及为什么选择当水手一直漂泊时，那个水手如此回答。所以，杰克船长最后的一句话是："现在朝那地平线出发！地平线是自由。"

对白一

原文

10 The Fighting

Jack: Did no one come to save me just because they missed me?

(Everyone looks around. Finally Jack the Monkey raises his hand.)

Jack: Why should I sail with any of you? Four of you have tried to kill me in the past.

(looks at Elizabeth)

Jack: One of you succeeded.

Lord Cutler Beckett: (Jack has a cannon aimed at Beckett) You're mad!

Jack: (grins) Thank goodness for that because if I wasn't, this had probably never work.

Barbossa: There was a time when a **pirate** was free to make his own way in the world. But our time is coming to an end. Our enemies are united; they **vow to** destroy us. The Pirate Lords from the four corners of the Earth must stand together.

Barbossa: (at a pirate gathering) There's not been a gathering like this in our lifetime.

Jack: And I owe them all money.

Lord Cutler Beckett: They know they face **extinction**. All that remains is where they make their final stand.

Tia: What would you do? What would any of you be willing to do? Would you brave the weird and haunted shores at world's end to fetch back wit' ye Jack?

Elizabeth: It would never have worked out between us.

Jack: Keep telling yourself that, darling.

Will: Will you marry me?

Elizabeth: (fighting a battle) I don't think now's the best time!

Will : Now may be the only time! I love you. I made my choice. What's yours?

Lord Cutler Beckett: You fight, and all of you will die.

(Giselle and Scarlett are fighting)

Jack: Ladies! Will you please shut it? Listen to me. Yes, I lied to you. No, I don't love you. Of course it makes you look fat. I've never been to Brussels. It is pronounced "**egregious**". By the way, no, I've never met Pizzaro but I love his pies. And all of this pales to utter insignificance **in light of** the fact that my ship is once again gone. Savvy?

(Giselle slaps Jack, Scarlett slaps Jack)

Captain Sao Feng: Welcome to Singapore.

Barbossa: (Captain Barbossa and Captain Jack Sparrow are both trying to give orders) What are you doing?

Jack: What are you doing?

Barbossa: No, what are you doing?

Jack: What are you doing?

Barbossa: No, what are you doing?

Jack: What are you doing? Hmm. Captain gives orders on the ship.

Barbossa: The Captain of this ship is **giving orders**!

Jack: (thinking) My ship, makes me captain!

Barbossa: They be my charts!

Jack: That makes you Chart-man!

Pintel: Stow it! The both of you! That's an order! Understand!

(they glare at him)

Pintel: Sorry, I just thought that with the Captain issue in doubt I'd just throw in my name for consideration. Sorry.

Young Elizabeth: Yo-ho, yo-ho, a pirate's life for me.

Jack: (to Beckett) Who am I?

(Beckett, who doesn't answer, looks confused)

Jack Sparrow: (rather hurt) I'm Captain Jack Sparrow.

Captain Sao Feng: Jack Sparrow, you have paid me a great insult.

Jack: That doesn't sound like me.

(Sao Feng punches Jack in the nose)

Barbossa: Everything we've ever done has lead to this.

Jack: My hands are clean of this.

Jack: We'll have to fight... to run away!

Elizabeth: Will you ever forgive me?

Jack: No.

Davy Jones: Do you feel dead?

Jack: You have no idea.

Barbossa: The only way for a pirate to make a living these days is by betraying other pirates.

Davy Jones: Are you prepared for what's next?

Jack: Should he be doing that?

(about Monkey Jack running around below decks)

Jack: I promise you will not be disappointed. Count on that!

(pointing his gun at Davy Jones crew)

Jack: (as he sees rock - like crabs) Now we're being followed by rocks. Never heard that before. You take the shore party; I'll stay with my ship.

Elizabeth: (watching a huge fight among the pirates)This is madness!

Jack: This is politics! Will you tell me something? Have you come because you need my help to save a certain **distressing damsel**? Er... rather damsel in distress? Either one. And that was without a single drop of rum!

译文

10 争斗

杰克:难道在你们这些人当中,没有一个只是因为想念我才救我的吗?

(每一个人都互相看了看,最后只有那只同样叫杰克的猴子举起了它的手)

杰克:我为什么应该告诉你们啊?要知道你们四个有一个算一个,过去都曾想过要杀我。

(看着伊丽莎白)

杰克:其中有一个还成功了。

卡特勒·贝凯特大人:(看到杰克将大炮对准了他)你疯了!

杰克:(咧着嘴一笑)感谢老天爷,因为如果我没有疯,可能永远都不会让你体验到被炮轰的恐惧。

巴伯萨:海盗们曾经以他们自己的方式在这个世界上存活着,但是我们的时代即将终结,我们的敌人团结在了一起,他们想要摧毁我们。来自于地球东南西北四个方向的海盗大佬们必须暂时将成见放在一边,共同战斗。

巴伯萨:(看着一名海盗在收钱)在我有生之年,从没看过这种收钱方式。

杰克:可能是因为我欠他们每一个人钱。

卡特勒·贝凯特大人:他们知道自己即将被消灭,所以他们要放手一搏。

蒂娅:你们想做什么?你们愿意做什么?你们足够勇敢到会去充满着神秘与恐惧、位于世界的另一边的海岸,把杰克接回来吗?

伊丽莎白:咱们两个不会有结果的。

杰克:记得时刻提醒自己,亲爱的。

威尔:你会嫁给我吗?

伊丽莎白:(打斗中)我认为现在不是说这个的时候!

威尔:现在可能是我唯一的机会!我爱你!我做出了我的选择,那么你的呢?

卡特勒·贝凯特大人:你们一旦参加战斗,就都得死。

(吉塞尔和斯嘉丽正在打架)

杰克:女士们!请停一下好吗?听我说,是的,我对你们撒谎了,是的,我不爱你们。当然,你身上的这件衣服让你看起来很肥。我从没去过布鲁塞尔,这些话听起来可能有点"惊人"。顺便再说一句,是的,我从没见过披萨罗,但我喜欢以他的名字命名的馅饼。然而现在说这一切都变得苍白无力且没什么意义了,因为事实上,我的船又丢了,了解了吗?

(吉塞尔扇了杰克一巴掌,斯嘉丽也扇了杰克一巴掌)

萧峰船长:欢迎来到新加坡。

巴伯萨:(杰克和巴伯萨都想当船长下达命令)你干什么呢?

杰克:你干什么呢?

巴伯萨:不,你干什么呢?

杰克:你干什么呢?

巴伯萨:不,你干什么呢?

杰克:你干什么呢?嗯,船长有权在船上下达命令。

巴伯萨:只有这艘船上的船长才有权下达命令!

杰克:(想了一下)我的船,当然我是船长!

巴伯萨:但这些航海图是属于我的。

杰克:那只会让你成为一个画图表的人。

皮泰尔:别吵了,你们两个,这是命令!明白?

(他们对他怒目而视)

皮泰尔:对不起,我只是想既然拿不准谁来当这个船长,那么是不是可以把我的名字考虑进去,对不起。

小时候的伊丽莎白:哟,哟,我的海盗人生。

杰克:(对卡特勒·贝凯特说)我是谁?

(卡特勒·贝凯特没有回答,但是看起来很困惑)

杰克:(有点受伤的表情)我是杰克·斯派洛船长。

萧峰船长:杰克·斯派洛,你给了我极大的侮辱。

杰克:你口中那个人好像不是我。

(萧峰打中了杰克的鼻子)

巴伯萨:我们做过的每一件事导致了这样的结果。

杰克:这可不是我偷的。我们不得不反抗……然后逃跑!

伊丽莎白:你会原谅我吗?

杰克:不会。

戴维·琼斯:你感觉到死亡了吗?

杰克:你肯定感觉不到。

巴伯萨:这些日子以来,海盗唯一能够采用的生存方式,就是背叛其他海盗。

戴维·琼斯:你准备好做下一个了吗?

杰克:它应该那么做吗?

(指猴子杰克在甲板上乱窜)

杰克:我保证你们不会失望的。看看我手中是什么!

(将他的枪对准了戴维·琼斯的船员)

杰克:(看到像岩石一样坚硬的螃蟹腿)现在我们正被一群石头跟着,真是闻所未闻。你参加你的海岸派对,我要和我的船待在一起。

伊丽莎白:(看着海盗们混战在了一起)这太疯狂了!

杰克:这就是政治!你是不是要告诉我什么事?你来是因为需要我的帮助,去拯救一位非常悲伤的少女?呃……或者是正在遭遇危险的少女?随便了。这里一滴朗姆酒都没有了!

注释

1. pirate['pairit] *n.* 海盗
2. vow to: 许愿;向某人立誓
3. extinction[ik'stiŋkʃən] *n.* 消失;消灭
4. egregious[i'gri:dʒəs] *adj.* 惊人的;过分的
5. in light of: 根据;鉴于
6. giving orders: 发出命令;下命令
7. distressing damsel: 痛苦的、正在遭遇危险的少女

对白二

原文

11 The Kidnapping

(Norrington approaches Elizabeth who is standing alone on the top of the **castle** looking over the sea.)

Norrington: May I have a moment? You look lovely, Elizabeth. I **apologize** if I seem forward, but I must speak my mind. This promotion throws me into sharp relief that I have not yet achieved a rear- riage to a fine woman. You have become a fine woman, Elizabeth.

Elizabeth: I can't **breathe**.

Norrington: Yes, I'm a bit nervous myself. And then they made me their chief. Elizabeth? Elizabeth! My God.

Subordinate: The rocks! Sir, it's a miracle. She missed them.

Jack: Will you be saving her?

Fat Soldier: I can't swim.

Jack: Pride of the King's Navy, you are. Do not lose these.

Fat Soldier: What was that? I got her! She's not breathing!

Jack: Move!

Fat Soldier: I never would have thought of that.

Jack: Clearly you've never been to Singapore. Where did you get that?

Norrington: On your feet.

Goy. Swann: Elizabeth! Are you all right?

Elizabeth: Yes, I'm fine.

Goy. Swann: Shoot him.

Elizabeth: Father.

Goy. Swann: What?

Elizabeth: **Commodore**, do you really intend to kill my rescuer?

Norrington: I believe thanks are in order. Had brush with the East India Trading Company, did we, pirate?

Goy. Swann: Hang him.

Norrington: Keep your guns on him, men. Gillette, fetch some irons. Well, well. Jack Spar-row, isn't it?

Jack: Captain Jack Sparrow, if you please, sir.

Norrington: Well, I don't see your ship, Captain.

Jack: I'm in the market, as it were.

Thin Soldier: He said he'd come to **commandeer** one.

Fat Soldier: Told you he was telling the truth. These are his, sir.

Norrington: No additional shot or powder. A **compass** that doesn't point north. And I have expected it to be made of wood. You are without doubt the worst pirate I've ever heard of.

Jack: But you have heard of me.

Elizabeth: Commodore, I really must protest. Carefully, Lieutenant. Pirate or not, this man saved my life.

Norrington: One good deed is not enough to **redeem** a man of a lifetime of wickedness.

Jack: Though it seems enough to condemn him.

Norrington: Indeed.

Jack: Finally.

(Throws his frons around Elizabeth's neck.)

Goy. Swnn: No. No! Don't shoot!

Jack: I knew you'd warm up to me. Commodore Norrington, my effects, please. And my hat. Commodore. It is Elizabeth, isn't it?

Elizabeth: It's Miss Swann.

Jack: Miss Dwaitn, if you'd be so kind. Come, come, dear. We don't have all day. Now if you'll be very kind. Easy on the goods, darling.

Elizabeth: You're despicable.

Jack: Sticks and stones, love. l saved your life. You save mine. We're square. Gentlemen, milady, you will always remember this as the day that you almost caught Captain Jack Sparrow.

译文

11 劫 持

(伊丽莎白独自一人站在城堡最高处,远望着辽阔的大海。这时诺林顿向她走来。)

诺林顿:能和你待会儿吗?你真美,伊丽莎白,我为我的鲁莽向你道歉,但我必须说出我的想法。这次晋升让我觉得前所未有的轻松。我该娶个好姑娘。你已经长成大姑娘了,伊丽莎白。

伊丽莎白:我喘不过气来了。

诺林顿:是的,我自己也有点紧张。他们还让我担任船长。伊丽莎白?伊丽莎白!我的上帝!

部下:礁石!先生,她居然没撞到礁石,真是奇迹!

杰克:你会去救她吗?

胖士兵:我不会游泳。

杰克:你可是皇家海军的精英!别弄丢了。

胖士兵:那是什么?我抓到她了。她没呼吸了。

杰克:走开!

胖士兵:我永远也想不到会发生这样的事情。

杰克:很明显,你没去过新加坡。这东西哪儿来的?

诺林顿:站起来。

斯旺总督:伊丽莎白,你还好吗?

伊丽莎白:是的,我很好。

斯旺总督:把他毙了!

伊丽莎白:父亲!

斯旺总督:怎么了?

伊丽莎白:准将,你真想杀了我的救命恩人吗?

诺林顿:我想我们应该感谢你。你和东印度公司打过交道,是吗,海盗?

斯旺总督:绞死他。

诺林顿:把枪瞄准他,伙计们。吉勒特,拿镣铐来。好,好,杰克·斯帕罗,是吗?

杰克:请叫我杰克。斯帕罗船长,如果你愿意的话,先生。

诺林顿:好吧,我怎么没看见你的船,"船长"。

杰克:可以说我正是来买船的。

瘦士兵:他说他是来抢船的。

胖士兵:我告诉过你,他说的是实话。这些是他的,先生。

诺林顿:没有备用枪支和弹药,一个指不到北的指南针,我还以为是木头做的。毫无疑问,你是我听说过的最差劲的海盗。

杰克:但你应该听说过我。

伊丽莎白:准将,我抗议。小心点,上尉。不管这个人是不是海盗,他救了我的命。

诺林顿:一件善举并不能抵偿一个人一辈子犯下的罪恶。

杰克:看起来善举让人受惩罚。

诺林顿:的确。

杰克:那只好如此了!

(他用手铐围住了伊丽莎白的脖子。)

斯旺总督:不,不,不要开枪!

杰克:我知道你喜欢海盗,诺林顿准将,请把我的东西,还有我的帽子还给我,准将!伊丽莎白,是吗?

伊丽莎白:是斯旺小姐。

杰克:斯旺小姐,如果你配合,我们不会在一起待很久的。只要你表现好。现在,别太紧张,亲爱的。

伊丽莎白:你真卑鄙。

杰克:棍棒和石头,亲爱的。我救了你,你又救了我,我们扯平了。先生们,女士们,你们会永远记得今天,因为你们差点捉住了杰克·斯帕罗船长。

(根据沪江英语网资料整理)

注释:

1. castle ['kæsl] *n.* 城堡
2. apologize [ə'pɔlədʒaiz] *v.* 道歉;认错
3. breathe [briθ] *v.* 呼吸;呼气

4. commodore['kɔmə'dɔr] *n.* 海军准将
5. commandeer[ˌkɔmən'dir] *vt.* 霸占；没收
6. compass['kʌmpəs] *n.* 指南针；罗盘
7. redeem[ri'dim] *vt.* 买回；赎回

影片五：《当幸福来敲门》(*The Pursuit of Happyness*, 2006)

赏析

美国电影《当幸福来敲门》(*The Pursuit of Happyness*)取材真实故事。故事的主角就是当今美国黑人投资专家克里斯·加德纳(Chris Gardner)(威尔·史密斯 Will Smith饰)。该片成功诠释出一位濒临破产、老婆离家的落魄业务员；讲述了一位如何刻苦耐劳地善尽单亲责任，奋发向上成为股票经纪人，最后成为知名的金融投资家的励志故事。该片获得2006年奥斯卡最佳男主角提名。

有趣的是，片中的小孩，其实正是威尔·史密斯现实生活中的儿子，给喜欢他的影迷带来了很大的看点。而片名中Happyness的拼写错误是别具匠心的，它暗指了片中一个意味深长的场景。影片中，威尔·史密斯看到墙上涂鸦中一个单词拼写错误，他说了这句话：There is no y in happiness, There is i.

有多少个美国人，就有多少个美国梦。Happiness。杰弗逊在美国的《独立宣言》上十三次提到这个词语。在那个时刻，这位伟大的美国开国元勋相信这是上帝指引他的梦想，于是他们拿起刀枪，不再高唱《上帝保佑女王》。生活是苦的，眼泪是咸的。卖掉那些白色的"时光机器"不足以维持一个很好的生活，却足以引起嬉皮士少女和精神病患者的目光。全球化把人缩小，电影又把人放大。幸福轻轻地敲门，而不幸和灾难却把门粗暴地踹开。于是我们看到了，平时彬彬有礼、看到幼儿园外墙上有fuck涂鸦都无法容忍的父亲，却被生活逼得像条疯狗：不付出租车费，为了十四美元和好友翻脸，还蛮横无理插队暴粗口。在社会底层挣扎太久，生存的本能无意中便远离了美德。活着，真是很辛苦的事情，却总有自己坚持的理由。就像片中的威尔·史密斯不停地对孩子和妻子说，我们一定会好起来，我们一定能够好起来的。在打篮球的时候，他还说："孩子，你一定要保护自己的梦想。"那一刻，我们都能看到，幸福的家庭和孩子才是他真正的信仰——没有繁文缛节的文艺腔，只有一个父爱温暖的硕硕冬阳。

对白一

原文

12 The Stockbroker

Chris: Man, I got two questions for you: What do you do? And how do you do it?

Man: I'm a **stockbroker**.

Chris: Stockbroker. Oh, goodness. Had to go to college to be a stockbroker, huh?

Man: You don't have to. Have to be good with numbers and good with people. That's it.

Chris: Hey, you take care. I'll let you **hang on to** my car for the weekend. But I need it back for Monday.

Man: **Feed the meter**.

Chris: I still remember that moment. They all looked so damn happy to me. Why couldn't I look like that?

Chris: I'm gonna try to get home by 6. I'm gonna stop by a **brokerage firm** after work.

Linda: For what?

Chris: I wanna see about a job there.

Linda: Yeah? What job?

Chris: You know, when I... When I was a kid, I could go through a math book in a week. So I'm gonna go see about what job they got down there.

Linda: What job?

Chris: Stockbroker.

Linda: Stockbroker?

Chris: Yeah.

Linda: Not an astronaut?

Chris: Don't talk to me like that, Linda. I'm gonna go down and see about this, and I'm gonna do it during the day.

Linda: You should probably do your sales calls.

Chris: I don't need you to tell me about my sales calls, Linda. I got three of them before the damn office is even open.

Linda: Do you remember that rent is due next week? Probably not. We're already two months behind. Next week we'll owe three months. I've been **pulling double shifts** for four months now, Chris. Just sell what's in your contract. Get us out of that business.

Chris: Linda that is what I am trying to do. This is what I'm trying to do for my family...for you and for Christopher.

Linda: What's the matter with you?

Chris: Linda. Linda. Linda. Linda!

译文

12 股票经纪人

克里斯:哇,老兄,请教你两个问题:你是干什么的? 你是怎么干的?

男人:我是股票经纪人。

克里斯:股票经纪人,哦,天哪。得上大学才能做股票经纪人,对吧?

男人:不用,只需要精通数字,会做人处世。就这么简单。

克里斯:嘿,保重。周末我这车就借你了,不过星期一得还我哦。

男人:付停车费去吧。

克里斯:我还记得那一刻,他们全都看起来超幸福的样子,为什么我不能也满脸幸福?

克里斯:我尽量在六点前回来,下班后要去一下证券行。

琳达:干吗?

克里斯:看看那里有没有工作。

琳达:哦,什么样的工作?

克里斯:你知道,我……我小时候,一星期就能把算数课本念完。所以我想去看看,有什么工作可做。

琳达:什么工作?

克里斯:股票经纪人。

琳达:股票经纪人?

克里斯:嗯。

琳达:不是宇航员?

克里斯:别用这种口气对我说话,琳达。我去看看情况,利用白天的时间。

琳达:嗯,你该打电话推销才对。

克里斯:还要你来告诉我,琳达,在办公室开门前,我就打了三通电话了。

琳达:还记得下星期就要付房租吗? 大概不记得了吧? 我们已经两个月没付了。下星期就欠三个月了,我已经上双份班四个月了!你就赶快把合约规定的数额卖完,咱们好脱身吧。

克里斯:琳达,我不是正努力那么做嘛! 努力来改善这个家,为你,为儿子。

琳达:你到底是怎么了?

克里斯:琳达。琳达。琳达。琳达!

注释

1. stockbroker['stɔk,brokə] *n.* (金融)股票经纪人
2. hang on to: 紧紧抓住;紧握
3. feed the meter: 付停车费
4. brokerage firm: 证券行;经济商行
5. pulling double shifts: 上双份班

对白二

原文

13 The Interview

Man: First in your class in school? High school?

Chris: Yes, sir.

Man: How many in the class?

Chris: Twelve. It was a small town.

Man: I'll say.

Chris: But I was also first in my **radar class**...in the Navy, and that was a class of 20. Can I say something? I'm the type of person...if you ask me a question, and I don't know the answer...I'm gonna tell you that I don't know. But I bet you what. I know how to find the answer, and I will find the answer. Is that **fair enough**?

Man: Chris. What would you say if a guy walked in for an interview......without a shirt on...and I hired him? What would you say?

Chris: He must've had on some really nice pants.

Twistle: Chris, I don't know how you did it dressed as a **garbage man**...but you **pulled it off**.

Chris: Thank you, Mr. Twistle.

译文

13 面 试

男人:克里斯,你在班上是第一名？高中？

克里斯：是的，先生。

男人：班上一共多少人？

克里斯：十二人，那是个小镇。

男人：我就说嘛。

克里斯：我在海军服役时是雷达班的第一名，那个班里有二十人。我能说几句吗？呃……我是这样的人，如果你问的问题我不知道答案，我会直接告诉你"我不知道"。但我向你保证，我知道如何寻找答案，而且我一定会找出答案的。这样可以吗？

男人：克里斯，如果有个人连衬衫都没穿，就跑来参加面试，你会怎么想？如果我最后还雇了这个人，你会怎么想？

克里斯：那他穿的裤子一定十分考究。

特维斯特：克里斯，我难以理解你穿成这样来面试，但是你刚才的表现很不错。

克里斯：谢谢，特维斯特先生。

注释

1. radar class: 雷达班
2. fair enough: 有道理；说得好
3. garbage man: 收垃圾的人
4. pulled it off: 圆满完成

对白三

原文

14 The Football Game

Chris: Wow, this is...This is the way to watch a football game here. Thank you very much for this, really.

Mr. Ribbon: Hey, it's my pleasure, Chris.

Chris: And, Mr. Ribbon, I also wanna thank you for giving me the opportunity to discuss the **asset management capabilities** of Dean Witter which we believe to **be far superior** to anything you got going over at Morgan Stanley. Really, I think you're gonna be **blown away**. **Point blank**, Dean Witter needs to be managing your **retirement portfolio**.

Mr. Ribbon: You know, I didn't have any notion that you were new there, I like you, but there's not a chance I'm gonna let you direct our fund. That's just not gonna happen anytime soon, buddy. So, you know, come on, relax. Let's play the game. Go, go, go! Yes!

Christopher: Yes! Yeah!

Jeff: Here you go.

Chris: All right. I've had a few ideas already, absolutely.

Man 3: Chris, I'll talk to you later. Nice to meet you, Chris. Give me a call.

Chris: I'm gonna give you a call. Yes, absolutely. Thank you.

Christopher: Bye.

Tim: Bye, Christopher.

Chris: After four months, we had sold all our **scanners**. It seemed we were making it. What's the fastest animal in the world?

Christopher: Jackrabbit.

Chris: It seemed we were doing good. Till one day...that day...that letter brought me back to earth.

译文

14 球 赛

克里斯：哇，这……呃……这才叫看球。真的谢谢您。

瑞本先生：别客气，克里斯。

克里斯：瑞本先生，还要感谢您给我机会向您介绍我们公司在资产管理方面的能力。我相信我们的能力会超过摩根史坦利投资公司，真的，您一定会很惊讶。坦白说，添惠公司该替您管理退休金的投资运用。

瑞本先生：我不知道你是那里的新员工。我很欣赏你，但是我绝不可能叫你来管理我们的资金。至少近期之内不可能，老兄。所以……轻松点。看球吧！快，快！好！

克里斯多夫：好呀！

杰夫：给你(名片)。

克里斯：好的。我已经想好几个方案了。

路人三：克里斯，回头和你再聊。很高兴认识你，给我电话。

克里斯：我一定会给你打电话的。当然，谢谢。

克里斯多夫：拜拜。

提姆：再见，克里斯多夫。

克里斯：四个月后，我们卖掉了所有的扫描仪，看起来我们正在向成功迈进。世界上最快的动物是什么？

克里斯多夫：长耳兔！

克里斯：看起来我们做得不错，直到有一天……那天……一封信又把我带回了现实。

注释

1. asset management capabilities: 资产管理能力
2. be far superior: 非常优秀
3. blown away: 吹走；驱散。此处指惊讶
4. point blank: 坦白说
5. retirement portfolio: 休金的投资运用
6. scanner['skænə] *n.* 扫描仪

对白四

原文

15 Demanding Repayment of the Loan

Chris: This part of my life is called "Paying Taxes". If you didn't pay them, the government could **stick their hands into your bank account**... and take your money.

Christopher: Dad.

Chris: No warning. Nothing. It can't be too late. That's my money. How is somebody just gonna just take my money? I was... I was...Listen, I... That's all the money that I have. You cannot go into my bank acc... No...

Chris: It was the 25th of September. I remember that day. Because that's the day that I found out...there was only 21 dollars and 33 cents left in my bank account. **I was broke**.

Chris: Dressed yet?

Christopher: No.

Ralph: Chris! Chris! Don't **jerk me around**, okay, Chris?

Chris: I'm not jerking you around, Ralph, all right? I'm gonna get it.

Ralph: I need that money now, not later.

Chris: When I get it, you get it, Ralph.

Ralph: Now!

Wayne: Hey, what's happening, man?

Chris: Wayne, I need to get that $ 14 from you.

Wayne: I thought I didn't owe you that now.

Chris: What? Why?

Wayne: Why what?

Chris: Why would you think you don't **owe** me my money?

Wayne: I helped you move.

Chris: You drove me two blocks, Wayne. That's 200 yards. It's been four months, Wayne.

Wayne: I have no money.

Chris: I need my money. I need my money. I need my money right now.

Wayne: I don't have it, man. I'm sorry.

Chris: Go get my money. Wayne, get my mo...

Wayne: I really don't, man. It's $ 14.

Chris: It's my $ 14! Go get my money!

Wayne: All of this for $ 14.

Chris: Get my money, Wayne.

译文

15 讨 债

克里斯：我人生的这部分叫作"付税"。如果你不付，政府就会把手伸向你的银行户头，然后强行拿走你的钱。

克里斯多夫：爸爸。

克里斯：事先没有任何警告。什么都没有。不会太迟的，那是我的钱。怎么能就这么拿走我的钱呢？我……我……听着，我……那是我全部积蓄。你们不能……从我账……不……

克里斯：那天是9月25日。我记得那天。因为就在那天我发现……我的银行账户只剩下21.33美元。我没钱了。

克里斯：穿好衣服了吗？

克里斯多夫：没呢。

拉尔夫：克里斯！克里斯！别耍我，好吗，克里斯？

克里斯：我没有，拉尔夫。我会给你，会付钱给你的。

拉尔夫：我要房费，现在就要！不是以后！

克里斯：我有了钱马上就付给你，拉尔夫。

拉尔夫：我现在就要！

韦恩：嘿，怎么了？

克里斯：韦恩，你得还我那十四块了。

韦恩：我以为不欠你钱了。

克里斯：什么？为什么？

韦恩：什么为什么？

克里斯：为什么你觉得不欠我钱了？

韦恩:不是帮你搬家了吗?

克里斯:你开车送了我两个街区,韦恩。也就两百码。都四个月了,韦恩。我需要那钱,我要我的钱,现在就要!

韦恩:我没有钱。

克里斯:把钱还我!把钱给我……

韦恩:我没有。对不起。

克里斯:给我钱,韦恩,给我钱……

韦恩:我真的没有,老兄,才十四块!

克里斯:那是我的十四块!把钱给我!

韦恩:就十四块。

克里斯:给我钱,韦恩!

(根据可可英语网资料整理)

注释

1. stick their hands into your bank account: 手伸向你的银行户头
2. I was broke: 我没钱了
3. jerking sb. around: 耍弄、糊弄某人
4. owe[əu] *vi.* 欠;欠钱

50句美国电影百佳台词

美国电影学会曾在2005年6月21日评选出了"美国电影百佳台词"。入选的100条台词由1500名评委从400条候选台词中选出,它们囊括了电影史上最精妙的双关语、论证语和最机智的回答。《乱世佳人》的克拉克·盖博口中的"坦白说,亲爱的,我一点也不在乎(Frankly, my dear, I don't give a damn.)"荣膺榜首。评选结果的影片涵盖面十分广泛,最早的可以追溯到1927年的第一步有声片《爵士歌手》,最近的则是2002年的《指环王2:双塔骑兵》。其中《乱世佳人》《卡萨布兰卡》《绿野仙踪》等经典老片在榜上占据了不止一席之位,而《卡萨布兰卡》凭借6句经典台词居首位。

据美国娱乐网站"Eonline"报道,这次评选标准包括台词给民族词汇带来的文化影响、是否对所属电影的流传起到作用等。值得一提的是,看似生硬的科幻电影也能出好台词。1977年,第一部《星球大战》中哈里森·福特的那句"愿原力与你同在(May the Force be with you)"成为鼓舞人心的良剂。

施瓦辛格在每部《终结者》最后总要说上一句"我还会回来的(I'll be back)",这句台词成为阿诺留给影迷的最好期待。

1982年的《E.T.外星人》中,学会英语的E.T.说的第一句话"E.T.打电话回家(E.T. phone home)"令人至今听来倍感温馨。

喜剧片方面,1996年的《甜心先生》中,小古巴·古丁常挂在嘴边上的“让我看到钱!(Show me the money!)”,这句话成了工薪阶层的口号。

惊悚片方面,童星海利·乔·奥斯蒙特在1999年的《第六感》中冒出的一句“我看到了死去的人(I see dead people)”确实让影迷害怕了一回。

入选台词中年代最久远的是1927年的《爵士歌手》中艾尔·乔森说的“等一下,等一下,你肯定听到了什么(Wait a minute, wait a minute. You ain't heard nothing yet!)”。

入选台词年代最近的是2002年的《指环王2:双塔奇兵》中格鲁姆常念叨的“我的珍宝(My precious)”。

美国电影学会总监费斯登堡认为,这些经典的电影台词已经成为美国语言文化的一个组成部分,评选的目的是重新激起人们对美国经典电影的热情。以下是从这100句最佳台词中精选部分台词,英汉对照,以飨读者。(以下的序号是台词的排名号)

1. Frankly, my dear, I don't give a damn.坦白说,亲爱的,我一点也不在乎。(《乱世佳人》1939)毫无疑问,即使那些没有看过《乱世佳人》的人,也会对白瑞德给郝思嘉的这句临别之言印象深刻。《乱世佳人》中这句经典的台词在评选中一举夺魁。此外,影片最后,费雯丽在阳光下说出了百折不挠的名句“毕竟,明天又是新的一天。(Tomorrow is a brand new day after all.)”而她另一句同样坚强的话语“上帝给我作证,我永远不会再挨饿。(As God is my witness, I'll never be hungry again.)”也位列其中。

2. I'm going to make him an offer he can't refuse.我会给他点好处,他无法拒绝。(《教父》1972)

3. You don't understand! I could had class. I could been a contender. I could've been somebody, instead of a bum, which is what I am.你根本不能明白!我本可以获得社会地位,我本可以是个竞争者,我本可以是任何有头有脸的人而不是一个毫无价值的游民!(《码头风云》1954)

4. Toto, I've got a feeling we're not in Kansas anymore.托托,我想我们再也回不去堪萨斯了。(《绿野仙踪》1939)朱迪·加兰在《绿野仙踪》中扮演的少女多罗茜对她的小狗托托说的这句话成了后来人们对无法回到鼎盛时期的感叹。

5. Here's looking at you, kid.就看你的了,孩子。(《卡萨布兰卡》1942)

同时,《卡萨布兰卡》里的台词还有几句入选,它们是:“路易斯,我想这是一段美好友谊的开始。(Louis, I think this is the beginning of a beautiful friendship.)”“我们永远怀念巴黎。(We'll always have Paris)”“世界上有那么多的城镇,城镇中有那么多的酒馆,她却走进了我的。(Of all the gin joints in all the towns in all the world, she walks into mine.)”还有一句是褒曼说的“弹吧,山姆。弹那首《时光流逝》。(Play it, Sam. Play *As Time Goes By*)”。

6. Go ahead, make my day.来吧,让我也高兴高兴。(《拨云见日》1983)

7. All right, Mr. De Mille, I'm ready for my close-up.好了,德米勒先生,我已经准备好拍摄我的特写镜头了。(《日落大道》1950)

8. May the Force be with you.愿原力与你同在。(《星球大战》1977)

9. Fasten your seatbelts. It's going to be a bumpy night.系紧你的安全带,这将是一个颠簸

的夜晚。(《彗星美人》1950)

10. You talking to me? 你是在和我说话吗?(《出租车司机》1976)

11. I love the smell of napalm in the morning. 我喜欢闻弥漫在清晨空气中的汽油弹味道。(《现代启示录》1979)

12. Love means never having to say you're sorry.爱就是永远不必说对不起。(《爱情故事》1970)

13. Made it, Ma! Top of the world! 好好去做吧,站在世界之巅!(《歼匪喋血战》1949)

14. I'm as mad as hell, and I'm not going to take this anymore! 我疯狂得如同地狱中的恶魔,我不会再这样继续下去了!(《电视台风云》1976)

15. Louis, I think this is the beginning of a beautiful friendship.路易斯,我认为这是一段美好友谊的开始。(《卡萨布兰卡》1942)

16. Bond. James Bond.邦德,詹姆士·邦德。(《诺博士》1962)

17. There's no place like home.没有一个地方可以和家相提并论。(《绿野仙踪》1939)

18. I am big! It's the pictures that got small.我是巨大的!是这些照片让我变得渺小了。(《日落大道》1950)

19. Show me the money! 让我看到钱!(《甜心先生》1996)

20. Play it, Sam. Play *As Time Goes By*.弹这首,山姆,就弹《时光流逝》。(《卡萨布兰卡》1942)

21. You can't handle the truth! 你不能操纵事实!(《义海雄风》1992)

22. I want to be alone.我想一个人待着。(《大饭店》1932)

23. (1) Land is the only thing in the world worth working for, worth fighting for, worth dying for. Because it's the only thing that lasts.土地是世界上唯一值得你去为之工作、为之战斗、为之牺牲的东西,因为它是唯一永恒的东西。

(2) I wish I could be more like you.我要像你一样就好了。

(3) Whatever comes, I'll love you, just as I do now. Until I die.无论发生什么事,我都会像现在一样爱你,直到永远。

(4) I think it's hard winning a war with words.我认为纸上谈兵没什么作用。

(5) Sir, you're no gentleman. And you miss are no lady.先生,你可真不是个君子;小姐,你也不是什么淑女。

(6) I never give anything without expecting something in return. I always get paid.我做任何事不过是为了有所回报,我总要得到报酬。

(7) In spite of you and me and the whole silly world going to pieces around us, I love you.哪怕是世界末日我都会爱着你。

(8) I love you more than I've ever loved any woman. And I've waited longer for you than I've waited for any woman. 我最爱的女人是你,等得最久的女人也是你。

(9) If I have to lie, steal, cheat or kill, as God as my witness, I'll never be hungry again! 即使让我撒谎、去偷、去骗、去杀人,上帝作证,我再也不要挨饿了。

(10) Now I find myself in a world which for me is worse than death. A world in which there is no place for me.现在我发现自己活在一个比死还要痛苦的世界，一个无我容身之处的世界。

(11) You're throwing away happiness with both hands. And reaching out for something that will never make you happy.你把自己的幸福拱手相让，去追求一些根本不会让你幸福的东西。

(12) Home. I'll go home. And I'll think of some way to get him back. After all, tomorrow is another day.家，我要回家。我要想办法让他回来。不管怎样，明天又是全新的一天。

(《乱世佳人》,1939)

24. I'll have what she's having.我会拥有她所拥有的。(《当哈里遇上萨莉》1989)

25. I'll be back.我会回来的。(《终结者》1984)

26. Today, I consider myself the luckiest man on the face of the earth.现在，我想我是这个世界上最幸运的人。(《扬基的骄傲》1942)

27. (1) Mama always said life was like a box of chocolates. You never know what you're gonna get. 妈妈说生活就像一盒巧克力，你永远都不知道你会得到什么。

(2) Stupid is as stupid does. 蠢人做蠢事。也可理解为傻人有傻福。

(3) Miracles happen every day. 奇迹每天都在发生。

(4) Jenny and I was like peas and carrots.我和珍妮形影不离。

(5) Have you given any thought to your future?你有没有为将来打算过呢？

(6) You just stay away from me please.求你离开我。

(7) If you are ever in trouble, don't try to be brave, just run, just run away. 你若遇上麻烦，不要逞强，你就跑，远远跑开。

(8) It made me look like a duck in water.它让我如鱼得水。

(9) Death is just a part of life, something we're all destined to do.死亡是生命的一部分，是我们注定要做的一件事。

(10) I was messed up for a long time.这些年我一塌糊涂。

(11) I don't know if we each have a destiny, or if we're all just floating around accidental? like on a breeze.我不懂我们是否有着各自的命运，还是只是到处随风飘荡。

(《阿甘正传》1994)

28. We'll always have Paris. 我们永远都怀念巴黎（那段美好的时光）。(《卡萨布兰卡》1942)

29. Oh, Jerry, don't let's ask for the moon. We have the stars.噢，杰瑞，不要再乞求能得到月亮了，我们已经拥有星星了。(《扬帆》1942)

30. Well, nobody's perfect.人无完人。(《热情似火》1959)

31. You've got to ask yourself one question: "Do I feel lucky?" Well, do ya, punk? 你应该问你自己一个问题："我是幸运的吗？"快点去做，年轻人，无知的年轻人。(《警探哈里》1971)

32. You had me at "hello". 当你说"你好"的那一刻起就拥有我了。(《甜心先生》1996)

33. There's no crying in baseball! 在棒球运动中没有哭泣！(《红粉联盟》1992)

34. A boy's best friend is his mother.一个男孩最好的朋友是他的母亲。(《惊魂记》1960)

35. Greed, for lack of a better word, is good.没有比"贪婪"更好的词语了。(《华尔街》1987)

36. Keep your friends close, but your enemies closer.亲近你的朋友,但更要亲近你的敌人。(《教父II》1974)

37. As God is my witness, I'll never be hungry again.上帝为我作证,我不会再让自己挨饿了。(《乱世佳人》1939)

38. Mrs. Robinson, you're trying to seduce me. Aren't you? 罗宾逊太太,你是在引诱我,对吗?(《毕业生》1967)

39. Of all the gin joints in all the towns in all the world, she walks into mine.世界上有那么多的城镇,城镇中有那么多的酒馆,她却走进了我的(酒馆)。(《卡萨布兰卡》1942)

40. Wait a minute, wait a minute. You ain't heard nothing yet! 等一会儿,等一会儿。你肯定听到了什么!(《爵士歌手》1927)

41. I have always depended on the kindness of strangers. 我总是非常依赖陌生人的仁慈。(《欲望号街车》1951)

42. Listen to them. Children of the night. What music they make.快点来听!黑夜中孩子的声音是他们缔造的美妙音乐。(《吸血鬼》1931)

43. I feel the need — the need for speed! 我感到一种需要,一种加速的需要!(《壮志凌云》1986)

44. Carpe diem. Seize the day, boys. Make your lives extraordinary.人生就应该是快乐的,要抓住每一天,孩子们。让你们的生活变得非凡起来。(《死亡诗社》1989)

45. (1) Outwardly, I was everything a well-brought up girl should be. Inside, I was screaming. 外表看,我是个教养良好的小姐,骨子里,我很反叛。

(2) We're the luckiest sons-of-××es in the world. 我们是真××走运极了。(地道的美国骂人)

(3) There is nothing I couldn't give you, there is nothing I would deny you, if you would not deny me. Open your heart to me. 如果你不违背我,你要什么我就能给你什么,你要什么都可以。把你的心交给我吧。

(4) What the purpose of university is to find a suitable husband. 读大学的目的是找一个好丈夫。(好像有些片面,但比较真实)

(5) Remember, they love money, so just pretend like you own a goldmine and you're in the club. 只要你装得很有钱的样子,他们就会跟你套近乎。

(6) All life is a game of luck. 生活本来就全靠运气。

(7) I love waking up in the morning and not knowing what's going to happen, or who I'm going to meet, where I'm going to wind up. 我喜欢早上起来时一切都是未知的,不知会遇见什么人,会有什么样的结局。

(8) I figure life is a gift and I don't intend on wasting it. You never know what hand you're going to get dealt next. You learn to take life as it comes at you. 我觉得生命是一份礼物,我不想浪费它,你不会知道下一手牌会是什么,要学会接受生活。

(9) To make each day count. 要让每一天都有所值。

(10) We're women. Our choices are never easy. 我们是女人,我们的选择从来就不易。

(11) You jump, I jump. 你跳,我就跳。

(12) Will you give us a chance to live? 能不能给我们留一条生路?

(13) God shall wipe away all the tears from their eyes, and there shall be no more death. Neither shall there be sorrow or dying, neither shall there be any more pain, for the former world has passed away. 上帝擦去他们所有的眼泪。死亡不再有,也不再有悲伤和生死离别,不再有痛苦,因往事已矣。

(14) You're going to get out of here. You're going to go on and you're going to make lots of babies and you're going to watch them grow and you're going to die an old, an old lady, warm in your bed. Not here. Not this night. Not like this. 你一定会脱险的,你要活下去,生很多孩子,看着他们长大。你会安享晚年,安息在温暖的床上,而不是今晚在这里,不是像这样死去。

(15) I'm king of the world! 我是世界之王!

(《泰坦尼克号》1997)

46. Save one life, save the world entire. 拯救一个人,就是拯救全世界。(《辛德勒的名单》1993)

47. A guy once told me: Don't have any attackments, don't have anything in your life you're not willing to walk out on in 30 seconds flat. 从前有个人对我说,别要任何附属品,在你的生命中,不应该有任何你不能在三十秒内抛弃的东西。(《盗火线》1994)

48. You are under arrest for so and so reason. You have the right to remain silent. Anything what you say can and will be used in the court of law against you. You have the right to an attorney. If you cannot afford one, one will be provided to you.你现在被捕了! 你有权保持缄默,但你说的每句话将成为呈堂证供。你有权要求见你的律师。如果你没有律师,我们将为你提供一名律师。(《神探亨特》1984)

49. (1) In all that sprawling city there was everything, except an end, there was no end. What I didn't see was where the whole thing came to an end, the end of them. 在那个无限蔓延的城市里,什么东西都有,可唯独没有尽头。根本就没有尽头。我看不见的是这一切的尽头,世界的尽头。

(2) All that world is weighing down on me, you don't even know where it comes to an end, and aren't you ever just scared of breaking apart at the thought of it. 那个世界好重, 压在我身上。你甚至不知道它在哪里结束,你难道从来不为自己生活在无穷选择里而害怕得快崩溃掉吗?

(《海上钢琴师》1998)

50. Don't tell me you are innocent, because it insults my intelligence.别跟我说你是无辜的,这让我愤怒。因为它侮辱了我的智慧。(《教父》1972)

(根据中青网资料整理)

20句迪斯尼动画经典台词

1. Let your heart guide you. It whispers, so listen closely. *The Land Before Time*

跟随你心的指引吧。它总是低诉着前进的方向,所以请仔细聆听。《大脚板走天涯》

2. "HAKUNA MATATA"...it means no worries. *The Lion King*

"哈库那马塔塔"……就是没有烦恼的意思。《狮子王》

3. The past can hurt. You can either run from it or learn from it. *The Lion King*

陈年往事固然伤人,但你可以选择从中吸取教训,或者远远地逃离。《狮子王》

4. If you live to be a hundred, I want to live to be a hundred minus one day, so I never have to live without you. *Winnie the Pooh*

如果你要活到一百岁,那么我只要活到一百岁差一天,这样我就不用度过没有你陪伴的分分秒秒。《小熊维尼》

5. Remember: Always let your conscience be your guide. *Pinocchio*

记住:要凭着你的良心做事。《木偶奇遇记》

6. You think the only people who are people, are the people who look and think like you. But if you walk the footsteps of a stranger, you'll learn things you never knew you never knew. *Pocahontas*

你自以为只有你那样的才算是人类,必须长得像你,同你一样思维。但倘若你愿跟随陌生人的脚步,你就会学到你从不明白的事情。《风中奇缘》

7. Nothing's impossible. *Alice in Wonderland*

没有什么是不可能的。《爱丽丝梦游仙境》

8. Hmm! Teenagers. They think they know everything. You give them an inch and they swim all over you! *Little Mermaid*

哼嗯!小屁孩。总是自以为是。得寸进尺,赶明儿就游你头上去了。《小美人鱼》

9. I'm not worthless — and I don't have fleas. *Aladdin*

我可不是一无是处——我身上也不带跳蚤。《阿拉丁》

10. All it takes is Faith and Trust. *Peter Pan*

只需要一些信仰和信念。《彼得·潘》

11. Look for the bare necessities. *The Jungle Book*

找到熊熊的生存之道。《丛林王子》

12. Dreams can come true! *Cinderella*

梦想是可以成真的。《灰姑娘》

13. A dream is a wish your heart makes. *Cinderella*

梦想是你的心许下的一个愿望。《灰姑娘》

14. It's kind a fun to do the impossible. — Walt Disney

做一些不可能的事情,其实挺好玩的。——华特·迪斯尼

15. To die would be an awfully big adventure. *Peter Pan*

死亡是一场华丽异常的冒险。《彼得·潘》

16. The world is my backyard. *The Aristocats*

世界是我们家后院。《猫儿历险记》

17. Reach for the sky! *Toy Story*

朝天空发射！《玩具总动员》

18. Even miracles take a little time. *The Fairy Godmother*

就算是奇迹也要花点时间才能发生的。《仙女教母》

19. Keep your chin up, someday there will be happiness again. *Robin Hood*

抬起头来吧，幸福快乐终有一天会重临。《罗宾汉》

20. What do you do when things go wrong? Oh! You sing a song! *Snow White*

事情不顺利的时候要怎么办呢？哦，就唱歌吧！《白雪公主与七个小矮人》

（根据沪江英语网资料整理）

参考文献

1. 黄哲."读"辟"曦"径——英语晨读素材精编[M].沈阳:白山出版社,2008.

2. 莎士比亚.莎士比亚十四行诗[M]. 辜正坤,译.北京:中国对外翻译出版社,2008.

3. 刘溶波. Selected Readings in British and American Literature[M]. 北京:高等教育出版社,2008.

4. 周建新.英语诗歌经典译析[M].南宁:广西人民出版社出版,2010.

5. 景晓莺.英语诗歌常识与名作研读[M].上海:上海交通大学出版社,2011.

6. 司炳月.英语诵读散文[M].大连:大连理工大学出版社出版,2009.

7. 张艳玲.最优美的诗歌[M]. 乌鲁木齐:新疆电子音像出版社,2010.

8. 孙毅兵,卞建华. 美国总统演讲集萃[M].天津:天津科学技术出版社,2012.

9. 马德高.英语演讲高手:名人演讲精选[M].济南,山东科学技术出版社,2008.

10. 刘荣,高洁. 励志演讲阅读经典[M].北京:国防工业出版社,2008.

11. 顾海兵. 英语演讲高手名人演讲精选精析[M].济南:山东科学技术出版社,2008.

12. 谢艳明.时代的强音——名人演讲及访谈精选[M].开封:河南大学出版社,2008.

13. 艾莉儿.世界上最伟大的演讲[M].北京:中国纺织出版社出版,2009.

14. Hendrik Willem Van Loon. The Story of Mankind[M]. 北京:中央编译出版社,2008

15. E. B. 怀特.夏洛的网[M].任溶溶,译.上海:上海译文出版社,2009.

16. 陶洁. 希腊罗马神话一百篇[M].北京: 中国对外翻译出版公司,1989.

17. 韦伯斯特.长腿叔叔[M]. 杜静斐,译.北京: 中国对外翻译出版公司,2005.

18. 夏洛蒂·勃朗特. 美丽英文 双语阅读——世界上最感人的书信[M]. 安娜,译.哈尔滨:北方文艺出版社,2009.

19. 朱维之. 圣经文学十二讲[M]. 北京:人民文学出版社,2008.

20. 杨周翰,吴达元,赵萝蕤. 欧洲文学史[M].北京:人民文学出版社,1985.

21. 罗选民. 英美文学赏析教程(散文与诗歌)[M]. 北京: 清华大学出版社, 2002.

22. 张蕾. 跟美国学生一起学英语(高级版)[M].广州:中山大学出版社, 2011.

23. 王炤. 英语名篇诵读与赏析[M]. 北京: 北京大学出版社, 2011.

24. 张艳玲.最经典的电影对白(上册)[M]. 乌鲁木齐:新疆美术摄影出版社,新疆电子音像出版社, 2010.

25. 张艳玲.最经典的电影对白(下册)[M]. 乌鲁木齐:新疆美术摄影出版社,新疆电子音像出版社，2010.
26. 卫岭. 英语影视欣赏[M]. 苏州：苏州大学出版社，2009.
27. 卫禹兰. 趣读英文影评[M]. 北京:外文出版社，2008.
28. 姜荷梅. 二十一世纪大学生英语晨读菁华[M]. 上海:复旦大学出版社，2012.
29.《英语学习》编辑部. 性情人生[M]. 北京：外语教学与研究出版社，2004.
30. 英语世界[J]. 北京：商务印书馆，2000年第8期.
31. 英语世界[J]. 北京：商务印书馆，2000年第11期
32. 英语世界[J]. 北京：商务印书馆，2001年第9期

后 记

经典，是通过个人独特的世界观和不可重复的创造，凸显出丰厚的文化积淀和人性内涵，提出一些人类精神生活的根本性问题。它们与特定历史时期鲜活的时代感以及当下意识交融在一起，富有原创性和持久的震撼力，从而形成重要的思想文化传统。在存在形态上具有开放性、超越性和多元性的特征。从价值定位看，经典必须成为民族语言和思想的象征符号。如莎翁之于英国和英国文学，普希金之于俄罗斯与俄罗斯文学，鲁迅之于中国和中国文学，他们的经典都远远超越了个人的意义，上升为一个民族，甚至是全人类的共同经典。

本书撷取了古今英美文学中的优秀之作，从莎士比亚的戏剧开始，荟萃了16到20世纪的名诗、散文佳作、名人信函、演讲以及经典影片中的经典片段，让您读后回味无穷，甚至有背诵佳句的欲望，这正是我们想要达到的目的。脍炙人口的名人名作和经典对白，让您领略英诗及演讲之瑰美，体会英语文章的幽默与严谨，感悟思辨哲学之智慧，感受到原汁原味的生活会话用语。通过赏析，让您了解相关背景知识及历史评价；通过译文和注释为您扫除英文学习中的难点和盲点。让您在学习中回顾经典，如饮一樽陈年美酒，芳香弥漫。又恰似漫漫长路永不泯灭的明灯或如茫茫沙漠一口清泉，给您指明前进的方向，让您享受甜美的滋味。同时在经典中学习，收获经典。

在创作本书的过程中，三位编者力求选取文字优美的英美文学名家名篇，内容涉及诗歌、散文、随笔、演讲、书信及经典台词等；同时译文力求名家译作；台词部分也尽量选取的是近20年内思想性艺术性评价较高的影视名片。赏析部分向读者提供了创作背景、写作方法和欣赏角度，有助于读者更好的理解其创作风格和遣词造句。当然，这些都只是抛砖引玉，更多的精彩在于原文。

此书由三位老师合作编写而成。张周瑞老师编著“名诗精选”和“名人演讲”部分，张洁老师编著“散文名篇”和“经典影片”部分，王宁老师编写“哲理故事”和“名人书信”部分。

为了给使用本教材的读者提供最真实准确的译文，我们在选编的过程中采用了诸位翻译名家的译本，在此真诚地感谢各位译者。英文经典的内容博大精深，历史文化内涵也极为丰富，在选编题材的过程中难免会存在着挂一漏万的现象。由于笔者的能力和水平有限，对原注的注释和理解恐怕也存在一些不妥之处，因此笔者衷心地希望广大读者、学生及专家批评指正，以便在今后的工作中进一步不断地完善和提高。